Third World Development

Problems and Prospects

Third World Development

Problems and Prospects

Edward G. Stockwell
and
Karen A. Laidlaw

Nelson-Hall nh Chicago

**For Margaret and Frank and
Elaine and John, for all
they have contributed to
our development . . .**

Library of Congress Cataloging in Publication Data
Stockwell, Edward G
  Third World development.

  Bibliography: p.
  Includes index.
  1. Underdeveloped areas. I. Laidlaw, Karen A.,
1949-1979, joint author. II. Title.
HC59.7.S827   330.9′172′4   79-24088
ISBN 0-88229-532-2

Contents

List of Tables

List of Figures

Preface

This book was written to fill the need for a general introductory volume dealing with the many facets of the complex development problem confronting the Third World nations of Asia, Africa, and Latin America. Although there are a number of good texts on this subject, neither of us is aware of one that adequately covers all major aspects of the development problem in a single volume. Most of the books that are available are too specific (i.e., they tend to focus primarily on a single aspect of the problem such as "the family in development," or "the military," or "economic dependence"); many others that purport to be general texts neglect one or more critical problem areas. We have tried in this book to provide a broad framework for studying Third World countries that encompasses all of the major aspects of the contemporary development problem.

Our book was not written for the seasoned scholar; professional students of social change and development will find nothing new in its pages. Rather, our intended audience is the beginning student or other nonprofessional who wishes to become acquainted with the many dimensions of the single most critical problem facing the world today. We make no claim to having included every relevant topic; however, we do believe that our book provides a good general introduction to the many and varied aspects of the problem of Third World development.

As is true with any effort of this kind, we owe a debt of gratitude to a great many people who have contributed directly and indirectly to the completion of this volume. There are of course the many scholars whose works we have read over the years and whose ideas have stimulated our interest in, as well as greatly enhanced our awareness and appreciation of the problems of Third World development. Works specifically referred to have been cited in the bibliography at the end of this volume; but these cited works by no means represent all that we have made use of, and we would like to acknowledge these unnamed scholars, past and present, for the indirect assistance they have given us. A similar acknowledgement is also extended to the many teachers and colleagues we have known over the years—particularly to Professors Sidney Goldstein, Jack Ray Thomas, and Vincent H. Whitney—who have contributed so much to our intellectual development.

A particular word of thanks is due to the following colleagues for reading and offering us many valuable comments on all or various portions of our manuscript: Roger C. Anderson, H. Theodore Groat, Joseph E. Kivlin, and Arthur G. Neal. We found their suggestions helpful and have incorporated many of them. However, we alone accept full responsibility for any errors or inadequacies that may appear in the text.

We wish also to express our appreciation to our respective universities for providing flexible teaching schedules and/or supporting released time requests that greatly facilitated the completion of our manuscript, and especially for providing a congenial atmosphere and intellectual climate favorable to the pursuit of academic achievement.

Finally, we owe a very special thanks to Patricia Carpenter, who bore by far the greatest burden of typing and retyping the many drafts of the manuscript.

Edward G. Stockwell   Karen A. Laidlaw
Bowling Green State   Indiana University
University   Northwest

Postscript to the Preface

Dr. Karen Laidlaw died on August 6, 1979, as this book was going to press. Her untimely death at the age of 29 represents not only a professional loss to the field of sociology but also a deep personal loss to those of us who knew her and worked with her. In all ways she will be missed very much.

Edward G. Stockwell
October, 1979

1

Introduction

The Problem

This book deals with the simple fact that anywhere from two-thirds to three-fourths of the people in the world today live in abject poverty and are hungry a good part of the time. Some of the more pertinent questions to which this situation gives rise are as follows:

What has brought about this situation?

What can or must be done to change this situation?

What obstacles are likely to impede efforts to change it; and how may these obstacles be overcome or circumvented?

What factors are likely to aid efforts to change this situation; and how can these factors be enhanced?

We do not pretend that we are going to offer definitive answers to all of these or to other related questions and thereby "solve" the most serious problem confronting mankind in the last two decades of the twentieth century. Rather, it is our intent in this book to outline for beginning students the basic dimensions of the development problem and to provide a simple framework for arriving at a better understanding of the specific problems facing particular regions or countries of the world.

The first step in arriving at a better understanding of the nature of the general problem of economic development is to become familiar with the more common characteristics of the so-called underdeveloped countries. This is necessary because one cannot take realistic measures to cope with any problem unless one has a thorough knowledge of the specific dimensions of the problem. This is especially true with respect to the problem of development because, as has been emphasized elsewhere (Stockwell, 1974), the various characteristics that generally differentiate underdeveloped areas from the more highly developed countries are often very closely related to the specific forces and circumstances which may be expected to handicap their economic development. To take a simple illustration, underdeveloped countries are generally characterized by population growth rates two or three times in excess of those commonly found in the advanced urban-industrial nations; during the past ten to fifteen years a rapid rate of population growth has been acting as a major obstacle to economic growth in many of the poorer countries of the world. As just indicated, then, a major prerequisite to studying the problems and processes of underdevelopment in the Third World nations today is a thorough knowledge of their distinctive characteristics.

The approach to be taken in this volume starts by identifying some of the major characteristics of the developing areas as a whole in terms of their present economic and demographic status, and then considers several noneconomic characteristics (e.g., culture, religion, social structure, education, political factors) in terms of how they may relate to or otherwise influence both economic and demographic behavior. The overall aim of the volume is to identify and describe some of the more general kinds of problems that the various developing countries may have to contend with in their present efforts to modernize and raise the level of living of their people. For the most part the approach will be descriptive, but in several instances specific suggestions or recommendations will be offered concerning things that we see as desirable or necessary in order to deal adequately with the problems of development throughout the Third World.

Before proceeding any further, however, it is desirable to make two points of clarification. First, we should recognize that the problem of economic development is an extremely complex one and that its solution is going to depend on much more than simply a better understanding of the characteristic features of underdeveloped areas. A simplistic view might assume that once the characteristics of an underdeveloped area are known, development is merely a matter of instituting programs to change particular unfavorable characteristics (e.g., if protein deficiency is a characteristic, just add a protein supplement to the diet). Such a view is untenable. In part this is because there is no prior way of knowing what kind of program is best suited to bring about a particular change in any given society; one man's meat is another man's poison, and introducing beef cattle as a potential food supplement is not going to alleviate protein deficiency among vegetarian peoples. Any cultural anthropologist can entertain people for hours on end with stories of how apparently rational plans of action in particular cultures or environmental settings were rejected completely when they were tried out.

The preceding view also ignores the basic fact that many of the distinctive characteristics of the underdeveloped countries are closely interrelated with one another, and a change in any single variable is likely to have ramifications throughout a society—ramifications that may or may not be beneficial for economic development. To take a simple illustration, instituting universal primary education may be a step toward reducing illiteracy, but it may also have other effects such as: (a) reducing the number of workers by putting children in school; (b) creating the need for changes in the occupational structure to provide jobs for a more highly educated labor force; (c) increasing the political awareness of the electorate; and (d) generating rising expectations which, if not satisfied, could result in increased frustration, discontent, and perhaps even violent action. Thus, simply knowing the major characteristics of an underdeveloped society is not a sufficient basis on which to build a development program. However, such knowledge is a necessary prerequisite for rational development planning, and acquiring this knowledge is a necessary first step.

The second point of clarification concerns the fact that the term "underdeveloped" covers a very large number of countries that often differ quite markedly from one another in both economic and noneconomic characteristics. For example, all underdeveloped areas have a low annual per capita income, but the variation is substantial. To illustrate, estimates prepared by the Population Reference Bureau (1978a) show that the 1976 per capita income in Mexico ($1,090) was roughly twice that of Morocco ($540), more than four times that of Togo ($260), and more than nine times that of Bangladesh ($110). Similarly, another major characteristic of underdeveloped areas is a low annual per capita use of inanimate energy (i.e., energy produced by fossil fuels such as coal or petroleum, as opposed to that derived from animal or human power). Here again, however, figures for the early 1970s prepared by the Environmental Fund (1975a) *(World Population Estimates, 1975)* show that per capita commercial energy consumption ranged from 10 to 12 kilograms of coal equivalent in Burundi, Rwanda, and Upper Volta to over 1,200 in Chile, Jamaica, Mexico, and Surinam. When one considers various socio-cultural characteristics such as religious beliefs, family structure, personality type, attitudes toward social change, acquisitive behavior, the ability to control ones destiny, etc., not to mention differences in topography, climate, and natural resources, the range of variation is even more substantial.

The signficance of this point is that the precise nature of

particular development problems will vary considerably from one region or country to another, depending on their unique characteristics and circumstances. In Latin America, for example, where most countries have been independent for much longer than the countries of Africa, there has evolved a rather conservative society in which the traditional authoritarian-elitist institutions have tended to be accommodative and absorptive, bending to change rather than being overwhelmed by it (Wiarda, 1973). Hence, these are societies which are more geared to maintaining the status quo than to any radical change, and in which whatever development has taken place has occurred in spurts with periods of growth alternating with periods of stagnation or even decline. In Africa, on the other hand, where the relative newness of independence is often coupled with racial conflict, the nations that are now just emerging from the colonial era are much more oriented toward radical or even revolutionary change.

It is of course true that the socioeconomic status of all underdeveloped areas is substantially below that of the more highly developed countries of Europe, North America and Oceania; hence there is some justification for considering them as a distinctive group of countries. Nevertheless, the fact remains that lumping all such areas together may conceal a great deal of internal variation, and such internal variation may be just as relevant for their development potential as the differences between the underdeveloped nations as a class and the more developed countries.

Approaches to the Problem

Since the end of the Second World War, an increasing number of scholars from a number of different fields have focused their attention on the development problems facing the emerging nations of the Third World; and a number of different approaches to or models for understanding the development process have been suggested. The more well known of these approaches can be grouped into three major categories: the psychological approach, the ideal type approach, and the diffusionist approach (Edari, 1976). A fourth approach, which has grown out of criticisms of the preceding three, is what may be called the dependency theory approach. Each of these will now be considered as a means of introducing the societal approach to be taken in the present volume. The discussion at this time will be very brief; however, most of the theories and/or models to be presented will be considered in greater detail in subsequent chapters.

The Psychological Approach

Those who take the psychological approach to the analysis of economic development basically seek to account for the presence or absence of economic growth in terms of some general personality trait or inner psychic state that is characteristic, to a greater or lesser extent, of a particular society. This approach, which is rooted in Max Weber's classical analysis of the emergence of the Protestant Ethic and the rise of modern capitalism in the Western world, would explain the lack of development in a particular society as being due to an insufficient number of persons who possess those traits that are seen as essential for development to occur. One of the foremost proponents of this psychological approach, perhaps, is David McClelland who explains economic growth in terms of what he calls the "need for achievement" (see chapter 5). According to McClelland, this can be conceived of as a desire to succeed as an individual, not so much for the sake of the recognition and rewards that success brings, but to attain an inner feeling of self-satisfaction from having accomplished something. Persons who are characterized as having a high achievement orientation "tend to work harder at certain tasks; to learn faster; to do their best work when it counts for the record, and not when special incentives, like money prizes, are introduced; to choose experts over friends as working partners, etc." (McClelland, 1963:76). Accordingly, societies in which a sufficiently large proportion of the population exhibits a high need for achievement will be more likely to undergo economic growth than a society in which the overall need for achievement level is low.

While McClelland's thesis has been found to have some validity in explaining past economic growth cycles in various parts of the Western world, it is derived in large measure from western religious and ideological thought; it has been found to have less relevance in nonwestern societies where the basic values have roots quite diverse from those of our Judeo-Christian heritage. Further, by stressing the inner need of individuals to attain self-satisfaction, the need achievement model is too narrowly focused to permit a full understanding of the complex problem of development facing the nations of Asia, Africa and Latin America.

A somewhat similar but broader approach is that taken by E. E. Hagen in his book, *On the Theory of Social Change* (1962) (see chapter 6). According to Hagen there are several personality traits that are associated with economic development. Among the more important are: (1) need for achievement (a predisposition to seek out and overcome challenges for the pleasure of it); (2) need autonomy (a feeling of self-reliance and confidence in one's self and one's ability to make decisions independent of the judgement of others); and (3) need order (a high tolerance for disorder and nonconformity). The basic problem facing most developing societies lies in the fact that they are "traditional" societies characterized by authoritarian social structures in which ascribed statuses are arranged in a hierarchial manner. Such societies tend to produce personality types that are the reverse of those needed for economic growth (Hagen, 1962:118-19). Specifically, the structure of such traditional societies tends to produce an authoritarian personality type that is characterized by a lack of self-confidence and a high level of anxiety when faced with the challenge of a new situation. Persons exhibiting such a personality configuration will tend to avoid new situations; they will take comfort in conforming to traditional rules and behavior patterns; and they will tend to have conservative attitudes that lean toward the preservation of the status quo. What is needed for development, according to Hagen, is a proliferation of persons who exhibit what he calls an innovative personality. In contrast to an authoritarian personality, an innovative personality is characterized by such things as a creative imagination, a high level of self-confidence, satisfaction in facing and solving problems, and a sense of duty or responsibility to achieve.

Again, as with McClelland's "need for achievement," the emphasis on personality traits is too narrow an approach to the topic of development (it excludes, for example, the importance of having some sort of natural resource base that can be developed). Further, Hagen's thesis is limited by the fact that traditional societies are not all "authoritarian and hierarchial" as he postulates (i.e., his model may fit the Latin American situation with its background of Catholic authoritarianism and its traditional two-class system epitomized by *patron-cliente* relations, but it would be much less applicable in the newly emerging African states). Finally, both of these psychological approaches suffer from an elitist or condescending view of non-Western societies which have not developed economically. That is, they "blame" their underdevelopment on the fact that they have not instilled the proper attitudes and personality traits into their members. Furthermore, the fact that people who are poor, hungry and generally deprived might desire to improve their objective economic situation can be understood without resorting to the motivational force of some inner psychic state.

The Ideal Type Approach

According to this approach, societies are grouped into various types on the basis of characteristics that are purported to be indicative of different stages of development. On the simplest level, countries are grouped according to some single index—such as annual per capita income, level of energy consumption, or rate of infant mortality. Such a procedure permits a researcher to rank countries in order to carry out statistical analyses of the various correlates of development status. It is limited, however, because of its reliance on a unidimensional index to measure a complex multidimensional phenomenon.

The approach taken by scholars such as Bert Hoselitz is on a somewhat higher level. Hoselitz utilizes part of the ''pattern variable'' scheme developed by Talcott Parsons to devise a dichotomous classification of developed and under-developed countries (see chapter 6). Very briefly, this approach identifies societies as developed or underdeveloped on the basis of: (1) whether rewards and prestige are allocated on the basis of *achievement* or of *ascription;* (2) whether the criteria used to evaluate a social object are *universalistic* or *particularistic;* and (3) whether social roles are functionally *specific* or *diffuse.* According to this model, the process of economic development in any society is associated with a shift away from a ''traditional'' social structure characterized by ascription, particularism, and functionally diffuse roles to a ''modern'' social structure characterized by achievement, universalism, and functionally specific roles. Again, however, one can view this model as an elitist oversimplification of the development problem that essentially says ''they'' (the people in the poor countries) are poor because they have different belief systems and different ways of thinking and behaving than ''we'' (the people in the rich countries) do. According to this approach, economic development would be seen as nothing more than a process of change in which ''they'' become more like ''us.'' Furthermore, even if it can be demonstrated that the development of the poor countries will depend on their becoming at least partially ''westernized,'' this model does not really tell us how the transition from a traditional to a modern society is supposed to take place. It does little more than identify some of the broader sociocultural features of some non-Western countries, and then explains economic under-development as a reflection of these broad features (the cause-effect direction may be vague but the association is stated very explicitly).

Another well-known variant of this ideal type approach is the "stages of growth" hypothesis such as that proposed by W. W. Rostow. In his book, *The Stages of Economic Growth: A Non-Communist Manifesto* (1960) Rostow identifies five stages in the process of economic development. These are (1) traditional society, characterized by such things as a low level of technology, a rigid social structure, fatalistic attitudes, and a low level of per capita output; (2) preconditions for take-off, which emerge as a traditional society is exposed to the scientific knowledge and technology of modern society, and in which the traditional values and practices begin to break down; (3) take-off, wherein the last remnants of the traditional culture are discarded and a period of sustained economic growth gets underway; (4) drive to maturity, in which a society undergoes rapid economic growth and becomes integrated into the larger international economic system; and (5) high mass consumption, which is the final stage of development and which is characterized by both a high standard and high level of living for the greater mass of the society. A closer look at this model reveals the same two polar types derived from the pattern variable approach: the "traditional" or underdeveloped society at one end of the continuum, and the "modern" developed society with its high level of mass consumption at the other end. The three intermediate stages are merely progressive stages of the development process that the underdeveloped countries are expected to go through in the process of becoming more like "us." Again, however, the inherent western bias aside, Rostow's approach also fails to indicate the specific mechanisms or factors that cause a society to move from one stage to another. Thus, while these ideal type approaches may have some value as schemes for classifying regions or countries according to their relative level of economic development, they fall short of being adequate theories for explaining the processes whereby any given society can be transformed from a state of underdevelopment to one of development.

Perhaps the strongest criticism that has been leveled at both the psychological and ideal-type approaches is that both seem to assume, albeit implicitly, that underdeveloped areas have only themselves to blame for their underdeveloped status. That is, "poor" countries are poor only because they do not have any worthwhile resources, or because the people lack the proper kinds of motivation, or because their culture or the structure of their society prevents them from adequately developing their resources. While it may well be that all these factors are important to one extent or another, emphasis on them alone leads to a neglect of various external factors that may be just as important (some would say more important) in impeding national development or modernization. For example, no consideration is given to the nature of the international economic system as a potential barrier to development, or to the idea that the underdevelopment of the poor countries may be an integral part of the development of the rich countries. The latter is the position taken by Marxists and the more recent dependency theorists such as A. G. Frank (see below) who locate the "causes" of underdevelopment not in the socio-cultural characteristics of a people but in the nature of the external economic relationships that the rich industrialized nations have historically established between themselves and the lesser developed countries.

The Diffusionist Approach

Although diffusion is generally conceived as a process whereby a cultural item that has its roots in one society is transmitted to another society, it has been used in a more narrow sense to refer to the process of modernization (Edari, 1976:45-46). In this narrower sense, diffusion is regarded as a process whereby an underdeveloped society adopts a particular item or items from a more advanced society in order to enhance its own development. In describing this approach

Edari deals with three categories of items: capital, technology, and social structure. To be brief, this approach starts by viewing underdeveloped societies as: (1) lacking the surplus capital needed to invest in development programs; (2) possessing a low level of technology that prevents the optimum utilization of both human and natural resources; and (3) having a social structure that is characterized by conservatism, ascription, particularism, low need for achievement, etc., and that is thus not conducive to capital accumulation or the adoption of technological innovations. According to this approach, development will be enhanced to the extent: (a) that underdeveloped areas are assisted in accumulating needed capital by means of grants and/or loans from the more highly developed societies; (b) that underdeveloped areas adopt modern methods of agricultural and industrial production; and (c) that they adopt those values, attitudes and behavior patterns that are associated with the social structures of the advanced urban-industrial nations of the Western world.

This diffusion model has much more merit for enhancing our understanding of the development problem than either the psychological or ideal-type approaches. However, it too has its limitations. For one thing, it contains an implicit assumption that the needed capital and technological aid is readily available through the kindness and generosity of the richer highly developed countries, and this assumption is not always warranted. For another thing, the diffusion of capital, technology and various elements of social structure from the advanced countries to underdeveloped areas has often hindered the development of the latter rather than promoting it (Frank, 1969). Finally, like the preceding approaches, this one also contains an ethnocentric notion that the developing societies have to become more like "us" with respect to their attitudes and values if they are to develop. While it may be true that many aspects of their cultural belief systems represent potential obstacles to development, the need for some modification in this respect does not require that they become "westernized." From the point of view of the societal approach to be taken in this volume, the diffusionist model is limited by virtue of the fact that it explicitly places heaviest emphasis on the economic and social structural aspects of the problem, while paying insufficient attention to what we regard as the equally important demographic dimension of the development problem.

Dependency Theory

The "dependency theory" approach to the problems of Third World development gained popularity during the 1960s in the writings of a number of Latin American scholars. It is basically a view that cites the historical appearance of colonialism and the emergence of western capitalism as the major factors accounting for the existence of so-called underdeveloped countries today (Wallerstein, 1974). One of the more articulate spokesmen for this point of view and a major critic of the preceding three traditional approaches to the problem of Third World economic development is Andre Gunder Frank. Although Frank's analysis of the problem of underdevelopment is based largely on the historical experiences of Latin America, the basic points can just as well be applied to Asia and Africa. According to Frank (1969) the causes of the underdeveloped status of Third World countries today are intimately related to the historical causes of development in the industrialized nations. That is, development and underdevelopment are seen as two aspects of the same process. Before there were developed countries there were no underdeveloped countries. All countries were at one time undeveloped; but beginning in the fifteenth century as the West Europeans spread out and colonized all parts of the world, the European countries (and those largely of European origin such as the United States) began to undergo rapid economic development largely because of their being in a position to exploit the resources (human as well as natural) of other nations who now began to emerge as underdeveloped. That is, the dependency theory approach asserts that the developed world has achieved its present high level of living largely at the expense of the now underdeveloped countries of Asia, Africa and Latin America.

An implicit assumption of many of the previously cited traditional approaches to underdeveloped areas is that such areas are relatively isolated from the rest of the world, and that this so-called isolation is one of the main factors affecting their lack of development. Dependency theory, however, argues the reverse; namely, that the problem lies in the fact that underdeveloped societies have been in *too close* contact with the developed world. Dependency theory argues that the problem of underdevelopment stems from the fact that the traditional societies of the Third World were destroyed some time ago upon contact with colonialist powers; their traditional ways of life were disrupted, economic assets were expropriated, and the underdeveloped countries were forced into close dependent relationships with colonial or imperialist powers. Furthermore, this economic domination of the underdeveloped areas by the industrial powers is seen as continuing today under the label of neocolonialism.

Fundamental to an adequate understanding of Frank's perspective is his concept of the ''metropolis-satellite'' relationship—a relationship in which one area (the metropolis) exercises economic dominance over and is exploitative of another area (the satellite). The metropolis may be either international or national. If it is being considered on an international level one may be referring to a particular country (e.g., the United States) while the satellite may be a particular region or another country (e.g., Latin America or Peru). On a national level, one may be referring to the capital city as the metropolis, and the rest of the country as the satellite region (e.g., Santiago and Chile). In either case the significance of the relationship for development (or the lack of development) is that the metropolis is clearly economically dominant with respect to the satellite, expropriating its natural resources and giving little if anything in return. In other words, ''contemporary underdevelopment is in large part the historical product of past and continuing economic and other relations between the satellite underdeveloped and the now developed metropolitan countries" (Frank, 1969:4).

An important aspect of this metropolis-satellite relationship lies in the area of industrialization. Specifically, according to Frank, it acts to retard industrialization. The multinational (foreign owned) corporations who control access to the major raw material sources have traditionally invested little of their profits in the satellite regions. Although much capital has often been generated within particular satellite countries, the surplus profits have generally been "exported" back to the metropolis or to the home countries/ regions of the multinational corporations. It is Frank's contention that the major satellite countries of Latin America have achieved the greatest amount of economic development and industrialization during periods of isolation from .the metropolis (i.e., the United States); for example, during the two world wars when the United States was occupied elsewhere.

Frank's critique of the current development problem is aimed specifically at the capitalist bloc nations which he sees as responsible for much past colonialism and imperialism, as well as continued neocolonialism; and he neglects the Soviet sphere of influence which may be having the same effect in many parts of the world today. Similarly, his theory is weakened somewhat by the fact that one can find examples of countries today where substantial economic development has taken place within a so-called satellite country operating under a capitalist economic system. Taiwan would be a case in point. Frank's basic conclusion, however, is a valid one; development and underdevelopment are two different sides of the same process. It is a fact that the economic growth and development of the capitalist nations was not an autonomous process. They drew, and they continue to draw heavily on the resources and raw materials of the so-called underdeveloped countries; and part of the solution to the development problem will necessarily entail a restructuring of this exploitative relationship.

A Societal Approach

The approach to be taken in this volume is essentially an elaboration of the diffusionist approach described above. At the same time, however, it is one that tries to incorporate into it certain useful features of the psychological and ideal type approaches, as well as many of the conclusions of the more recent dependency theorists. The problems of development confronting the Third World today are so vast and so varied that no single model or theory will be adequate to explain them. What we hope to do with our approach, rather than try to provide answers to all the many questions pertaining to the complex development problems facing the world today, is to present a general framework for looking at the more specific problems of particular regions or countries.

To begin with, the problem of underdeveloped areas in general is here broadly conceived of as a three-dimensional problem. It is first and foremost an *economic* problem in that the majority of the world's people today live in areas where abject poverty (and all that this entails) is a pervasive and persistent way of life. Many underdeveloped areas are also characterized by a scarcity of natural resources, especially arable land; this limited resource base is further aggravated by a low level of technology and primitive modes of production and by a labor force whose productive efficiency is severely curtailed by high rates of illiteracy, by ill health, by lack of technical skills, etc. In short, from an economic perspective, underdeveloped countries are in very dire straits; due to their low incomes, the inferior quality (if not outright scarcity) of productive resources, and their low state of technological development, most underdeveloped areas are not able to provide adequately for the development needs of their people. The problem is further exacerbated by the fact that the economies of many countries are agrarian or possess certain natural resources which are in great demand by the industrialized nations. Such countries developed export economies that were dependent on the world market situation; as demand fluctuated in the industrialized nations, so too did local prices, thus creating a basically unstable economic structure in the export countries which continues today to be a major factor contributing to their state of underdevelopment.

Second, there is a *demographic* dimension to the overall development problem. Many underdeveloped areas tend to de-emphasize this aspect of the problem and to regard the "population issue" as a smoke screen the rich countries are throwing up to hide what the former see as the real problem—inequitable access to the world's resources, especially food. Nevertheless, the fact of the matter is that most underdeveloped areas today are still characterized by high birth rates in the face of low or rapidly declining death rates, resulting in very rapid rates of population growth and high ratios of consumers to producers—both of which represent a serious obstacle to efforts to alleviate the basic economic problem.

Finally, and most significantly, the major aspect of the development problem as conceived here is the *sociocultural* dimension. By this we mean that underdeveloped areas in general tend to have traditional value systems and institutional structures that frequently function to aggravate both the economic and the demographic dimensions of the problem. For example, underdeveloped areas often have antiquated systems of land tenure (e.g., fragmented holdings which prevent an optimal use of existing land resources); or they have religious beliefs that are conducive to nonproductive or even wasteful uses of resources (e.g., the practices of hoarding wealth to finance an elegant funeral, and the Hindu's reverence for the cow); or they have strong familistic societies in which the positive value on having many children (especially sons) encourages the persistence of a high level of fertility. The implication of this is that such things as massive capital assistance, a more equitable distribution of the world's wealth, and the cessation of the exploitation of poor by rich nations that is still prevalent in many parts of the world are necessary if we are to eliminate the economic inequalities that presently exist; but they alone will not suffice to "solve" the pressing problems facing the underdeveloped nations. Rather, it is the thesis of this volume that the solutions to the development problem are to be found in the sociocultural dimension; and if (when) these kinds of obstacles can be overcome or otherwise circumvented the way will be open for sustained economic growth throughout the underdeveloped world. It could be said that the economic problem will be "solved" by a more productive utilization of existing resources; and the demographic problem could be "solved" by a decline in fertility and a stabilization of the rate of population growth. But, these solutions will not be forthcoming until the many and varied sociocultural problems are "solved," or until a way is found to mitigate the negative influence of sociocultural factors on development programs.

It is important to remember that the developing nations of the Third World do not exist in isolation but are part of a larger international economic system that is dominated by the western capitalist (First World) and socialist bloc (Second World) industrialized countries. In many respects, then, the problem of Third World development is a political problem. A major component of the sociocultural dimension concerns this political dimension, and a crucial factor determining the success of national development programs in the poor countries will be the strength of the government and the nature of the policies it adopts to deal with the realities of the international economic-political situation.

Summary Comments

We are well aware of the difficulty, if not impossibility, of developing a model which adequately explains all aspects of development or the lack of development. The preceding review of the various approaches points out that the major theories and explanations have either been too general or too narrow in scope. The advantage of our approach is that while it regards underdeveloped areas as similar in their underdevelopment, it recognizes that they do not constitute a homogeneous group. It further recognizes that the problem is not one for which there is a single, unidimensional solution. Instead the solution will have to be a multidimensional effort which takes many aspects into account. Modernization is not strictly a political or economic or cultural phenomenon, but one that encompasses all sections of society. Accordingly, our approach looks at all sections of society. In our approach we will also question traditional assumptions (e.g., that the extended family hinders development, or that capitalism and democracy are necessary to achieve development), and discuss outside interference into a nation's economy and political life. This latter is particularly important. Much of the recent literature on development has been written by social scientists from the United States, and we feel it suffers from a particular cultural bias; while we do not pretend to have overcome all our biases we have at least tried to be aware of them. The practical or policy problem linked to this is that the United States has been insistent that underdeveloped countries follow the path of the western capitalist "first world of development" (Horowitz, 1972); if they do not, it has been our policy to refuse foreign aid or to apply other economic pressures which are detrimental to economic development and modernization. In point of fact, however, the development path that most of the present industrialized nations followed, which relied heavily on the existence of large tracts of empty land for settlement as well as the presence of other countries to act as suppliers of the basic resources and raw materials for development, cannot be followed by those Third World countries that are presently trying to develop. Some other path has to be followed, but there is little basis at this time for generalizing about what path would be most appropriate for what country. Rather, what we need to do is to thoroughly study the various institutions and structures of the individual underdeveloped countries, identify specific problems, and point out potential obstacles to development. At the same time we must be fully aware that each country will have to elect its own path to development, and we must recognize that we may not always agree with the path they do elect. For those in the "First World," there must be this recognition of individual choice and a willingness to cooperate with the nations of the developing world. In a very pragmatic sense, the futures of both the developed and developing worlds are linked closely together, and it is in our own best interest to encourage the development process in the poorer countries of the world in every way we can.

Our approach is admittedly an oversimplified conception of an exceedingly complex problem, and it is necessary to stress that it is offered primarily as a means of establishing a general framework for analyzing the specific development problems of a given area. Not all underdeveloped areas will have a scarcity of natural resources, for example (although many will); not all such areas will be characterized by an inefficient use of those resources that do exist (although many will); not all underdeveloped areas have economies that are based on an historically exploitative relationship with the more advanced nations (although many do); and not all underdeveloped countries are in the midst of a demographic nightmare (although many are). Rather, the combination of specific sociocultural factors (and their positive or negative influence on economic and demographic behavior) can be expected to vary considerably among the different countries of the world. In fact, if there is any generalization that can be made with a high degree of confidence it is this: *the precise nature of the development problem, hence its most likely solution(s), will be situationally determined.* That is, each underdeveloped nation will be characterized by its own unique combination of circumstances relevant to its level of economic development; and each underdeveloped nation will have to be considered separately in order to arrive at a thorough understanding of what its particular problems are, and of what are likely to be the best solutions to its problems. The main point to stress, however, is that an adequate assessment of the nature of the development problem facing any given area must take into consideration these three separate dimensions of the problem: the economic, the demographic, and especially the sociocultural.

A Note on Terminology

The reader will have noted, and perhaps been confused by the different terms used to refer to the same status and/or process (e.g., some countries are rich, highly developed, modern, industrialized, etc., while others are poor, underdeveloped, traditional, etc; and the latter are attempting to go through a process of economic growth, economic development, modernization, etc., to become more like the former). We confess that such terms have been used interchangeably in this and the following chapters, and it is hoped that knowing this will minimize any confusion. We also want to emphasize that terms such as "poor" or "underdeveloped" are not used in a pejorative sense; nor do we mean to imply that a country wanting to "develop" or "modernize" has to become "Westernized" (i.e., has to become like "us"). Our basic position is that the countries of the world today can be arranged along a continuum at the ends of which there are two distinct polar types. At one end there are countries that are very rich and whose citizens are thriving at the highest levels of living that any society has ever enjoyed. At the other end there are countries that are very poor and whose citizens are suffering badly and barely subsisting at some of the lowest levels of living the world has ever seen. It makes little difference what one calls the countries at the opposing ends of the continuum; nor does it matter what we label the process whereby countries move away from the low end toward the high end. The important point is that these pronounced differences in living levels exist, and those who are located toward the low end of the continuum are in the midst of a struggle to overcome a wide variety of problems and obstacles in an attempt to move toward the high end. It is with the nature of this struggle and the problems associated with it that our book is concerned.

Organization of the Book

Following the three-pronged focus of the societal approach to understanding the situation in the Third World today, the remainder of the book will be divided into several chapters, each dealing with a specific aspect of the development problem. The next two chapters will present a general description and analysis of the first two basic dimensions of the problem—the economic dimension (chapter 2) and the demographic dimension (chapter 3). In each of these chapters the emphasis will be on a general description of their present economic and demographic characteristics, although some attention will also be given to the identification of some of the things that need to be done to aid the developing countries in their efforts to raise their current low economic status and to modernize their demographic situation.

Because the third (sociocultural) dimension is such a broad one, and because we see it as the most significant aspect of the problem, several chapters are devoted to its consideration. Following the description of the economic and demographic characteristcs of underdeveloped societies there is a chapter on the importance of various aspects of culture for economic development (chapter 4), and a chapter devoted to the special role of religion in relation to economic and demographic behavior (chapter 5). Chapter 6 will then discuss various aspects of social structure as they relate to the development process (e.g., the family, stratification systems, status and role of women in society), and chapter 7 will look at the important place of education in development planning. The next chapter will focus on the all important role that the state can and must play in guiding national development programs (chapter 8), and chapter 9 will consider the special case of the military as a potential agent of modernization. In all of these chapters the discussion will be divided into two broad sections—one focusing on the economic aspects of the development problem and one on the demographic aspects. In this way it is hoped to illustrate more clearly the particular relevance of each of the several sociocultural variables to the twin problems of economic growth and demographic modernization facing the Third World countries today. Finally, chapter 10 will draw together what has gone before and present a brief summary statement of the kinds of problems that must be faced and the kinds of programs that must be implemented to assist the emerging nations of Africa, Asia and Latin America as they strive to develop during the last decades of the twentieth century.

2

Economic Aspects of the Development Problem

In many respects, the economic aspect of the development problem is *the* development problem. That is, the most outstanding characteristic of underdeveloped areas is widespread poverty and an associated low level of living; the basic problem of development is one of reducing poverty and raising the living levels of the masses of the population in these countries. In this chapter we shall begin by presenting a working definition of an underdeveloped country, and then proceed to a more detailed description and discussion of some of the more common economic characteristics of such countries and the problems associated with them.

Definition of Underdevelopment

The initial task in an undertaking such as this is to define the unit of investigation. In this case the task becomes one of answering the question, What is a developing area? The answers to this question are many and varied and include consideration of such factors as climate, topography, natural resource base, level of technology, population growth rates,

various characteristics of the population (e.g., literacy, occupational skills), degree of urbanization and/or industrialization, level of political development, and the general
quality of life. Virtually all such definitions, however, have
one important element in common: more than anything else
an underdeveloped country is a poor country. It is one in
which the most obvious and outstanding characteristic is
widespread poverty that is chronic, not the result of some
temporary misfortune, and in which the majority of the population subsists at a very low level of living. In fact, poverty is
the outstanding characteristic of underdeveloped areas.

The significance of this economic dimension of the development problem is further emphasized by the common
practice of using some measure of a nation's average income
level, such as per capita income or per capita gross national
product as an index of its relative economic status. This
practice is illustrated by the data in Table 2.1 which show the
substantial size of the income gap that separates the countries of North America (Canada and the United States) from
the poorer countries of Africa, Asia, and Latin America.

Table 2.1 Per capita gross national product in U.S. dollars for the major regions of the world: 1976.*

World Regions	Per Capita Gross National Product
World	$1,650
Africa	440
Asia	610
Latin America	1,100
U.S.S.R.	2,760
Europe	4,420
Oceania	4,730
North America	7,850

Source: Population Reference Bureau, *1978 World Population Data Sheet,* Washington, D. C. 1978.

*The term "gross national product" refers to the sum of all the goods and services produced by a nation in a given year. *Per capita gross national product* is an indicator of the average income level of a nation, and reflects the share of a nation's wealth that each member of the population would receive each year if the gross national product was divided evenly among all the inhabitants of a nation.

There are, of course, numerous limitations to using national income data as an index of economic development.
For example, national income statistics do not include factors such as food grown for home consumption; nor do they
take into consideration the way in which income is distributed within a country. That is, there is no way to tell from
such average income levels the degree to which a nation's
income may be shared more or less equally among all its
citizens, or whether it is concentrated in the hands of a few
very wealthy families leaving the masses of the population
living in abject poverty. This problem can be illustrated by
reference to Romania and Venezuela. Both of these countries fell into the same development category in terms of per
capita income in 1970, but the proportion of the nation's
income that was concentrated in the hands of the richest 5
percent of the population was 40 percent in Venezuela as
compared to only 6 percent in Romania. At the other extreme, the lowest 20 percent of the population accounted for
only 2 percent of Venezuela's income in contrast to 24 percent in Romania. Thus, because of a more equitable distribution of its income, the average level of living in Romania
would be higher than in Venezuela, even though the latter
had a higher per capita income (International Bank, 1976).

Granted that these are indeed serious limitations, most
scholars in the field today would agree that per capita annual
income is an acceptable indicator of a nation's level of
economic development—particularly if it is used to make
only gross distinctions rather than as a basis for any precise
ranking of specific countries. To illustrate, one could justifiably conclude that the two countries of North America, both
of whom had per capita incomes in excess of $7,500, were
substantially more developed than the countries of West
Africa where comparable income levels ranged from $100 in
Mali to $610 in the Ivory Coast (Population Reference
Bureau 1978a). Within West Africa, however, it would be
difficult to justify the conclusion that Upper Volta with an
annual per capita income of $110 was "more developed"

than Mali, or that Senegal ($390) was more highly developed than Nigeria ($380) but less developed than Liberia ($450). Thus, while the existence and significance of various limitations to the use of income statistics as precise measures of economic status is acknowledged, such statistics can nevertheless be regarded as useful and meaningful indicators of gross differences in levels of economic development, especially when such statistics are used to identify extreme groups.

Levels of Living

There is one other limitation to the use of income statistics; defining underdevelopment solely in terms of a low per capita income glosses over the real characteristics of an underdeveloped area and ignores the miserable, poverty-stricken lives that most of the people in such areas lead. For the masses of the people living in Third World countries, underdevelopment is much more than a low income. It is being often hungry and having to subsist on a diet that is not only low in calories but frequently deficient in basic nutrients; it is a high rate of morbidity associated with malnutrition and the lessened ability of the body to resist various disease-causing microorganisms; it is a high level of infant and child mortality; it is an acute shortage of medical and paramedical personnel to provide needed health care; it is a high rate of illiteracy and a shortage of schools and teachers to remedy this situation; it is living in shanties and hovels that lack electricity, running water, toilet facilities, or even such basic home furnishings as chairs, beds, and cooking and eating utensils. In short, underdevelopment is a state of severe deprivation with respect to virtually everything that we in the United States and the other developed countries would regard as essential for maintaining a minimally adequate level of living. It is often difficult for a person who has not actually seen and smelled poverty to understand how depressing and debilitating it can be; yet the majority of the people in the world today live under such conditions. The reason for making this point is two-fold: first, to try and add a qualitative or subjective dimension to the quantitative indexes of development that are noted elsewhere in this volume; and second, to stress that the problem of underdevelopment is a human problem, not a statistical one, and that economic development entails much more than a simple increase in per capita income. It involves a substantial improvement in the social, economic, and personal well-being of the peoples now living in the underdeveloped areas of the world.

Scope of the Problem

Given the basic definition of a developing country as a poor, low-income country, the next question to be considered concerns how many underdeveloped countries there are, and what proportion of the world's population lives in such countries. In other words, "What is the scope of the problem of development?" The answer to this question obviously relates back to the definition of what constitutes a developing area. If we regard (as some do) all of Africa, Asia (excluding Japan and the Soviet Union), and Latin America as underdeveloped, then in 1978 approximately 3.1 billion people (73 percent of the world's population) were living in underdeveloped areas. In terms of the present income definition, the answer would depend on where one establishes the cut-off between "rich" and "poor." For example, if $800 (approximately one-half of the average income for the world as a whole) is selected as the level below which annual per capita income must fall if a country is to be classified as underdeveloped, then as of 1978 there were eighty-one underdeveloped countries inhabited by 2.6 billion people representing 61 percent of the world's population (Population Reference Bureau 1978a). Both of these definitions are somewhat arbitrary—the former would exclude Albania with a per capita GNP of $540, whereas the latter would exclude countries like Tunisia and Mexico with per capita GNP's of $840 and $1,090 respectively. Even with these qualifications, however, it is clear that anywhere from 2.5 to 3 billion people in the world today live in countries that by one definition or another would be classified as underdeveloped. Thus, the opening sentence of chapter 1 referring to "anywhere from two-thirds to three-fourths of the people in the world" seems amply justified. In any event, the reader is cautioned to be aware of the fact that statements about the extent of poverty and underdevelopment in the world today depend entirely on how one defines the cut-off point between poverty and affluence. At the same time, however, it should be clear that the problem with which we are dealing in this book is a very important one, and that it involves a clear and substantial majority of the world's population.

Economic Characteristics of Underdeveloped Areas

The term *underdeveloped* is a relative one, and when it is used to characterize a given country it means that the country so designated differs markedly in certain respects from some other country that would be regarded as "developed." In point of fact, we generally have a wide variety of criteria or standards of comparison in mind when we characterize a given country as being economically underdeveloped. Underdevelopment is a phenomenon or state that permeates a society. In this section we will examine a number of characteristics of two widely contrasting groups of countries— those that lie at the two extremes of the development continuum. In line with our basic three-fold conception of the development problem, the characteristics of developing countries can be divided into three basic categories: economic characteristics, demographic characteristics, and sociocultural characteristics. The discussion in this chapter will focus on the economic characteristics of underdeveloped areas, while the next chapter will be devoted to a detailed discussion of the demographic dimension of the development problem, and the several remaining chapters will be concerned with the various social and cultural aspects of the problem.

We will look at the economic characteristics of underdeveloped countries in terms of three factors: (1) income and savings performance; (2) the level of industrial development; and (3) the quality of human resources. Tables 2.2 through 2.5 show the wide differences between developed and developing countries with respect to selected economic characteristics. Although the data shown in these tables refer to the end of the 1960s and beginning of the 1970s (a circumstance necessitated by the time lag in the production and publication of all national statistics), the data that are available for more recent dates (International Bank, 1976) suggest that the basic patterns of differentiation have not changed very much since then.

Income and Saving

As has already been indicated several times, poverty—and extreme poverty at that—is the most outstanding characteristic of the developing countries of Africa, Asia and Latin America. Moreover, their very low incomes represent a major barrier to economic growth and development. To illustrate, one of the major consequences of this low income is that the domestic accumulation of capital is bound to be slow (Gill, 1967). Because income is the source of savings, a low per capita income necessarily means that per capita savings will also be low; and a low per capita savings performance necessarily means that savings will contribute a correspondingly smaller proportion to a nation's gross domestic product. The extent to which this phenomenon does in fact characterize development status is clearly revealed by the first characteristic presented in Table 2.2. Here it is readily apparent that the more highly developed countries, as measured by level of annual per capita income, save a far greater fraction of their total income than do the underdeveloped countries; and within this latter group the poorest countries, those with annual incomes of less than $100 per capita, have by far the poorest domestic savings record. The explanation of this relationship is relatively simple; among the poor countries the meager incomes must nearly all be spent on meeting basic consumption needs (e.g., food, clothing), and there is generally nothing left over to save. Translated to the societal level this means that little surplus income is available for investment in national development programs. In other words, the developing societies not only have much lower incomes than the more highly developed countries, they also have to use a larger share of that lower income for day-to-day maintenance expenses; the lower the economic status of a country the more pronounced this situation is.

A somewhat related issue or problem concerns the use to which savings are put. In many cases, as will be illustrated more fully in subsequent chapters, the savings that are accumulated are frequently invested in nonproductive areas: they are often used to purchase land or gold and jewelry for the purpose of enhancing individual wealth; or they are used for some religious or ceremonial purpose (e.g., financing a pilgrimage to Mecca). The problem then is not only one of scarce capital and a low rate of saving; it is also one of how savings and potential investment capital are actually used.

One of the major corollaries of a low saving performance is a low rate of investment and, consequently, a low rate of economic growth. Again, this is clearly revealed by the sec-

Table 2.2 Selected income characteristics of developed and developing countries: circa 1970.*

Income characteristics	Developed Countries	Developing Countries	
		Total	Poorest
Gross domestic savings as a percent of gross domestic product	24.3	14.7	10.3
Annual rate of increase (percent) in gross domestic product.	3.4	2.3	0.9

Source: Adapted from E. G. Stockwell, "The Dimensions of Development: An Empirical Analysis," *Population Review*, 18 (1974):35-51.

*The development classification is based on the following 1969-70 national per capita income levels: *Developed countries*, $1,500 or more; *Developing countries—total*, less than $500, *poorest*, less than $100.

ond item listed in Table 2.2 (the annual rate of increase in per capita gross domestic product). Considering this characteristic, the important point to note is *not* that all three groups of countries have experienced an increase in income as measured by each individual's share of the gross domestic product. Rather, the important point is that the data clearly suggest that the gap between the rich and the poor countries has been increasing. World economic development means more than a simple increase in the average income levels of the poor countries. It involves particularly a narrowing of the international income gap and a leveling of the economic differences among countries. Clearly this has not been happening. During the 1960s, to which the rates in Table 2.2 refer, the richer developed countries experienced an average increase in per capita gross domestic product (GDP) of 3.4 percent a year compared to only 2.3 percent for the developing countries. Among the poorest of the developing countries the annual rate of increase of GDP per capita was less than one percent. In other words, although all countries would appear to have gained in absolute terms, the fact that the poorest countries experienced the slowest rate of increase in their income means that the already sizeable gap between the "have" and "have not" nations of the world actually became wider. Thus in *relative* terms, rather than there being any trend toward an equalization of international economic differences, the rich have been getting richer and the poor have been getting poorer.

In pointing to the widening gap between the rich and poor countries it is also necessary to note that the same trend can often be observed *within* a developing country. That is, although per capita income may be increasing for a nation as a whole it is not uncommon to find it increasing faster among the higher income groups, thus contributing to a progressively greater maldistribution of wealth within a country. In the previously cited case of Venezuela, for example, the proportion of the national income received by the wealthiest 5 percent of the population rose from 20 percent in 1960 to 40 percent in 1970; and in Mexico during the same period it rose from 29 to 36 percent. In the United States, by contrast, the proportion of the nation's income concentrated in the hands of the wealthiest 5 percent fell from 16 to 13 percent between 1960 and 1970 (International Bank, 1976). Thus, while the level of income may be increasing for a country as a whole it is important to keep in mind that not all segments of the population may be benefiting equally from the increase, and that in many cases it will be creating a wider gap between the rich and poor groups, thus increasing the extent of relative poverty within a country. Such widening income gaps can contribute to the growth of jealousy and frustration, and be a source of potential conflict not only between nations but within them as well.

Getting back to the widening of international economic differences, what we have in effect is a situation in which the low income status of the underdeveloped countries is acting as one of the major obstacles to their economic development: the underdeveloped countries are poor because they do not develop, and they do not develop because they are poor. This situation is most aptly illustrated by the concept of the vicious circle of poverty. This concept can be diagrammed simply as in Figure 2.1.

That is, a low income means that there is a small capacity to save and thus a low rate of saving; a low rate of saving in turn means that there is a shortage of investment capital; a shortage of investment capital means that investment and consequently productivity will be low; and low productivity serves to perpetuate the low income situation.

Figure 2.1 Diagrammatic illustration of the "vicious circle of poverty."

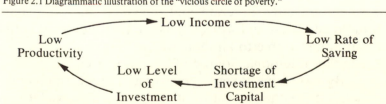

Sources of Capital Given that most developing countries can be characterized as capital-poor, and given that this
lack of capital is one of the major factors thwarting economic
development, it necessarily follows that one of the most
important tasks facing a developing country is to create the
necessary investment capital. Some of the more fortunate
developing nations have *natural resources* for which there is
a big world demand (oil would be a good example here); and
such nations (e.g., Nigeria, Venezuela, many of the Arab
states) can accumulate capital through the sale of these resources. Other less well endowed nations must rely on other
means for acquiring the capital needed to finance development.

From a traditional economic perspective, there are a
number of policies that might be adopted to create the capital
needed to raise the rate of investment (Gill, 1967:92-94). For
example, where there is an oversupply of labor, as is often
the case in the poor countries, capital can be accumulated by
increasing the labor input in the industrial sector at the same
time that wages are held down (The experience of the
People's Republic of China is a case in point). In this way,
both output and profits can be increased, and the higher
profits are available for investment. In any given case, however, this assumes that the government has sufficient control
or influence over industry to ensure that the increased profits
are in fact reinvested rather than used to widen the gap
between industrial owners and the workers. This approach
also suffers from the disadvantage that much of the supposed
oversupply of labor may be needed to increase agricultural
output and, hence, is not really available for industrial expansion. Further, even if not needed in agriculture, rural
workers are often illiterate and unskilled and often have
traditional beliefs and work habits, so that they may not be
easily transferrable to an industrial setting.

Another traditional source of investment capital is taxation. By increasing taxes a government can create capital
which it can either invest on its own or make available to

private investors. However, although taxation played a major role as a source of investment capital in the historical development of many nations (notably Japan and the U.S.S.R.), and although there is very likely a potential for raising taxes in many developing countries today, this too is limited as a method of capital accumulation. For one reason, higher taxes may act as a disincentive to investment (i.e., people may be unwilling to work harder to increase productivity if the extra income earned is taken away in the form of higher taxes). More important, however, these countries are by definition poor countries. Income levels are often barely adequate to meet basic subsistence needs, and as such do not represent a realistic tax base for increasing government revenues. Further, very often the bulk of the taxes that are collected are indirect taxes (International Bank, 1976). They are derived from import duties, or they are built into the cost of various goods rather than being levied on incomes; since all classes have to pay the same price for the same products, this situation means that the poor have to pay proportionately more taxes than the rich. In many Third World countries, then, one of the reforms needed is a change in the basic tax structure to spread the costs of development more equitably among the population.

Finally, governments in developing areas may accumulate capital by increasing government deficit spending. An increase in government deficit spending causes prices to rise (i.e., creates inflation), and rising prices mean rising profits which act as a stimulus to private investment. The problem here, however, especially for poor countries, is that the inflation spiral can easily get out of hand and be more harmful than beneficial. As prices increase, wages also have to increase so that workers have money to purchase goods; and as wages increase profit margins go down and the rate of capital accumulation falls off. Efforts to balance this by further price increases lead to still higher wages, declining profits, still further price increases, and so forth until prices for consumer goods are so high they cannot compete on the world market and a serious balance-of-payments problem may result. Thus, while most economists would likely feel that some inflation may be useful to stimulate investment, it is a very risky means of accumulating capital—especially in underdeveloped countries where personal incomes are so very low.

The Importance of Foreign Aid Given the widening economic gap that separates the rich from the poor countries, and given the difficulties just noted with respect to domestic capital formation, it can be argued quite strongly that outside capital assistance in the form of foreign aid will be a major prerequisite for economic growth in the present underdeveloped countries.

In the past, most developing countries have financed the bulk of their development programs by themselves, and most of them will continue to obtain the major portion of their development capital from domestic sources. However, this does not mean that these countries do not also need outside capital aid. In point of fact, the United Nations at one time defined an underdeveloped country as one that required external capital aid to help finance its development, and most countries that today fall into the underdeveloped category will depend heavily on foreign capital assistance for some time to come if they are to achieve any improvement in the living levels of their growing populations. The poorer a country is, the more outside capital aid it will need. This is because the poorest countries are not only in the worst position with respect to their ability to generate domestic capital, they are also the ones who are least able to cope with price fluctuations in the international economic system. What are "inconveniences" for the more highly developed countries are often stark tragedies for the poor countries. A good illustration of this point is provided by the tremendous increases in the price of oil that were levied by the Organization of Petroleum Exporting Countries (OPEC) during the early 1970s. Gasoline prices and home heating costs rose sharply in developed nations such as the United States, but the impact of these price hikes was much more devastating in those poor countries that were relying heavily on petroleum-based fertilizers, pesticides and herbicides to enhance their agricultural productivity. In commenting on this situation *Time* magazine noted that the increase in the price of petroleum products "critically undermined" the much heralded "Green Revolution." The new hybrid seeds that had produced the bumper crops of the late 1960s require, among other things, large amounts of fertilizer and pesticide, and by the time the developing countries had paid for their oil imports (up from $3.7 billion in 1972 to $15 billion in 1974) they had little capital left to buy the other chemicals and nutrients that their high-yield, intensive farming required. A country like India, for example, was able to afford only half the fertilizer that it needed to maximize agricultural output in 1974 (*Time*, November 11, 1974).

Over and above the need that the developing countries have for capital assistance is the idea that the richer nations have a moral responsibility to furnish this assistance. The basic argument in this case is that the poor nations played a major role in the historical growth of the western nations through the provision of labor, often in the form of slavery, and through the provision of a wealth of natural resources. Thus, it is only just that the countries who in the past benefitted economically from the exploitation of others should today bear the major responsibility for financing the economic growth and development of those nations that were (and in many cases still are!) major suppliers of raw materials for the industrialized world. As noted in the earlier discussion of dependency theory, development and underdevelopment have historically been dynamically interrelated in a single process. The economic growth and development of the western industrialized nations was facilitated and is still partially supported by their ability to draw heavily on the resources and raw materials of the underdeveloped countries. Part of the solution to the development problem will necessarily entail a restructuring of this exploitative relationship. The end of this exploitative relationship will mean that the developing countries will be in a much better position to accumulate their own development capital from domestic sources and will, accordingly, have less need for external capital assistance.

With respect to this issue of moral responsibility, some scholars believe that economic blocs that emerge within the developing world can (or even should) adopt policies that will be less harmful to other poor countries than the above cited OPEC price increases. For example, such blocs could establish a differential price structure for their raw materials, making the rich countries pay proportionately more and the poor countries proportionately less for the products in question. This would be an indirect way in which the industrialized nations could be "encouraged" to meet their responsibility for aiding the economic development of the Third World. For the present, however, largely because they have such a long way to go to catch up, and because of their particularly vulnerable position with respect to international economic changes such as the OPEC price increases, extensive direct foreign aid will continue to be a major prerequisite for economic development in many of the Third World countries.

Limitations of Foreign Aid Although it is generally accepted that foreign assistance is necessary to alleviate the shortage of investment capital in the underdeveloped areas, and although many of the developed countries have foreign aid programs of one kind or another, it is important to recognize that external capital aid will not in itself be sufficient to generate sustained economic growth. One of the reasons why this is so relates to the demographic situation in many of the aid recipient countries (see following chapter). In many of the developing countries the initial impact of any improvement in the level of living will be a drop in the death rate, particularly the infant death rate. This means that a larger proportion of the babies that are born will survive and contribute to an increase in the population. This situation, often referred to as the Malthusian Dilemma (see below) means that instead of having a positive economic effect, foreign aid may have only a demographic effect; instead of raising the level of living of a fixed number of people, foreign aid ends up being used to support a larger population at the old low level of living. Thus, to the extent that their populations continue to increase, it will seriously limit the value of foreign aid to the developing countries.

Even if active steps are taken to lower the birth rate and forestill the Malthusian Dilemma there are a number of other reasons why external capital assistance will not by itself solve the problem of economic development. For one thing, the amount of capital that a nation can absorb into its economy depends in part on how much it already has. Providing diesel engines and a fleet of railway cars is not going to do much to enhance the transportation system if there are no tracks; nor are trucks of much use in countries which lack a network of interconnected highways, or where heavy rains or floods make major roads impassable during much of the year. An automobile factory requires not only a skilled labor supply but also the development of other auxiliary industries such as steel mills to furnish the necessary parts and raw materials. What this all means is that both the underdeveloped areas and the donor nations will have to work actively to create a situation in which to fit incoming capital. This goes back to what was said earlier about developing countries having to generate a major share of their investment capital from domestic sources. To this we can now add that the value of foreign aid will increase directly with the extent to which a country is successful in accumulating domestic capital.

A second limitation derives from the fact that low income countries are not the most attractive places in which to invest capital. Hence, they have difficulty attracting it from external sources, particularly from private investors seeking short-run profits. This problem often results from the fact that many underdeveloped countries are characterized by an unstable political situation. Where this is the case capital investment may be discouraged for fear that it will be lost, as, for example, when newly emerging nation states have expropriated or nationalized the holdings of foreign based multinational corporations. While there is definitely something to be said in favor of such expropriation, the existence of such a threat is not likely to encourage an inflow of private investment capital. This possibility should not, however, be a major deterrent where national governments are concerned, especially if the donor nation has accepted the moral obligation to "repay" the developing world for its past contributions to the economic growth and development of the industrialized nations. And there is some evidence that the richer nations may be willing to assume part of this responsibility, at least to the extent of increasing the size of their foreign aid programs. A number of European countries, for example, have reached or surpassed the target of "one percent of gross national product" for foreign aid recommended by the United Nations General Assembly in 1960. There are even signs that the United States may be contributing a larger share of its wealth to the developing nations—the $7.4 billion that President Carter requested for foreign aid for the 1978 fiscal year represented more than a 100 percent increase over the amount expended on foreign aid a decade ago (Pearson, et al., 1969).

But there is one other problem that needs to be mentioned in connection with foreign aid, and that concerns the uses to which such aid is put. There are many ways that incoming capital may be used in developing nations, not all of which will be beneficial for economic growth (Novack and Lekachman, 1969: especially pp. 348-74). To illustrate, if the foreign aid is used to build up the military establishment (as has happened in some countries, notably in South Korea and a number of Latin American countries), or if it is used to construct ostentatious symbols of development to generate national pride (as when Sukarno diverted a lot of Indonesia's development capital for the construction of a modern hotel, a stadium complex, department stores and monuments), or if it is used as a form of bribery to obtain favors of one kind or another (such as trade concessions, a favorable vote in the United Nations, or permission for the donor country to establish and maintain military bases in the recipient country), then such aid is not likely to have much of an effect in promoting overall economic development. A specific case in point is the changing composition of U.S. foreign aid since the end of World War II. According to data published by the U.S. Bureau of the Census in the 1976 *Statistical Abstract of the United States*, the total amount of American foreign aid was approximately the same—$35-36 billion—for the two periods 1946-52 and 1971-74. However, the proportion of total aid dollars earmarked for economic programs has declined dramatically. In the immediate postwar period 89 percent of foreign aid funds were for economic aid, but in the more recent period this proportion was down to 43 percent. The proportion that went for military aid, on the other hand, rose from only 11 percent in 1946-52 to 57 percent for the years 1971-74 (Smith, 1978). Such a trend is not likely to be in the best interest of the developing countries. What is really needed in this respect is not simply foreign aid, but foreign aid that is (1) given with no strings attached so that the recipient nations can use it for whatever development program it wishes, and foreign aid that is (2) used by the recipient country to finance domestic development programs aimed at increasing per capita productivity and raising the living level of the population.

Industrial Development

Another characteristic commonly associated with under-developed areas is that they are predominantly agrarian societies with a very low level of industrial development. This lack of industrial development is in fact a major determinant of their generally low productivity and low incomes discussed in the preceding section. The low level of industrialization characterizing the countries of the Third World is clearly illustrated, first of all, by the very large proportion of the labor force in developing areas that is engaged in agricultural activities (see Table 2.3). In contrast to the most highly developed countries where an average of 14 percent of the adult working population is engaged in agriculture, fully two-thirds of the work force in the developing nations is engaged in some kind of agricultural activity. Among the poorest countries—those with an annual per capital income of less than $100—agricultural workers comprise fully 85 percent of the economically active population.

The overriding significance of agriculture in the economies of the underdeveloped areas is further revealed by the fraction that the agricultural sector contributes to a nation's income. Again referring to Table 2.3 it can be seen that agriculture accounts for an average of 32 percent of the gross domestic product in the developing countries as compared to only 7 percent among the richer nations; and in the poorest group of developing countries the low income producing agricultural sector accounts for just over half of the annual gross domestic product.

Two other measures have been included here to illustrate

Table 2.3 Selected industrialization characteristics of developed and developing countries: circa 1970.

Industrialization characteristics	Developed Countries	Developing	
		Total	Poorest
Percent of economically active population in agriculture	14.0	67.2	84.6
Percent of gross domestic product contributed by agriculture	7.1	31.7	50.7
Annual per capita consumption of energy (kgs. of coal equivalent)	5,211	329	55
Annual per capita consumption of steel (kgs.)	471	28	6

Source: Adapted from E. G. Stockwell, "The Dimensions of Development: An Empirical Analysis," *Population Review*, 18 (1974):35-51.

the pronounced differences between developed and under-developed countries with respect to their level of industrial development, namely, the amount of commercial energy and steel that is consumed. Considering energy first, it has been suggested recently that the replacement of animate by in-animate sources of energy (e.g., the replacement of human and animal power by coal or electricity) is one of the most notable characteristics of economic development (Weller and Sly, 1969). The magnitude of this association is clearly revealed in Table 2.3 where it can be seen that on the average the most highly developed countries consume nearly sixteen times as much energy per capita in a year than the developing countries taken as a whole, and nearly one hundred times as much as that consumed in the poorest group of countries! A similar pattern characterizes the level of steel consumption. In this case the average person in the high income countries consumes approximately seventeen times as much steel in a year as the average inhabitant of the developing world, and roughly eighty times as much as the average person in the poorest group of undeveloped countries.

Natural Resources A discussion of the level of indus-trial development of a nation or group of nations necessarily has to consider the issue of natural resources—not only the raw materials and energy sources needed for industrial ac-tivities, but also land, the basic agricultural resource. In some developing countries, there is just not much usable farm land available in relation to the size of the population, and such countries may face a very real problem in providing an adequate food supply for their inhabitants. Egypt is an especially significant case in point. In that country, accord-ing to recent estimates, the level of agricultural density (i.e., the number of persons per square kilometer of arable land) was 1,172 (International Bank, 1976). This figure contrasts sharply with the 47 inhabitants per square kilometer in the United States at the same time and with the 239 estimated for the industrialized nations as a whole. Other developing countries with an even higher agricultural density were the

Republic of Korea (1,337) and the Republic of China (1,610). Among the industrialized nations only Japan, with one of the most highly developed systems of intensive agriculture in the world today, has an agricultural density of this magnitude (1,610 in 1970). For most industrialized countries the agricultural man-land ratio is well below 300 persons per square kilometer.

Aside from quantity (availability) of agricultural land, the basic problem in many developing countries is often one of quality. For example, according to one estimate (Gill, 1967), fully one-fourth of the total land area which is being or has been cultivated in Latin America has lost its topsoil through erosion. In Africa, overgrazing has resulted in such massive degradation of the soil that some countries are already facing a crisis situation. The seriousness of this problem was most alarmingly illustrated in the late 1960s and early 1970s when the poor soil conditions were aggravated by a prolonged drought and a number of African countries, notably those in the Sahel region—Senegal, Mauritania, Mali, Upper Volta, Niger, and Chad—experienced devastating food shortages (DuBois, 1974).

Another important point that needs to be made in relation to agriculture and the production of food concerns the nature of the crops that are planted. This problem can be viewed in part as another legacy of colonialism. Historically, many of the Third World countries were looked upon by the western industrial nations as sources of cheap raw materials and as markets for manufactured goods. Hence, they were encouraged to develop an agriculture based on export crops (coffee, cocoa, copra, rubber, etc.) rather than on food products. In many parts of the Third World the advent of commercial farming has led to the consolidation of land holdings into large estates or plantations, and land that might otherwise have been available for domestic food production was converted to the cultivation of these export cash crops. Further, as demand for these export products has increased over the years, larger and larger areas of land have been put into cultivation to produce them, and this has often resulted in increasingly smaller areas being available to grow food for local consumption. Consequently, many underdeveloped countries that were once major exporters of food have in recent years come to rely heavily on food imports to sustain their growing populations.

Even where agriculture has not become commercialized, many of the developing countries are characterized by systems of land tenure that are not conducive to increasing agricultural output. In many parts of Asia, for example, it has long been the custom for all sons to inherit an equal share of the family land holdings upon the death of the father, and a system of fragmented land holding has evolved in which the land a man owns is subdivided into so many small plots scattered over such a wide area that it is virtually impossible to farm efficiently since such small scattered holdings are not amenable to modern agricultural technology such as the use of tractors and other mechanized equipment. In still other areas a long-standing landlord-tenant situation may exist which is characterized by such things as exorbitant rent fees for the landlord and the absence of security of tenure for the tenant. A tenant who has no guarantee that he will be able to continue farming a given piece of land, or who has to pay a higher rent if his output is increased (usually a fixed proportion of the crop) is not likely to have much incentive to try to develop and improve the land. Related to these land ownership problems are a wide variety of problems concerning such things as confusion over water rights and land titles, inadequate agricultural credit systems, tax rates that are geared to output levels, laws requiring the sale of a portion of the crop to the government for less than the prevailing market price, etc., all of which seriously aggravate the land resource problem and clearly point out another major need that most developing countries face today—the need for substantial agrarian reform programs. The importance of such reforms, and the desire for them among the agricultural classes, is clearly revealed by the fact that all political movements in the Third World, revolutionary or otherwise, list agrarian reform as one of their primary objectives.

With regard to other natural resources such as fossil fuels, metal ores, and forest products, the developing countries are generally better off than they are with respect to land and agricultural productivity. On the one hand, many of them are very well endowed with supplies of particular resources. The oil reserves in several of the low income countries is a prime example (e.g., Nigeria, Venezuela, and several of the Middle East Arab nations), but it is far from being the only one. Other nations have large and valuable reserves of such mineral resources as bauxite, copper, zinc, manganese, tin and other metals for which there is a large and growing world demand. In fact, as noted above, it was often the presence of these particular resources that led to the colonial domination and exploitation that is at least partly responsible for their current underdeveloped state. Many of the present developing countries are not exploiting the natural resources they have available only because they have not developed the industries to process them. Rather, they have historically been developed by the present industrialized countries to serve as suppliers of rather than users of their raw materials. The problem in this regard, then, is not so much one of an inadequate supply of important natural resources in the developing countries as it is one of achieving greater control over and a more appropriate utilization of existing resources to benefit their own economies rather than those of the more highly developed industrial nations. Once again, the establishment of OPEC to control the price and distribution of oil resources can be cited as an illustration of how the developing countries can make better use (for themselves) of their particular natural resource base.

Another reason why nonfood resources are not such a serious issue for the developing areas today (even for those nations that are not particularly well blessed in this regard) lies in the fact that so many major technological advances have been made in the world. This means that many resources that were once very important will play a much more limited role in economic development in the future. Progress in transportation, for example, makes it much easier today to redistribute basic resources and raw materials from one area to another. To cite another illustration, the development of synthetic substances has greatly reduced the significance of some raw materials (e.g., rubber). Further, continued progress in technology can be expected to reduce the importance of still other natural resources in the years to come. The development of either nuclear or solar energy, for example, will greatly reduce the economic significance of petroleum and other fossil fuels. Much of this optimism with respect to nonfood resources is of course predicated on the assumption that the richer developed countries will take more active steps (e.g., by removing trade barriers or expanding foreign assistance programs) to share their knowledge, wealth, and technology with the less developed countries. It also assumes that the various mineral resources will not be soon exhausted as world consumption levels continue to increase. Whether or not either of these assumptions is justified remains to be seen. Nevertheless, it can be concluded that while the scarcity of nonfood resources may limit a country's development, this need not be the case in today's modern world. As noted earlier, however, the food situation appears to be much less optimistic, and may in fact be approaching a crisis state in many developing countries. Because this is such a crucial issue in the world today it is discussed more fully in the following section.

The Food Crisis The problem of feeding the people of the world is as old as mankind itself, and there is every indication that it is going to remain a problem for some time to come. According to recent estimates of the Food and Agricultural Organization of the United Nations the years between 1970 and 1985 will see the population of the developing countries increase by 49 percent. During this same period it is estimated that food production in these areas will increase by only 39 percent (Environmental Fund, 1975b).

These two trends clearly reveal what is perhaps the major problem facing the world's underdeveloped areas today— the problem of finding ways to feed their large and rapidly growing populations. One of the first scholars in the modern era to call attention to the problem of the relationship between population growth and the food supply was the British clergyman-economist, Thomas Robert Malthus. Writing in England at the close of the eighteenth century, Malthus formulated a "principle of population" that was based on two postulates and one assumption. The two postulates were: (1) people cannot live without food; and (2) the human sex drive, which shows no sign of diminishing, is so strong that the human race will always be in danger of increasing its numbers at a faster rate than it is able to increase the food supply. More specifically, Malthus *assumed* that population was capable of increasing exponentially, doubling itself every twenty-five years or so, whereas the best one could anticipate with respect to food production was an arithmetic rate of increase. In Malthus' own words:

> . . . the power of population is infinitely greater than the power in the earth to produce subsistence for man. Population, when unchecked, increases in a geometrical ratio. Subsistence increases only in an arithmetical ratio. A slight acquaintance with numbers will show the immensity of the first power in comparison of the second. (Malthus, 1959:5)

The "immensity of the first power in comparison of the second" is clearly illustrated by the following progressions:

```
Population:  1 ........2 ........4 ........8 ........16 .......
      Food:  1 ........2 ........3 ........4 ........5 ........
```

In the second term of the above progressions the increase in the food supply is keeping pace with the growth of population; but the third term is obviously untenable as it indicates a population size (4) in excess of the food supply (3). Clearly, something has to happen to prevent population from growing beyond the number that can be sustained by the available food supply.

In order to keep the size of the population within the limits set by the ability to produce food, Malthus believed that some check to population growth would always be necessary. He explicitly recognized two such checks: positive checks (e.g., war, famine, disease), or those checks which held population size down by increasing the number of deaths; and preventive checks (by which he meant "moral restraint," or such things as delayed marriage and total sexual abstinence outside of marriage), or those checks which controlled population size by reducing the number of births.

Based on his two postulates, the assumption, and the associated perceived need for checks to curtail population growth, Malthus formulated a three part "principle of population" which can be summarized as follows:

1. The size of the population is limited by the size of the available food supply.
2. Because of the strong human sex drive, any increase in the food supply will be followed by an increase in population unless something happens to prevent it.
3. The various things that can happen to prevent population from increasing fall into one of two categories—"moral restraint" (preventive checks) or "vice and misery" (positive checks).

Although implicit in this "principle of population" is the clear provision that people could, by exercising moral restraint, keep population size within the limits set by the food supply, Malthus himself was not very optimistic about this happening. He regarded the human sex drive as so powerful that people would be unlikely to exercise such moral restraint. Hence, he foresaw a world where war, disease, and periodic famine would always be with us to curb the tendency to increase population beyond the maximum number that could be supported by the available food supply.

Needless to say, the Malthusian "principle of population" was not received with open arms when it was first published in 1798. The late eighteenth century in European history was a period of widespread optimism concerning man's future,

and philosophers and social critics were coming to believe
that people were perfectible and easily capable of creating a
better world for themselves. In this atmosphere, the virtually
unmitigated pessimism of "Parson Malthus" was decidedly
unwelcome, and its appearance generated a literary con-
troversy that carried over into the field of economics and
lasted well into the nineteenth century. During the late
nineteenth century, however, a declining death rate and
increasing rates of population growth were accompanied by
tremendous social and economic advances which contributed to substantial increases in the level of living. In light of
these developments there seemed little justification for
bothering with the doomsday theories of an eccentric English clergyman, and the world appeared more or less to forget
Malthus. But developments during the years since the end of
World War II have reawakened concern over the old Malthusian hypothesis that the human race was doomed to a
miserable existence because of the ever-present tendency
for population to outstrip the food supply.

  According to one recent estimate (Kanthi et al., 1976), the
seriousness of the situation today is revealed by the fact that
more than 2.5 billion people already subsist on diets that are
well below the optimal levels required for survival. Combine
this figure with what since 1970 has been a downward trend
in the size of the world's fish catch, extended drought and
crop failures in many parts of the world, serious flooding that
has destroyed food crops in other parts, and a steady increase in the number of people that have to be fed, and the
food crisis assumes seemingly insurmountable proportions.
The very real potential of the Malthusian crisis is illustrated
further by the data presented in Table 2.4. Taking the underdeveloped areas of the world as a whole it can be seen that
there has been little change in the rate of population growth
in recent years; the average rate of increase in population
was 2.4 percent per year during both 1960-65 and 1965-73. By
contrast, there was a notable decline in the annual rate of
increase in agricultural production—from 4.4 percent during

1960-65 to 3.0 percent between 1965 and 1973. Taking these areas as a whole, then, it is apparent that the rate of increase in agricultural output had managed to stay ahead of population growth. However, there is room for some question as to how long this situation can continue, especially if the annual rate of increase in food production were to continue to decline (see the earlier cited projections of the Food and Agricultural Organization of the United Nations that foresee population overtaking and exceeding the food supply in the developing countries during the 1980s). More significantly however, when one looks at specific regions and countries, it is clear that the situation has already reached a crisis state. In both the Middle East and in the Latin American countries of the Western Hemisphere the most recent period has seen the average annual rate of increase in agricultural production fall below the rate of population growth, and in Africa food production increases have just managed to keep pace with population growth. The problem is clearly most serious in those African nations of the Sahel region that were so hard hit by the severe drought conditions that prevailed during the early 1970s. In all six of these nations, the annual rate of agricultural output has *declined* since 1965, in spite of continued high rates of population growth. The results here have been critical food shortages, widespread hunger and malnutrition, a substantial rise in the death rate, and a catastrophic upsetting of (and perhaps an end to) the traditional ways of life in this part of the world.

Although not many underdeveloped nations are as yet as bad off in this respect as those of the Sahel region (not many have experienced declines in agricultural productivity), a large number have recently entered a period of potential Malthusian crisis. Between 1965 and 1973, for example, the annual rate of population growth exceeded the annual rate of increase in agricultural production in at least forty-two of the developing countries in Asia, Africa, and Latin America (International Bank, 1976); and, as of the summer of 1978, a reported twenty-six countries encompassing some 230 mil-

Table 2.4 Recent annual growth rates for population and agricultural production: selected developing areas.

| Developing areas | Annual rate (%) of increase in: | | | |
| | Population | | Agricultural production | |
	1960-65	1965-73	1960-65	1965-73
All developing countries	2.4	2.4	4.4	3.0
Middle East	3.0	3.0	5.1	2.9
Africa	2.5	2.4	2.7	2.4
South Asia	2.4	2.3	1.4	3.4
East Asia	2.5	2.4	8.2	3.6
Western Hemisphere	2.9	2.8	3.9	2.7
Sahel Region:				
Chad	1.5	2.0	0.7	−3.7
Mali	2.5	2.0	3.2	−2.5
Mauritania	1.2	2.5	2.9	−2.2
Niger	2.8	2.6	5.3	−4.5
Senegal	2.0	2.2	2.5	−3.6
Upper Volta	2.2	2.1	5.2	−0.6

Source: International Bank for Reconstruction and Development, *World Tables, 1976*, Johns Hopkins Press, 1976, pp. 392-95.

lion people were experiencing abnormal food shortages, mostly as a result of shortfalls in food production during the preceding year (Population Reference Bureau, 1978b). This situation cannot go on for long, and it clearly emphasizes the need for continued concerted efforts to increase agricultural output throughout the world.

Although increases in agricultural output are essential, and although there are many ways in which food production can be increased—expanding the amount of acreage under cultivation, increasing per acre yields through the use of hybrid seed, developing new foods such as algae derivatives, etc.—it must be stressed that such measures alone are not going to alleviate the world food crisis. One difficulty here is the fact that the potential consumers of any food increases are already alive. Since a large portion of the world's people are already living close to bare subsistence levels, any increases in food production will be quickly absorbed by the already existing surplus population. Moreover, as population continues to grow—and one of the ironic aspects of the situation is that such growth is facilitated by the mortality reductions that generally accompany increases in the quantity and quality of the food supply—the level of food consumption in the developing countries could fall even lower in the years ahead. These facts clearly emphasize the need for some sort of check on population growth. If they are to be of any value in reducing world hunger, any increases in food production must be accompanied by declines in the rate of the population growth (i.e., by declines in the number of births). In fact, some experts are of the opinion that significant improvements in per capita food supply are not likely to be achieved until population growth rates in the developing countries have been reduced (Johnson, 1976). Although many authorities anticipate being able to maintain existing levels of per capita food production through the end of the century, after that it will become more and more difficult for food output growth to keep pace with continuing population growth.

One other point needs to be made in relation to the world food supply and that concerns the consumption levels in the developed countries. A simple example will serve to illustrate this point. It is estimated that the average American consumes about 2,000 pounds of grain per year, most of which is consumed indirectly in the form of meat, poultry, eggs and milk (i.e., animals are first fed the grain and we then eat the animal products). In a country like India, by contrast, the average person consumes about 400 pounds of grain per year, most of which is consumed directly in the form of bread and cereal products. In other words, the average American consumes roughly five times as much grain per year as the average Indian. The difference of course is due to the fact that it takes several pounds of grain to produce a single pound of animal product (e.g., approximately eight pounds of grain are needed to produce one pound of beef); and one implication of this differential is that even a slight modification in the diet of Americans and other industrialized peoples, such as eating one pound of meat less per person per month, could theoretically free up millions of tons of grain per year for export to the developing societies. While such a proposal may sound utopian in that it ignores various political-economic problems, as well as the logistical problems of distribution, the fact remains that a significant dimension of the present world food crisis (and the crisis with respect to many of the earth's other resources as well) can be traced to the extraordinarily high consumption levels in the industrialized countries.

To summarize briefly, a major task confronting the poorer countries of the world today is to prevent population from increasing at a faster rate than the projected rate of increase in food production; this will entail a reduction in fertility through a wider adoption of modern birth control techniques. The alternative will be a continuation of and perhaps even an increase in the poverty, misery, and hunger characterizing the lives of the majority of the world's population. It should be eminently clear that the problem of achieving the needed increases in food production today and in the years ahead would be made substantially easier, and the risk of failure would be considerably diminished, if the rate of population growth in the developing countries would slow down and if the level of consumption in the developed countries would be reduced. All of the experts who have studied the situation agree on this key issue. In fact, many would go a step further and say that unless the growth of population does slow down and slow down considerably in the near future, there is a real danger that the present abject conditions of life in many of these countries will become even worse. Indeed, there is evidence that they were already getting worse in the early 1970s when a number of poor countries experienced at least temporary upturns in the death rate associated with increasing hunger and nutritional stress (Brown, 1976). In any case, as long as the tendency persists for population to grow more rapidly than the food supply, all the talk about using the wonders of science to increase food production and to raise levels of living in the underdeveloped world borders on fantasy.

The major difference between the advanced nations of the Western world and the underdeveloped countries today is that when the former industrialized they had relatively small populations and seemingly unlimited resources. The developing countries, however, often have large and rapidly growing populations; in many cases their resources have been depleted to provide raw materials for western development. The dilemma they face today is truly a monumental one. They are characterized by inadequate levels of industrialization, and they are facing serious problems of increasing their agricultural output in order to meet the needs of their growing populations. It is going to be difficult, if not impossible, to do one without the other. Since it is through the application of industrial technology—e.g., chemical fertilizers and pesticides, farm machinery—that agricultural production will be increased, industrial development is needed for agricultural development. At the same time, an agricultural surplus is needed to provide both the investment capital and the labor for industrial development. In many cases a decision may have to come down to either sacrificing the living standards of the people in order to promote industrialization or to delay industrial development in order to meet some of the consumption demands of the people—that is, a choice between "bread or steel" (De Castro, 1967:56). All too often it is a decision that may have to be made at the same time they are trying to contend with the problems of rapid population growth that are aggravating what is already a bad situation in many countries. While it may be true to say that hunger will be conquered only through development, it is also true that the present world food crisis stands today as a major obstacle to development. To ignore this situation, to ignore the need to slow down population growth rates, is to court disaster for the struggling peoples throughout the Third World.

An end to population growth will certainly not, by itself, solve this or any other aspect of the development problem, but it will make the eventual solution that much easier; the longer it takes to slow down the rate of population growth the longer will be the delay in alleviating the present world food crisis, and the longer the process of economic development will take.

Human Resources

It is conventional for economists to speak of productive resources in terms of three basic categories: (1) land, or natural resources; (2) labor, or human resources; and (3) capital. As we have noted in the preceding pages of this chapter, the problems most commonly associated with capital and land resources are primarily quantitative—they are often in short supply, particularly capital resources. This is certainly not the case with respect to labor. On the contrary, human resources (people) are one commodity that most poor countries generally have in large supply. Rather than being quantitative, the problems associated with human resources are more likely to reflect questions of quality and efficiency of utilization. Some of these problems, such as cultural attitudes that may effect work productivity, will be discussed in later chapters. In the remainder of this chapter we shall consider those objective characteristics of the labor force (i.e., skill, training and health) that directly affect productive efficiency.

Before discussing some of these problems, however, it is worth noting that at least one country—the People's Republic of China—has taken good advantage of its human resources to foster economic development. When the government of Mao Tse-tung came to power it was well aware that the country was poor in capital but rich in people, and a major part of its development program was based on the mobilization of its human resources. While Westerners may lament the loss of freedom and severe regimentation that accompanied this forced collective effort, the fact remains that the intensive use of human labor was the means by which millions of miles of dikes were repaired and constructed and millions of miles of irrigation canals were built, thus permitting a substantial increase in the amount of land available for agricultural cultivation (De Castro, 1967:31-32). While the scarcity of data from China makes it difficult to measure accurately the economic progress that has been made, the point is that the government did rely heavily on the one outstanding resource at its disposal—a large population—in its post-World War II efforts to stimulate the growth of the national economy.

While it is possible that other countries with large populations might also be able to enhance their development by means of a fuller utilization of their human resources, there is one serious limitation that needs to be considered. Specifically, although many underdeveloped areas have large populations, they often have a relatively smaller labor force than do the more advanced countries. That is, as the first entry in Table 2.5 indicates, the less developed countries are characterized by a smaller proportion of adults that are economically active; for example nearly 60 percent of the adult males in the developed countries are economically active in contrast to just under half the males in both of the underdeveloped groups. Since these data refer to the "nonchild" population (generally persons age fourteen or over, although in some cases the age limit may be as low as six or seven years), the observed differences cannot be accounted for in terms of possible differences in age composition. These differences in the relative size of the working population suggest that at least part of the development problem may be traced to the fact that in the poorer countries a smaller number of producers has to support a larger number of dependents. The potential seriousness of this problem may be emphasized by noting that the statistics here refer only to the number who are counted as being economically active without any regard for the amount of activity in which they are engaged or for its productivity. That is, no consideration has been given to the possibility of underemployment among the economically active population (i.e., persons working well below their productive capacity, such as only a few hours a day, or only one or two days a week, or working at nonproductive tertiary activities); and such underemployment has long been recognized as a major factor effecting productivity in the underdeveloped countries (Nagi, 1971).

Not only do underdeveloped areas commonly have a smaller labor force relative to the size of the total population, but also, at least in terms of particular technical skills, the smaller number of workers are qualitatively deficient as well. This is aptly illustrated by the second entry in Table 2.5. Here one can see that there is a clear-cut direct association between development status and the percentage of economically active males who possess some skill or who have had some kind of technical training. This relationship would suggest that many of the skills necessary for the development of a modern industrial state are in extremely short supply in many of the world's underdeveloped countries.

Still another indicator of the quality of the labor force is its educational status, particularly its level of literacy. The im-

Table 2.5 Selected socioeconomic characteristics of the population of developed and developing countries: circa 1970.

| | | Developing Countries | |
Socioeconomic Measures	Developed	Total	Poorest
Percent of males who are economically active	58.8	49.5	49.7
Percent of working males with some kind of skill or technical training.	47.7	19.5	6.3
Percent illiterate	0.9	63.7	83.2
Average per capita daily calorie consumption	3,089	2,231	2,089
Percent of calories derived from animal protein	41.3	9.8	6.1

Source: Adapted from E. G. Stockwell, "The Dimensions of Development: An Empirical Analysis," *Population Review*, 18 (1974):35-51.

portance of a certain threshold of literacy and the generally positive role of education in economic development has been discussed at length in the literature (see chapter 7). In general, it may be said that education derives its importance in part from the enrichment of the lives of individuals and in part by improving their earning potential. This latter function is especially significant for economic development because it is one of the principal means of expanding the productivity of the economy. The problem of course relates to the fact that the overall level of educational attainment is quite low among the poor countries—the poorer the country, the lower its educational status. Again referring to the statistics presented in Table 2.5, one can observe a pronounced inverse relationship between economic status and educational attainment as measured by the percent of the population that is illiterate. In this instance the range is from just under 1 percent in the developed countries to 83 percent among those poorest countries where per capita incomes are less than $100 a year. Although there are many limitations to these data (stemming largely from international differences in the definition of such basic concepts as "literacy" and "adult population"), the marked differences that are revealed with respect to this characteristic can only be interpreted as highlighting the decidedly disadvantaged position of low income countries in terms of the overall educational attainment level of their population.

To the preceding must be added the "brain drain" problem that has plagued many developing countries during the post-World War II era. The migration stream from the Third World to the more advanced nations during this period has been dominated by skilled labor and scientific personnel. In many cases, as in the United States, this has been encouraged by immigration laws that give preference to persons possessing marketable skills such as scientists, engineers, and physicians; the developed countries have benefited enormously from the economic contribution of these new immigrants. At the same time, however, the developing countries have suffered a severe economic loss: often having invested heavily in their education and training, they have not been able to reap the benefits of their potential productivity. In summary, then, their generally low levels of educational attainment, coupled with frequent losses to emigration among the educated few, represents still another of the many and varied problems that must be overcome by the developing countries in their continuing struggle to achieve a higher level of living.

One final variable influencing the productive efficiency of "human resources" in the developing countries is their health status. One of the more important indicators of health status is the nature of the diet, specifically the quantity and quality of the food consumed. Once again the data presented in Table 2.5 clearly point to the thoroughly disadvantaged position of the poorer countries. In the first place it can be seen that the average daily calorie consumption among the more highly developed countries (3,089) is 38 percent higher than among the underdeveloped areas taking as a whole (2,231), and as much as 47 percent higher than in the poorest of the undeveloped countries (2,089).

One might argue with some justification that statistics on average calorie consumption levels cannot be accurately evaluated without reference to variations in caloric need as determined by such things as age, sex, and body structure. Thus, these data cannot by themselves be used to indicate the existence of dietary deficiencies in the poor countries. However, of even greater potential seriousness than the implied general caloric deficiency among peoples in the developing areas is the "hidden hunger" gap. By this is meant that the problem may not so much be that people in the poor countries do not get enough to eat as it is that the food they do consume is derived largely from starchy grains and tubers and is often grossly deficient in a number of basic nutrients. The most serious problem here concerns the lack of protein in the diet, especially animal protein. To illustrate, among the countries for whom data is presented in Table 2.5 the proportion of total calories that is derived from animal protein ranges from a high of 41 percent for the highly developed countries down to roughly 10 percent for the underdeveloped areas as a whole, and to a low of 6 percent among the poorest countries in this underdeveloped category. A marked protein deficiency characterizing the population of the developing areas not only represents a major health problem, but may also serve as a major factor impeding their economic development. It has been shown, for example, that a woman who suffers nutritional deficiencies during gestation will generally give birth to a child who will be weaker, smaller, less resistant to disease, and less intelligent than a child whose mother was well nourished during her pregnancy. Similarly, it has been shown that children who suffer from malnutrition will grow up into weaker, smaller, less healthy, and less intelligent adults than those who never suffer from nutritional deficiency. The obvious economic implication here is that those countries that have a high incidence of malnutrition will have populations that are generally less healthy and less productive than the populations in those countries where malnutrition is relatively rare (Belli, 1971). It is also apparent from this discussion that alleviating the present food/hunger problem is going to involve much more than a simple increase in the total food supply. For many people throughout the Third World the problem is not only one of undernourishment (not enough food to eat) but also one of malnourishment (a nutritionally inadequate diet). Thus, the solution calls for an increase in the nutritional quality of the diet as well as in increase in food quantity.

The implication of the preceding relationship pertaining to the human resources of developing countries, particularly with respect to food consumption, is that many of these countries are faced with the need to spend a proportionately larger share of their national incomes on consumption items such as food, health services, and education. Diverting funds to meet these consumption needs means that less capital will be available for other productive enterprises. On the other hand, failure to do so means that these conditions will continue to deteriorate, especially as population continues to grow, and it is difficult to see how any kind of national economic progress can be made in the face of a continuously worsening social situation and the political and economic instability that this would imply. Rather, it is likely that where it is necessary to divert potential development capital to meet food and other consumption needs, it will slow down the rate of national economic development. How much it will be slowed down will depend in large part on how soon runaway population growth is brought under control.

Summary

By way of brief summary it may be noted that the economic status and associated levels of living in the developing countries, no matter how they are measured, are extremely low. More important, however, the nature of the economic resource base in many of these areas is such that it may represent a major obstacle to development. In attempting to assess the development potential of the Third World resource base in general, as well as that of particular countries, there are three considerations to keep in mind: the availability of resources, the way in which available resources are used, and the various aspects of the sociocultural environment that may influence both resource availability and utilization.

(1) The problems of resource availability may be both quantitative and qualitative. On the one hand, most developing countries are characterized by severe shortages of one or more of the three basic economic resources of land, labor, and capital—particularly land and capital. On the other hand, often the resources that are available are of inferior quality. The inadequacy of the capital stock can be illustrated by such things as roads that are impassable when it rains, the existence of competing railroad systems with tracks of different gauges, and schools that do not have enough books or other essential educational equipment.

Much of the available land consists of mountains, arid deserts or jungle rain forests. Finally, the populations are characterized by such things as high incidences of malnutrition and poor health—all of which reduce productive potential.

(2) The crucial question often will not concern what resources are available, but the manner in which they are used. Land that is severely fragmented or that is consolidated into large estates for the cultivation of export crops, capital that is hoarded, natural resources (as well as capital) that are drained off by the more developed countries, and a labor force that is unemployed or underemployed in either agriculture or tertiary service activities all represent inefficient uses of potential productive resources.

(3) Finally, in line with the basic societal approach taken in this volume, a major dimension of the economic problem in many developing countries may be found in the general sociocultural system. This third point is especially important because it can determine both what resources are available and how they are used. Cows, for example, cannot be considered as a potential resource in India where cattle are regarded as sacred; laws or customs that require that all sons inherit equal portions of land leads to excessive fragmentation; rigid caste systems such as can still be found in India, as well as traditions that subjugate women in society, inhibit the effective utilization of labor; and religious values that encourage such things as extensive gift giving or financing a pilgrimage to Mecca lead to nonproductive uses of capital.

Clearly, the problem of Third World development is an economic problem in that poverty is widespread, levels of living are extremely low, and basic resources are often both in short supply and inefficiently used. Beyond this, however, it is a sociological problem in that a wide variety of sociocultural factors play a major role in determining both the availability and utilization of resources. The bulk of this volume (chapters 4 through 9) will be concerned with the role of these noneconomic factors in Third World development.

First, however, the following chapter will examine what we consider to be one of the most serious obstacles to development in these countries: their demographic situation, particularly their rapid rates of population growth.

3

Population and Development

The demographic dimension of the development problem encompasses a wide variety of specific variables ranging from the more general size and growth rates of a population to the levels of the particular components of growth rates (fertility, mortality, and migration), to various measures of population composition (age, ethnicity, sex) and population distribution (density, degree of urbanization). The present chapter will identify some of the more significant demographic characteristics of underdeveloped areas. In each case attention will focus first on a description of the general situation in the developing countries as a whole, and second on how the various demographic characteristics are related to the problems and processes of economic growth and modernization. A final section will present a more detailed discussion of the harmful effects that continued rapid population growth could have for economic development throughout the several regions of the Third World.

Demographic Characteristics of Underdeveloped Areas

The major demographic characteristics of most developing areas can be noted briefly as follows: (1) a relatively high but rapidly declining death rate; in combination with (2) a still relatively constant high birth rate; resulting in (3) rapid and/or accelerating rates of population growth and (4) the emergence of a youthful age composition. Further, (5) the rapid rate of population growth, coupled with the increasing utilization of modern agricultural technology, is displacing large segments of the rural population from the farm labor force and leading to rapid rates of urbanization. Each of these characteristics and their significance for economic development in the Third World will now be considered in greater detail.

Death Rates

The overall mortality level of a population is generally measured by the *crude death rate*, which for any area is defined as the number of deaths in a calendar year per 1,000 population. For the most part, the crude death rates in the underdeveloped countries of the world are substantially higher than those presently found in the more developed areas of North America, Europe, and Oceania. To illustrate, estimates prepared recently by the International Statistical Programs Center of the U.S. Bureau of the Census indicate that, with the exception of the Latin American mainland and the Caribbean Islands, crude death rates in the less developed regions range from about 40 percent (Asia) to more than 100 percent (Africa) above those currently prevailing in the more developed regions (see Table 3.1). Death rates in developing areas are lowest in Latin America and the Caribbean, where an earlier start on mortality decline has produced a fairly young population; and they are highest in those African countries that have only recently begun to experience economic development. Compared to a crude death rate of 18 to 21 per 1,000 for Africa as a whole, at least six countries on that continent have death rates in excess of 25 per 1,000. These are Chad, Guinea-Bissau, Mali, Mauritania, Spanish Sahara and Upper Volta. The highest crude death rate, estimated at 28 to 29 per 1,000, is found in

Upper Volta, although it may range even higher to levels of 30 or more in parts of some countries (U.S. Bureau of the Census, 1976). Although substantial progress has been made in reducing mortality throughout much of the underdeveloped world (see the section on population growth below) it is clear from these data that most countries in this group are still characterized by relatively high death rates.

The adverse mortality conditions in the less developed regions are revealed especially by the association between development status and the *infant mortality rate* (defined as the number of deaths to infants under one year of age in a calendar year per 1,000 live births). Whereas the average crude death rate of the underdeveloped group as a whole is roughly 50 percent greater than that of the more developed regions, the former's infant mortality rate is nearly five times higher than that characterizing the high status group. This relationship is so pronounced and has been observed so consistently that, in the absence of more direct measures, the infant mortality rate may be used as an indirect index of the overall level of well-being characterizing the population of a given country, if not its level of economic development

Table 3.1 Birth and death rates for the major regions of the world: 1974.

World Regions	Births per 1,000 population	Deaths per 1,000 population	Infant deaths per 1,000 live births
World	29-31	12-13	90
More Developed Regions	*16-17*	*9*	*23**
North America	15	9	19
Europe	16	10	24
Australia/New Zealand	19	8	17
Less Developed Regions	*35-37*	*13-14*	*113**
Asia	32-33	13	132
Africa	44-48	18-21	158
Latin America	36-38	9-10	79

*Weighted arithmetic means calculated by authors.

Source: U.S. Bureau of the Census, International Statistical Programs Center, *World Population, 1975: Recent Demographic Estimates for the Countries and Regions of the World,* ISP-WP-75 (June 1976). Infant mortality rates were obtained from the 1973 edition of this same report: ISP-WP-73 (May 1974).

(i.e., the higher the infant mortality rate, the lower the level of social and economic development).

To the extent that mortality rates are an indicator of overall health status, it is clear that the underdeveloped countries have populations whose level of physical well being is substantially below those prevailing in the rich nations. The significance of this situation, as far as economic development is concerned, lies in the relationship between high rates of illness and the impairment of productive efficiency. Although the evidence is sketchy, it may well be that poor health, by contributing to such things as general physical weakness and higher rates of absenteeism from work, is an important factor underlying the low productivity of the labor force in many underdeveloped areas.

Birth Rates

There are two basic points to make concerning the fertility characteristics of underdeveloped areas: (1) fertility levels are high; and (2) the culture and social structure tend to be such that they generally either encourage a high level of fertility or, at the very least, contain few elements that might serve to induce a decline in the level of fertility.

With respect to the first point, the *crude birth rate* (the annual number of live births in an area per 1,000 population) is well below 20 in the more developed regions taken as a whole, but it is well above 30 in the major regions of the underdeveloped world (see Table 3.1). As was the case with death rates, the highest fertility of any region is found in Africa where there were an estimated 44 to 48 births per 1,000 population in 1974. Twenty African nations had crude birth rates that are estimated to be around the level of 50 per 1,000 while in at least two (Mali and Rwanda) the birth rate is between 50 and 52 per 1,000, and may be even higher in parts of several other countries (U.S. Bureau of the Census, 1976).

Considering the second point, the substantially higher levels of fertility among underdeveloped areas are generally explained in terms of certain structural features or cultural values that are conducive to the maintenance of a high birth rate (see chapters 4, 5, and 6). A major factor frequently cited in this regard relates to the structure of the family (Davis, 1955). Many underdeveloped countries are still largely peasant agrarian societies characterized by a strong familistic orientation rather than an individualistic orientation. In such societies there is a great deal of emphasis on promoting and maintaining the strength and solidarity of the extended kinship group, and this subordination of the individual to the larger kinship unit has several consequences that would serve to encourage a high birth rate. For example, in such a setting the economic burden of caring for children does not rest solely on the young parents but is spread among all members of the family, as is the time and effort involved in caring for young children. More important from an economic perspective, however, is the simple arithmetic fact that the more children that are born in a family, the more "workers" there will be to contribute to the common family treasury. Further, in societies that lack formal old age retirement systems (such as Social Security), the more children a couple have, especially the more sons, the more secure they can feel about being taken care of in their old age.

An additional influence on fertility in such familistic societies is the traditional sharp differentiation between the roles of men and women, with women being confined largely to the household where they are identified primarily with the tasks of housekeeping and the bearing and raising of children. All of these factors combine to create a setting in which early marriage coupled with early and regular childbearing are strongly encouraged, in which the prestige and security of women in the family is often directly determined by the number of children she has borne (especially by the number of sons), and in which barrenness is among the worst "sins" of which a woman can be guilty.

Some scholars have suggested that this high fertility syndrome would be modified downward if women in underdeveloped areas were provided with alternatives to marriage as a means of obtaining economic security, and in fact there is evidence to indicate that those countries that have taken active steps to raise the status of women and have encouraged female employment have also met with some success in reducing national birth rates (see chapter 8). Such alternatives for women generally do emerge among the societal changes that accompany the process of industrialization and development, and their emergence may eventually facilitate fertility declines. So far, however, the available data continue to point to a high level of fertility as a major characteristic of most developing countries. In spite of the fact that a number of people have suggested that a significant downward trend in non-Western birth rates is either already underway or imminent (Bogue, 1967; Kirk, 1971) the available statistical evidence clearly indicates that for many developing areas such a decline has not as yet made much headway. Nevertheless, it should still be stressed that energetic action to bring down the birth rate must play a major role in any realistic development plan, and further, that the success of any development plan may very well depend in large part on the success of programs to reduce fertility.

Population Growth

One of the most frequently cited demographic correlates of economic development is the rate of population increase. The nature of this relationship is negative, that is, rates of population growth in the poor countries of Asia, Africa, and Latin America are frequently two or three times greater than corresponding rates in Europe and North America (see Table 3.2). According to estimates recently prepared by the International Statistical Programs Center of the United States Bureau of the Census, the population of the less developed regions, taken as a whole, had an annual growth rate during the early 1970s that was nearly three times as high as the overall annual growth rate characterizing the more developed regions. At these rates the number of people living in the more developed regions will double in 85 to 90

Table 3.2 Annual population growth rates for the major regions of the world: 1974.

World Regions	Annual rate (percent) of population growth
World	1.7—1.9
More Developed Regions	0.8
Europe	0.7
North America	0.9
Oceania	1.7—1.9
Less Developed Regions	2.1—2.3
Africa	2.4—2.9
Asia	1.9—2.1
Latin America	2.6—2.9

Source: U. S. Bureau of the Census, International Statistical Programs Center, *World Population 1975: Recent Demographic Estimates for the Countries and Regions of the World*, ISP-WP-75 (June 1976).

years, whereas it will take only 30 to 35 years for a doubling of population to occur in the poorer, less developed regions of the world.

The demographic contrasts become even more dramatic when individual countries are considered. The United Kingdom, for example, with an annual growth rate of only 0.1 percent, will require nearly seven hundred years to double its population. In sharp contrast to this, a number of low income developing countries (e.g., Honduras, Iraq, Jordan, Kenya, Mexico, and Nicaragua), have population growth rates approaching 3.5 percent per year. If these unprecedented high growth rates persist these countries can expect a doubling of their population in approximately twenty years (i.e., within a single generation). Such a projected numerical increase will obviously intensify the pressures and strains on their already overburdened economies and will seriously increase the magnitude of the development problems they are presently struggling to overcome.

The Demographic Transition In order to appreciate fully the current pattern of population growth in the world's developing areas it is necessary to be familiar with the concept of the "demographic transition." Very briefly, the term "demographic transition" refers to the historical transformation of a society from an era in which it is characterized by what can be called a *primitive demographic balance* (with birth and death rates fairly stable and in a relative balance with each other at a high level) to a *modern demographic balance* (with birth and death rates fairly stable and in relative balance with each other at a low level). Both of these two demographic types (primitive and modern) are characterized by relatively slow rates of population growth, but the dynamic growth component is different. In the primitive type the high birth rate remains relatively constant, and it is primarily fluctuations in the death rate that effect changes in the rate of growth. In the modern type, however, it is the low death rate that is constant, and the rate of population growth and changes therein are determined by the level and trend of the birth rate. The transition from the former to the latter begins when the old primitive balance is upset by the emergence of a sustained downward trend in the death rate, and it ends when a subsequent decline in the birth rate restores a balance at the low modern level. The intervening period is marked by fairly rapid and substantial increases in the size of the population.

So far, only a small group of countries have made this transition, and these are confined largely to the industrialized developed regions of the Western world. Furthermore, those industrialized nations that have completed the transition and have achieved a modern demographic balance between relatively low birth and death rates have only done so fairly recently. Throughout most of the vast time span of human existence on earth, the brutally harsh conditions of life made survival an extremely precarious affair, and a new born infant had only about a fifty-fifty chance of surviving to adulthood. Although population data prior to the modern era are very scanty for all parts of the world, the evidence that can be obtained from various anthropological and archeological sources indicates that the death rate of ancient peoples was very high, and that the average length of life could not have been more than twenty to twenty five years (Stockwell, 1968:26-28). In the face of such high death rates, a high level of fertility was a necessary condition for the survival of the species, and birth rates often approached their biological maximum. As human culture developed over the ages, however, the chances of survival tended to improve. The first great advancement came with the neolithic cultural achievements of agriculture and the domestication of animals, roughly eight thousand years ago. With the provision of a more stable food supply, the base was laid for the maintenance of a larger population. However, the widespread prevalence of disease resulting from poor nutrition and the extremely unsanitary conditions of life continued to keep death rates high; and although population began to increase, it grew so slowly and gradually as to appear almost stationary by modern standards.

It was not until the eighteenth century that any substantial reductions in mortality occurred, and that the modern population explosion really got underway. Although it was at one time popular to locate the causes of this mortality decline in the development of modern medicine and public health programs, it now seems clear that the initial declines in the death rate were associated with an increase in the quantity and quality of the food supply. More and better food significantly improved the nutritional status of the population and increased people's ability to resist many of the microorganisms which cause disease and death (McKeown, 1976); as the food supply started to improve in the early eighteenth century death rates began to decline. The initial mortality reductions that followed the improvements in diet were, however, substantially enhanced by the tremendous cultural advances that accompanied the Industrial Revolution. The Industrial Revolution brought with it the emergence and advancement of modern science; and with this development, the mortality pattern of a million years was finally broken. The discovery of vaccination for smallpox by Edward Jenner in 1796 was the first in a long line of discoveries and inventions that were destined to improve substantially the chances of survival, particularly among infants and young children. This and other applications of the scientific method to biology and medicine, the continued improvements of agricultural technology, the development of better means of transportation and communication, improvements in the sanitary condition of the physical environment, and all the social, economic, and psychological changes that accompanied the emergence of an urban-industrial civilization, combined to set in motion forces which dramatically lowered death rates and substantially increased human reproductive efficiency.

Although death rates began to fall during the eighteenth century, the birth rate continued to remain at fairly high levels. In fact, there is some evidence to indicate that the initial response of fertility to the profound societal changes taking place was an increase (Tabbarah, 1971). The same improvements in nutrition and health status that contributed to mortality decline also contributed to such things as a reduction in involuntary sterility and greater fetal survival (i.e., fewer miscarriages); and these general health improvements were enhanced by a number of societal changes such as the breakdown of the old apprentice system and increased agricultural productivity that made it possible for more people to marry, and to marry at a younger age. As a consequence, the birth rate in many countries of Western Europe tended at first to increase in response to the rising levels of living associated with the early stages of modernization, and this contributed to an even greater difference between levels of fertility and mortality. This widening spread between levels of fertility and mortality (which was created both because more babies were being born and because an increasingly larger proportion of births survived and lived through adulthood), is commonly referred to as the *demographic gap*. It is the opening of this gap that marks the beginning of rapid population growth.

As noted above, this gap generally began to open in

Europe in the eighteenth century, and it continued to widen during several decades of declining mortality, thus producing steadily increasing rates of population growth. Eventually, however, as social and cultural values shifted from an emphasis on the welfare and development of the group to an emphasis on the welfare and development of the individual, as the economic base of the society shifted from rural-agrarian to urban-industrial, and as continued technological progress provided the means for the more effective control of fertility, the birth rate also began to decline. A new demographic balance between low birth and death rates was ultimately achieved, and the rate of population growth—at least in the industrial nations of the Western world—slowed down considerably. It is this shift from the old preindustrial demographic balance between high birth and death rates, through a period of sustained growth as a declining death rate creates an imbalance between fertility and mortality, to a new modern demographic balance between low birth and death rates as an eventual fertility decline narrows the gap created by the earlier and more rapid fall in the death rate, that is referred to by the term ''demographic transition''; and it is the completion of this transition that marks the end of rapid population growth.

In order to illustrate more clearly the nature of the classical demographic transition model just described, a graphic representation of a hypothetical set of birth and death rates over time is depicted in Figure 3.1. It may be helpful in understanding this transition process to look at this model in terms of some readily identifiable growth stages as follows:

Stage 1. This is the primitive or preindustrial stage in which birth and death rates are fairly stable at relatively high levels, and in which fluctuations in the generally low rate of population growth are largely the result of fluctuations in the death rate (i.e., the death rate alternately declines in times of plenty and rises in times of disaster due to such things as crop failures and related food shortages, war, or the outbreak of epidemic diseases). This is the stage that characterized all

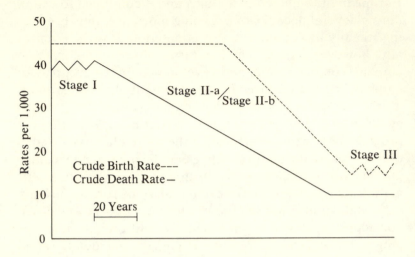

Figure 3.1 Graphic representation of the classical demographic transition model.

human populations until the late seventeenth and early eighteenth centuries, at which time the West European nations began to enter the second or "transitional growth" stage.

Stage 2. The transitional phase of rapid population growth, which lasted anywhere from one hundred to two hundred years, can be subdivided into two separate phases in terms of whether the rate of population growth is accelerating or slowing down. In stage 2A, the early or expanding growth phase is characterized by a persistent high birth rate in conjunction with a declining death rate, so that the demographic gap is becoming wider and the rate of population growth is accelerating. In general, the countries of Western Europe began to enter this accelerating growth phase sometime during the period 1650-1750. In stage 2B, the late or contracting growth phase of this transitional period begins when the birth rate starts to decline (generally several generations after the start of mortality decline). The onset of fertility decline was traditionally regarded as a natural accompaniment of the broad socio-economic transition from a rural-agrarian to a modern urban-industrial society, and as the declining birth rate caught up with the earlier fall in the death rate it brought about a slowing down in the overall rate of population growth. Although the precise timing of the onset of fertility decline and the subsequent slowing down in the rate of population growth varied among the several West European nations, this contracting phase generally began around the middle of the nineteenth century and lasted until the second or third decade of the present century.

Stage 3. This is the modern stage where birth and death rates are in relative balance at a fairly low level, and where fluctuations in the generally low rate of population growth are due to fluctuations in the birth rate. This stage, which marks the completion of the transition and the end of runaway population growth, has characterized the industrialized advanced nations of the Western world since the 1930s.

The problem being faced today derives from the fact that with few exceptions (most notably Japan) only the European countries and those of European settlement in North America and Oceania have completed their demographic transition. The majority of the countries in the developing world have only recently entered the early accelerating growth phase of stage 2. Furthermore, the gap that has opened between levels of fertility and mortality in these countries has opened faster and is substantially wider than the gap that characterized the European countries during their transition, and many of these poorer countries are today in the midst of what is truly a monumental population explosion.

The explanation of the present situation in the developing regions lies primarily in the trend with respect to the death rate. In contrast to the European experience, where the decline of the death rate took place gradually over several generations, the ability to make immediate use of modern techniques for postponing death (techniques that took years to develop and perfect) means that the decline of mortality in the less developed areas of the world today has been more pronounced and has taken place much more rapidly than it did in the demographic history of the present highly developed countries. Whereas it took one hundred or more years for the crude death rate of most European nations to decline from levels of thirty or thirty five to around ten per one thousand population, the years since the end of World War II have witnessed comparable reductions in many underdeveloped areas in the space of ten to fifteen years, sometimes even less. Fertility, on the other hand, has in many countries shown little signs of declining—in some countries, as was the case in Europe historically, birth rates have in fact risen—and the rapid and substantial mortality decline in conjunction with a high, perhaps slightly increasing birth rate has produced unprecedented rates of population growth in many of the world's developing countries in recent years.

The general nature of the fertility-mortality gap that has recently emerged in many of the less developed countries is graphically illustrated in Figure 3.2. The significance of this recent gap can best be appreciated by comparing it to the gap that characterized the classical transition pattern depicted in Figure 3.1. In the demographic history of the European world, the gradual decline in the death rate meant that fertility decline was able to get underway before mortality reached its lowest levels, and this in turn meant that the rate of natural increase seldom exceeded 1.5 percent a year. Today, however, the rapid and substantial mortality declines that are possible have frequently resulted in growth rates on the order of 3.0 to 3.5 percent a year (or rates that would lead to a doubling of population in about twenty years)! So far, fertility has shown very little inclination to decline in these areas, and until it does they will continue to be characterized by the rapid rates of population growth that so frequently act as a major obstacle to economic development.

To take a more specific illustration, the contrast between the classical demographic transition model and the growth pattern that has characterized much of the developing world

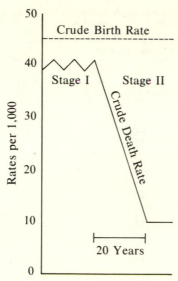

Figure 3.2 Graphic representation of the demographic gap in the developing countries.

since the end of World War II is revealed dramatically by Table 3.3 which compares birth and death rate trends for Sweden and Sri Lanka (formerly Ceylon). In the former case it took well over one hundred years for the crude death rate to decline from an annual level of 25 to 10 per 1,000; most significantly, the slow pace of mortality meant that by the time the death rate had fallen below 20 per 1,000, the birth rate had also begun to decline. Thus, at no time during its transition did Sweden's annual rate of natural increase exceed 15 per 1,000 (or 1.5 percent per year). In Sri Lanka, however, the death rate fell from about 25 to below 10 per 1,000 in less than thirty years, reaching this low level far in advance of any downward trend in fertility. Consequently, in the case of Sri Lanka, the crude rate of natural increase was between 25 and 30 per 1,000 per year until the most recent period when a slight fall in the crude birth rate has led to an annual growth rate of 2 percent.

Further consideration of Table 3.3 indicates that the traditional transition pattern may be undergoing another modifi-

Table 3.3 Comparative vital rate trends for Sweden and Sri Lanka.

| Dates | Sweden | | | Sri Lanka | | |
| | Crude rates of: | | | Crude rates of: | | |
	Birth	Death	Natural Increase	Birth	Death	Natural Increase
1818-22	34	25	9	—	—	—
1828-32	33	26	7	—	—	—
1838-42	31	22	9	—	—	—
1848-52	32	21	11	—	—	—
1858-62	34	20	14	—	—	—
1868-72	29	19	10	—	—	—
1878-82	30	18	12	—	—	—
1888-92	28	17	11	—	—	—
1898-02	27	16	11	38	28	10
1908-12	25	14	11	38	31	7
1918-22	21	14	7	38	32	6
1928-32	15	12	3	39	24	15
1938-42	16	11	5	36	20	16
1948-52	18	10	8	40	15	25
1960	14	10	4	37	9	28
1970	14	10	4	29	8	21
1973-74	14	11	3	28	8	20

Source: Historical data from Warren S. Thompson, *Population Problems*, 4th ed., McGraw-Hill, 1953, pp. 162 and 236. Data for 1960 and 1970 were obtained, respectively, from the 1966 and 1971 *Demographic Yearbook* of the United Nations. Rates for 1973-74 were obtained from U. S. Bureau of the Census, International Statistical Programs Center, *World Population: 1975*, ISP-WP-75 (June 1976).

cation. The birth rate in Sri Lanka has also started to decline in recent years; and the magnitude of the decline as of 1973-74 (down 25 percent since 1960) further suggests that, as was the case with mortality, the fertility transition may take place more rapidly than it did in Sweden. A number of countries have in fact gone through the transition faster than was generally the case for the West European countries. That is, some countries (notably Japan, the USSR, and some East European countries) went through an "accelerated transition" in which fairly rapid declines in mortality were followed shortly by equally rapid declines in the birth rate — with the latter being facilitated by fairly widespread reliance on induced abortion (Omran, 1977). These countries, whose accelerated transition pattern is graphically illustrated in

Figure 3.3, were thus able to complete their transition without going through such an extended period of rapid population growth as that which characterized most West European countries during the eighteenth and nineteenth centuries, and the existence of such an alternative model may be
an encouraging sign with respect to the present demographic
situation prevailing throughout much of the Third World.

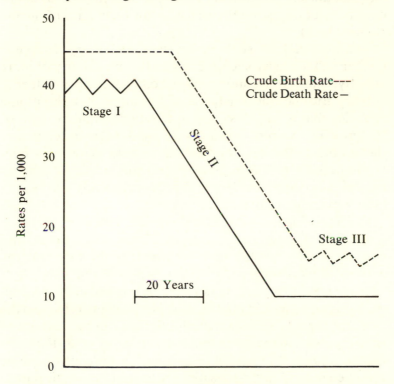

Figure 3.3 Graphic representation of the accelerated transition model.

If it is indeed possible that the present developing countries may undergo a more rapid fertility decline than the
European countries who went through the classical demographic transition, the future would then look less pessimistic than initially suggested; a number of contemporary
demographers (Bogue, 1967; Kirk, 1971) regard this as a very
real possibility. For example, Kirk (1971) has noted in a

recent study that birth rate declines have been observed among underdeveloped peoples of widely diverse cultural backgrounds. Moreover, just as mortality decline has occurred faster in the post-World War II years than it did in the Western world, the evidence suggests that the more recent the onset of fertility decline the faster it is likely to take place, and that the less developed countries could therefore experience a faster transition from high to low birth rates (Tsui and Bogue, 1978).

The potential for such an accelerated fertility decline is further enhanced by such factors as the availability of more effective means of contraception today than in nineteenth century Europe, the existence of a number of international agencies that offer assistance to family planning programs, the growing awareness among national political leaders of the problems for development that could arise from continued rapid population growth, and the increased willingness of national governments to become actively involved in family planning efforts.

Before taking too optimistic a position, however, there are a number of qualifying points that need to be taken into consideration—not the least of which is the fact that the national leadership in some countries may not be so ready to endorse fertility programs as would be implied in the preceding paragraph (see chapter 8). Another problem relates to the fact that there is a fundamental difference in the amount of active public cooperation required to achieve fertility decline as opposed to mortality decline. Death control can be achieved in large measure with very little effort on the part of the masses of the population simply by the implementation, by the state, of various public health and sanitation improvement programs such as swamp drainage, the widespread use of pesticides, the purification of public water supplies, etc. That is, the success or failure of many death control programs does not rest on the conscious decision of hundreds of thousands of people to participate actively in them. The success of birth control programs, on the other hand, does require the active participation of hundreds of thousands of couples who, acting independently of one another, make a conscious decision to take specific steps to control the size of their own individual families. It will obviously be much more difficult to generate widespread public cooperation and get people to take deliberate steps to control their fertility than it is to bring about declines in mortality by superimposing death control programs on a society from above.

Over and above this fundamental difference in the degree of individual participation required for the success of fertility control programs, there are a number of structural differences between the developing countries today and the countries of Europe a century ago that could mitigate against any rapid reduction in the birth rate. Among the more significant of these differences would be the following (Teitelbaum, 1975:421-23):

1. Western Europe was characterized by a pattern of relatively late marriage and extensive nonmarriage, whereas early and nearly universal marriage prevails in most contemporary developing societies.

2. Reflecting these marriage patterns, the birth rates in most developing countries today are substantially higher than those that prevailed in Europe at the start of the classical transition; hence, the former rates have much further to decline in order to close the demographic gap.

3. The countries of Western Europe had higher rates of literacy and had already made fairly substantial progress in raising the level of living before the declines in fertility really got underway toward the end of the nineteenth century. This same situation characterized those industrialized countries that experienced the accelerated transition, and those non-Western countries that have more recently shown some progress toward fertility decline (e.g., Singapore, Taiwan, South Korea) have also been characterized by higher rates of literacy and urban-industrial development than are found in the majority of Third World countries.

4. The very rapid declines in mortality in recent years, in conjunction with persistent high birth rates, have produced a very young population (see following section), thus creating a far greater momentum for further growth in the developing countries—even if fertility were to decline immediately to a bare replacement level, the population in the developing countries would continue to increase for another fifty to sixty years.

All of the preceding characteristics of the developing societies (near universal marriage, high birth rates, low urban-industrial status, youthful age composition) are likely to work against any rapid declines in fertility in the immediate future. The big question obviously concerns whether these negative factors will exert more or less influence than the earlier noted factors that are likely to promote an accelerated fertility decline (i.e., improved contraceptive technology, growing government concern). The issue is basically one of timeliness. Birth rates will decline at some point, and population growth rates in the Third World will slow down. But how rapidly will birth rates fall? How soon will runaway population growth come to an end? Will population growth rates slow down in time to ease the process of development and avert many of the calamities such as widespread famines, depletion of natural resources, increasing domestic unrest and violence, and a return to the higher death rates of the past that some observers have been predicting will be the outcome of continued rapid population growth? These are questions for which there are no precise answers. Although some professional demographers are more optimistic than others about the future course of population growth and its effects in the developing world, almost all would agree that waiting for the ''natural'' gradual decline in fertility of the classical transition model that paralleled the socioeconomic development of Western Europe during the nineteenth century would be a naive and unrealistic response to the present world demographic situation. Further, most would also agree that continued rapid population growth represents a major obstacle to economic development programs, and that specific policies and programs to reduce fertility and the rate of population growth should continue to be an important aspect of national development plans.

There is one other point that needs to be made before ending this section on population growth: as high as they already are, there is a possibility that the future will see even higher growth rates. For one reason, many of those underdeveloped nations where mortality is still fairly high are in the midst of ambitious programs for improving sanitation, public health, and medical care, and there is a possibility that they will achieve further substantial mortality reduction in the years ahead. As long as birth rates remain high, these mortality reductions will mean an even greater widening of the current demographic gap and will increase the rate of population growth in the countries concerned. Such a development would clearly intensify the already critical population obstacle to economic growth in the underdeveloped world. On the other hand, an even worse tragedy would be a deterioration in the economic situation caused by too rapid population growth and a consequent failure to achieve the additional mortality gains that are biologically possible.

In this same connection it must also be re-emphasized that many of the modernizing forces now in progress could in some cases lead to even higher birth rates (Petersen, 1975:642-43)! As noted earlier, the same improvements in health status that could bring about further mortality declines could also enhance fertility by reducing the rate of miscarriage and the incidence of involuntary sterility. Again, the resulting increases in the rate of population growth would seriously aggravate the demographic and economic problems confronting the areas affected.

Age Composition

The influence of demographic factors on the economic development of the poor countries of the world is not limited solely to the size and rate of growth of the population.

Another important aspect of this problem relates to the age structure of the population. The distribution of its members according to age is in fact one of the most important characteristics of a population. On the one hand, virtually every aspect of human behavior, from subjective attitudes and physiological capabilities to objective characteristics such as school attendance, health status, labor force participation, occupation, and income may be expected to vary with age. On the other hand, many of the special needs and problems of a particular society, both now and in the future, will be influenced by the age structure of its population. A population with a high proportion of young persons may be expected to differ from one that has a high proportion of older persons in its productive capacity, in its consumption needs, and in its outlook and mode of life. Labor force efficiency and productive capacity are in part a function of the number of persons within the active adult ages in relation to the number of persons outside these ages, both young and old. The adequacy of facilities or services such as housing, schools, and pension plans depends, respectively, on the number of young people who are marrying and starting their families, the number of children at the school and preschool ages, and the number of older persons. From a demographic perspective, both birth and death rates, and hence the rate of population growth, are partly influenced by the age distribution of a population. For reasons such as the preceding, a knowledge of the current age structure, how it came into being and what consequences it is likely to have for future population trends, is essential for adequately understanding the nature of the demographic dimension of the contemporary development problem.

To make a somewhat oversimplified generalization concerning the relationship between age composition and economic growth in low income countries: the younger the population the more capital will have to be diverted from production to consumption purposes, and the more difficult will be the overall development problem. The available data, which indicate that the population in the less developed regions is considerably younger than that of the more highly developed areas of the world, clearly reveal the seriousness of this aspect of the demographic obstacle to development. According to recent estimates (see Table 3.4) only 24 percent of the population in the more developed regions is under fifteen years of age, as compared to 39 percent in the less-developed regions. Among the latter the proportion of the population that falls into this youthful group ranges from 38 percent in Asia to 44 percent in Africa. In a great many countries this fraction exceeds 45 percent, and in twelve of the major underdeveloped countries the proportion under fifteen years of age was 48 percent or higher. These twelve were Algeria, Botswana, Dominican Republic, Iraq, Jordan, Libya, Mali, Nicaragua, Rhodesia, Surinam, Swaziland, and Syria. In the South American country of Surinam an estimated 50 percent of the population fell into this youthful age group.

The explanation for the pronounced youthfulness of the Third World populations must be sought in the present pattern of rapid population growth resulting from declining mortality, especially in infancy. When death rates decline,

Table 3.4 Age composition and level of urbanization for the major regions of the world.

World Regions	Percent under age 15	Percent Urban
World	36%	38%
More Developed Regions	24*	66*
North America	26	74
Europe	22	65
USSR	26	60
Australia/New Zealand	28/30	71/81
Less Developed Regions	39*	29*
Asia	38	26
Africa	44	24
Latin America	42	59

*Weighted arithmetic means calculated by authors.

Source: Population Reference Bureau, *1977 World Population Data Sheet*, Washington, D.C., 1977.

especially death rates among infants and young children, but birth rates remain high the effect is to bring about a marked increase in the number and proportion of youth in the population. Since young people are primarily consumers (not only of food, but also of other essential services such as health and education), such an increase in the number of youth greatly intensifies the dependency burden on the rest of the population. It means that a smaller proportion of adult workers has to bear a larger burden of support, and it also means that resources that might otherwise have been used directly to support various other development programs must be diverted instead to provide for the consumption needs of the young. Furthermore, after a few years when the increased number of surviving infants reaches adult working ages, it creates (and will create) a corresponding increase in the problems of unemployment and underemployment already found in many developing societies.

Finally, it may be noted that the present heavy burden of youth dependency may not only be creating serious social and economic problems in the underdeveloped areas by putting greater pressure on limited educational facilities, or by diverting potential developmental capital to necessary maintenance expenses; it may also have serious political implications. It is the young people with their youthful ideals and ambitions that are the least committed to the maintenance of the traditional status quo; it is this most volatile segment of the population in the underdeveloped world that is most likely to react violently to a situation in which continued failure and increasing frustration are the major byproducts of the so-called revolution of rising expectations. Uncommitted and dissatisfied young people have in the past been a major source of social unrest and political instability in many countries, and their rising numbers pose the same threat today in many areas of the developing world. Since internal political stability is an important requisite for national economic development (see chapter 8), the present age structure of the population in many Third World countries must be regarded as an especially serious aspect of the overall development problems they face. Moreover, this heavy burden of youth dependency will remain as long as fertility remains high—when the recent birth cohorts reach adulthood they will have proportionately more children, if fertility does not fall, and the increasing population will be characterized by the same high ratio of children to adults. Hence, there is even greater urgency to reduce the level of fertility in today's developing nations—not only to slow down the *present* growth rates, but also to alter the youthful composition of the population and thereby lessen the momentum for continued rapid growth in the years to come.

Migration and Urbanization

The term "urbanization" refers to an increase in both the number and proportion of the population living in cities, and such an increase has traditionally been the normal accompaniment of the economic transformation of a society from an agricultural to an industrial state. Since this shift in the distribution of the population is brought about primarily by the voluntary movement of people away from farm areas to search for nonagricultural employment in the cities and towns, it is common to consider the two topics of migration and urbanization together.

When one compares the developed countries with the lesser developed areas of the world with respect to their level of urbanization, it is apparent that the former are much further advanced in this respect. According to the extensive study of world urbanization levels and trends carried out at the University of California at Berkeley (Davis, 1972), approximately two-thirds of the population of the more developed regions were living in urban areas in 1970 in contrast to slightly below one-fourth in the less developed areas. Since the level of urbanization has long been recognized as a major correlate of economic status, this is the relationship one would expect to find. A significant point to note, however, is that even though levels of urbanization are still much lower throughout the developing areas than in the more highly developed countries, the former have experienced a pronounced intensification of the urbanization process in recent years. The rapidly declining death rate that has already been cited as being characteristic of so many developing areas today has created, among other things, a serious problem of overpopulation in the rural areas of the developing regions; the past fifteen to twenty years has seen hundreds of thousands of illterate, poverty-stricken, technologically untrained agricultural peasants flocking to urban areas throughout the developing world. Again referring to the University of California study cited above, it is estimated that the rate of urbanization in the less developed areas during the 1960s was nearly twice as great as that observed in the developed regions—the urban population increased by 24 percent for the former as compared to only 13 percent for the latter. This phenomenon is further indicated by the data presented in Table 3.4 which show that by the middle of the 1970s the urban fraction in the less developed countries had risen from less than one fourth in 1970 (Davis, 1972) to nearly 30 percent, whereas it had remained relatively constant at two-thirds in the more developed regions. In other words, the process of urbanization is today preceeding rapidly in many of the developing nations of the world.

Although the rapid growth of urban areas is a fairly general phenomenon throughout the developing world, there are substantial differences among regions and particular countries (Beier, 1976). There are some areas, notably in Latin America, where urbanization is already well advanced and where the problems associated with rapid urban growth such as high levels of unemployment, marked inequalities in the distribution of wealth, and massive and overcrowded slum areas are already fairly widespread. Continued rapid population growth in these countries during the years ahead will encourage higher levels of urbanization and will exacerbate the already existing problems and add to the overall burden of development. On the other hand, there are some countries, particularly in sub-Saharan Africa, where urbanization has barely begun and where sufficient land resources are still available so that urbanization can be expected to proceed at a relatively slower rate and where, accordingly, the process and problems of urban growth may not be so pressing. Despite the existence of such differences (which are essential to consider when dealing with the development problems of a particular country), the general outlook for the remainder of this century is that urban growth will continue to be a major phenomenon throughout most of the Third World.

Urbanization and Economic Development In the historical experience of the industrialized nations of the Western world, the growth of cities was so closely associated with the process of economic growth that urbanization came to be regarded as both an index of and a stimulant to economic development. On the one hand, since large population aggregates cannot exist without some means of livelihood, the growth of cities indicates, at the very least, some minimum development of opportunities for nonagricultural employment. On the other hand, the growth of cities provides concentrations of the manpower needed for the further growth and expansion of nonagricultural activities. Given this Western experience, the rapid urbanization now taking place in many of the less developed areas might be regarded as an indicator that economic growth is taking place and as a potential stimulus to continued economic growth. However, closer examination of the nature of the urbanization process currently underway in many of these areas reveals that this is not necessarily the case, and that the role of the city in relation to economic growth needs to be reassessed. Pursuing this issue further, it is possible to distinguish at least three ways in which the urbanization process now taking place in the less developed areas differs from the historical experience of the Western world: these relate to cause, type, and effect.

Although migration continues to be a significant component of urban growth in the less developed countries today, there has been a major change with respect to the underlying *causes* of the basic rural-to-urban migration stream. When people move they usually do so in order to find better opportunities for themselves, and any migration stream can generally be explained in terms of a combination of "push" factors (factors such as a high level of unemployment that motivate people to leave one area), and "pull" factors (those, such as an abundance of employment opportunities, that draw people to another area). In the historical experience of the more developed countries both sets of factors were generally present, so that the rural-to-urban migration stream performed the dual function of reducing overpopulation in rural areas at the same time that it provided the workers needed for the expanding urban industries. The problem with respect to many developing countries today, however, arises from the fact that the traditional rural push is as strong as ever (if not stronger, given the much higher rates of population increase prevailing throughout the developing world); but the existence of the urban pull forces is more felt than real. That is, rural peasants are flocking to the cities in search of jobs that are not there. The sad truth is that in many cases the process of industrialization is proceeding so slowly that opportunities for nonagricultural employment are not being created fast enough to absorb the hordes of rural-to-urban migrants.

This phenomenon, whereby the rate of increase in the size of the nonagricultural population exceeds the rate of increase in meaningful nonagricultural employment opportunities, is referred to as "over-urbanization," and represents a serious obstacle to economic growth and development. Lacking opportunities for productive work in the modern sector, people moving from the country to the city are often forced to find employment in peripheral occupations where they neither contribute much to the economy nor receive much from it, and often the overflow of rural distress into urban areas is the most outstanding characteristic of urbanization in underdeveloped areas. In contrast to the past, when economic development and the growth of industry was the underlying cause of rural-to-urban migration, the present situation in many parts of the developing world is one where rural-urban migration not only takes place in the absence of comparable industrial development, but also where this same rural-urban migration could seriously retard the overall development process (see below).

In addition to a shortage of nonagricultural employment opportunities, the larger cities in the developing world also lack many of the services such as health and education facilities to meet the basic needs of the new migrants. A major problem in this respect is lack of housing (Lakshmanan, et al., 1976). Part of this problem relates to the housing supply, and part relates to the public services one commonly associates with adequate housing—energy for heating and lighting, running water, waste disposal, etc. Although most people in developing countries have some kind of house in which to live (extreme exceptions such as the "pavement dwellers" of Calcutta notwithstanding) the quality of the housing environment—particularly for the poor in the massive slum and squatter settlements that are one of the most distinguishing characteristics of Third World cities today—ranges from poor to appalling. Much the same can be said for other basic facilities and services, and, as will be seen below, the need to provide these facilities and services often results in scarce capital being diverted away from more productive development programs.

In summary, then, the shortage of nonagricultural employment opportunities as well as the lack of many essential urban services means that city growth in many developing countries today is often little more than an expansion of dilapidated shantytowns filled with underemployed, poverty stricken rural peasants.

A second key difference associated with the urbanization trend in many of the less developed countries today relates to *type*. In the West, the process of urbanization generally

involved the growth and development of a great many different cities, many of which were characterized by a more or
less specialized function, such as government administration
(Washington, D.C.), commerce (Boston and New Orleans),
heavy industry (Detroit, Gary, and Pittsburgh), or insurance
and finance (Hartford and New York). The result was the
development of a functionally integrated urban network, or
system of cities. In marked contrast to this pattern, much of
the urban growth that has been taking place in many underdeveloped areas in recent years has been concentrated in a
single large city—what have come to be called "Primate
Cities." To illustrate, data compiled for the late 1960s reveal
that among the highly developed countries an average of 32
percent of the urban population was living in the single
largest city, but in the group of underdeveloped countries an
average of 55 percent of the urban population was concentrated in the largest city (Stockwell, 1974). Furthermore, it is
likely that this situation will persist for some time to come.
That is, rather than generating many new cities, the rapid
growth of the urban population in the developing countries
will take place largely through the expansion of already
existing cities (Beier, 1976:8-9). This is mainly because most
choice locations for cities have already been taken, and it
will be much easier and cheaper to expand existing cities
than to build new ones. Some new cities will likely grow up
where newly discovered resources are located, and in a few
cases new cities may be established for political reasons—
Brasilia in Brazil is a case in point, although the problems
encountered in this effort are likely to discourage similar
ones. However, such new city development is likely to be
limited by economic considerations, and even if they are
built they are likely to attract only a small fraction of overall
urban population growth. One reason for this is that the bulk
of the rural-to-urban migrants will likely continue to be attracted to the older, more familiar and well-established
cities.
    Another reason that the larger established cities have been

and will continue attracting a disproportionate share of the rural migrants reflects a change in the traditional migration process. In the early stages of urbanization, migration generally took place in a series of moves—from a rural area, to a small town, to a city, and then to a large urban area. Today, however, as Beier (1976) has noted, rural migrants in the developing countries are increasingly by-passing the intermediate stops and moving directly to large urban centers. Two factors have been cited to explain this trend: a decline in transportation costs and the presence of friends or relatives among earlier migrants. The former "has facilitated movement back and forth between rural and urban areas, improving information and lowering the risk of resettlement" (Beier, 1976:11). The latter means simply that friends and relatives who migrated earlier provide not only information but also a base of support for newer migrants until they can get settled.

The significance of the preceding "cause" and "type" differences in the urbanization process taking place in many developing areas today lies in their *effect* on national economic growth. Despite certain advantages such as a location that has ready access to world markets, or the presence of a large labor pool, a great deal of evidence has been amassed concerning the potential detrimental effects of the tendency for a single large city to draw a disproportionate share of the rural-to-urban migrants. To illustrate, these so-called Primate Cities tend to monopolize the professional and skilled personnel (teachers and doctors, for example), leaving other areas without needed services; by draining off rural resources while returning little if anything to the rural markets they tend to command more than their fair share of the national income; because of the strong attraction in terms of the available labor pool they discourage industrial dispersion and the growth of other cities; and they tend to be the center of all major cultural activities (theaters, colleges and universities, museums, etc.), leaving the rest of the country in a barren state.

One of the major problems is that the earlier noted short-age of nonagricultural economic opportunities has often meant that the rural-to-urban migration stream often does little more than effect a transfer of rural poverty to urban areas; in many cases it has even contributed to greater urban poverty. When there are only a limited number of unskilled low-paying jobs and a surplus of poor workers competing for them, the effect is to depress incomes even more, and the hundreds of thousands of unskilled urban laborers and service workers are constantly finding their low wages bid even lower by the waves of new migrants that are flocking to the cities from depressed rural areas. This problem is further exacerbated by the age composition of the rural-to-urban migrants. For the most part they are younger than the general population; hence, the previously discussed problems of age structure (high dependency burdens and potential economic-political instability) tend to be most pronounced in the larger cities of the developing areas:

> Studies of urban population in developing countries show that low income groups usually have the lowest median age and highest dependency burden within the total population. Since younger workers are likely to have less education, training, experience, and job seniority, and therefore are likely to have lower paying jobs, the advancement of poor urban families is hindered by their disproportionate number of young workers, in addition to high dependency ratios. (Beier, 1976:16)

In addition to flooding the labor market, depressing wages, and increasing the ranks of the unemployed, the rapid growth of the urban population may have a more direct harmful effect on national development programs. In many countries, the growth of a large urban proletariat has created needs and demands that must be met, often at the expense of more productive investments. That is, funds that might otherwise have been used to finance various programs to promote national development must be diverted to the provision of food and other basic services such as public health, housing, and education for the masses. This is in fact what happened in Peru during the late 1960s. At that time, the constitutional government of Fernando Belaunde was faced

with the task, among others, of increasing agricultural productivity and raising the level of living of the rural population
through a variety of land reform programs. At the same time
it had to satisfy the needs of the growing urban masses in
order to maintain their political support. The latter was done
by greatly increasing expenditures in the social sector (education, public health, etc.) at the expense of other productive
development programs—particularly at the expense of agricultural development. That is, political expediency dic-
tated that investments be made in consumption areas rather
than in productive ones. This situation has recently been
described by Laidlaw who noted:

> What has happened in Peru (and in other Latin American countries
> as well) has been a massive migration from rural to urban areas,
> particularly to metropolitan Lima-Callao. This has led to a substantial
> growth of a new class of urban poor with greater political potential, and
> whose demands exert a greater influence on economic policymaking
> than those of the rural poor. . . . In other words, a politically weak
> peasantry was more or less kept in line by a start in the direction of land
> redistribution, whereas an increasing share of government resources
> was diverted to programs to benefit the urban poor who represented a
> potentially more serious threat to overall economic stability. Viewed in
> connection with the watered-down land reform bill that came out of the
> opposition-dominated congress, it seems clear that Balaunde's need to
> adapt to the realities of the political situation lie at the bottom of the
> lack of any real success of the agrarian reform programs of his govern-
> ment. (Laidlaw, 1976:67-68)

The case of Peru illustrates a problem that all constitutional governments face—the problem of maintaining sufficient popular support to stay in power—and it anticipates
one of the conclusions to be made later in this volume to the
effect that successful development in today's world may well
depend on the presence of an authoritarian type of central
government (see chapter 8). As one scholar has recently
noted with respect to Asia, but which may apply to other
regions of the Third World as well, successful national
economic development may well have to be achieved at the
expense of personal consumption:

> If we imagine that whatever gains are made by the total economy are

used to make the collectivity work and to increase its competitive power, then personal consumption at a high level is not only unnecessary but dangerous because it is not controlled by the officials. . . . Further massive growth in urban populations rules out a democratic, consumer-sovereign adaptation, leading instead to a minutely regulated communal dictatorship with lower personal consumption and high collective use of whatever resources and surpluses are available. (Davis, 1975:85)

Based on these observations, it can be concluded that the relation between city growth and economic development is no longer as clear cut as was once believed. Whether or not urbanization promotes economic development will depend on its nature and on the type of city that emerges. It can also be concluded that when city growth occurs in the absence of sufficient industrial development, and when it is concentrated in one or two large Primate Cities (as indeed appears to be happening in many of the developing areas), then its influence on economic development is more likely to be negative rather than positive.

Urbanization and Fertility In examining the historical demographic transition in the countries of Western Europe it will be noted that when fertility declines occurred they followed large scale rural-to-urban migration (Weinstein, 1976). Given this historical correlation, there might seem reason to regard the present widespread urbanization trend throughout the developing world as the predecessor of the much sought after reductions in fertility and in the rate of population growth. Some of the factors that might support this thesis would include (1) the urban-rural fertility differential (since urban birth rates are lower than rural, an increasing proportion of the population living in urban areas should be reflected in a lowering of the overall birth rate); (2) the economic character of the city (large families, which may be economically beneficial in rural areas, are a drain on family economic resources in non-agrarian settings, and as the growing urban population adjusts to this fact fertility levels should drop); (3) the social psychology of city life (in an urban setting traditional attitudes and values are replaced by modern rational modes of thinking and evaluation, and the birth of a child becomes more the result of deliberate calculation rather than chance). In summing up this "urban growth thesis" as a correlate of the downward transition in fertility Weinstein has observed:

> Economic activity and/or the level of sensory stimulation in nonurban settings do not promote abstract thought or intellectualization. Thus, most activities, and especially childbearing, are subject only to physical and traditional parameters in the countryside. With the shift to urban society, rational calculation becomes the dominant sensory mode, and fertility practices become understandable in economic terms. Since large families entail high costs, urban residents limit family size. (Weinstein, 1976:78)

As Weinstein goes on to point out, however, this urban growth explanation is not only an oversimplification of a very complex process, it also suffers from at least two serious weaknesses. In the first place, both urban growth and fertility decline were part of a much broader societal transformation that included such other things as the emergence of capitalism, colonial expansion, the industrial revolution, a decline in the importance of the family as an economic unit of production, an increasing secularization of social values, and a general rise in the overall standard of living. While all of these profound societal changes took place in conjunction with the rapid growth of the urban population, it is virtually impossible to specify what is causing what. And in particular it becomes impossible to say for certain that any single phenomenon such as urbanization was responsible for the decline in fertility.

A second weakness lies in the situation discussed in the preceding section; namely, major differences in kind exist between the urbanization process in eighteenth and nineteenth century Europe and the one that is taking place in the developing nations today. For example, the lack of a real urban pull in terms of available opportunities for nonagricultural employment has meant that a high proportion of urban dwellers throughout the Third World have maintained traditional peasant lifestyles—one aspect of which is a high fertility level. Another key difference is that the larger Primate Cities that have been attracting the bulk of the rural-to-urban migrants are often cities that were either founded or expanded by European colonists, and their growth was largely determined by the needs of the European economies. That is, the indigenous cities in the non-Western world grew and expanded as part of the historical development of the European economic system; they did not develop, as cities in Europe did, as an integral part of a larger indigenous social transformation:

> Lacking an indigenous social origin, cities in the underdeveloped areas have failed to produce the effects on traditional institutions to the same degree as have cities eleswhere. In particular, traditional fertility norms have not, as yet, succumbed to the priorities of urban life and economy. (Weinstein, 1976:93)

It can thus be suggested that the sought-after declines in fertility within the developing countries are not going to come as a response to such a simple change as a redistribution of the population from rural to urban areas. Rather, the causes of the fertility transition that followed urbanization in the West must be sought in those other social changes that were an integral part of the growth of cities—the shift away from traditionalism to rationalism, increased literacy, improvements in the status of women, rising levels of living, declines in the social and economic importance of the extended family system, removal of traditional class barriers and increases in socioeconomic mobility, and so forth. In other words, the determinants of fertility behavior are to be found in the fundamental attitudes and values of people, in their traditional modes of behavior, and in the institutional structure of their societies—not in their place of residence—and it is through these other aspects of cultural and social life that changes in fertility behavior will have to be effected.

Population Growth and Economic Development

It should be clear from the preceding discussion that the

demographic characteristics of the low-income countries in Asia, Africa, and Latin American constitute a major dimension of the overall development problem. Perhaps the most crucial and most hotly debated aspect of this dimension concerns the question of the relationship between population growth rates and economic development. On the one hand, many Third World nations regard the so-called population problem as a smoke screen set up by the more highly developed countries to divert attention away from the more basic political and economic roots of underdevelopment (see chapter 8). On the other hand, while it is generally recognized that the high fertility levels and rapid growth rates in the poor countries are in large part an effect of their low income status, rather than its primary cause, the majority of scholars who have studied this topic tend to take the position that continued rapid population growth in these countries will seriously hamper their national development efforts. As one writer has noted:

> If an economy is growing but the population remains unchanged in size, then any increase in goods and services, minus that needed for reinvestment purposes, is available for improving the level of living of the people. . . . On the other hand, if there is any amount of population growth, then the increase in goods and services, minus that needed for reinvestment, when divided amongst a larger population, will result in smaller gains per capita in the level of living. (Jaffe, 1960:529-30)

Not everyone shares this view to the same extent, however. There are some, for example, who take the more optimistic view that diminishing returns is not a necessary result of rapid population growth in a technologically advanced world (Kuznets, 1967; Barnett, 1971). Further, there are even a few who would take an extreme contrary position that rapid population growth is desirable, and may even be necessary to stimulate economic progress (Clark, 1960). In spite of the fact that there are such differences of opinion (and in fact there are actual differences in the nature of the population growth/economic development relationship among various parts of the world, as well as during different time periods), it

Table 3.5 Average annual rates of increase in per capita income in low income countries grouped
by population growth rates, 1960 decade.

Average annual rate of population growth	Average annual rate of increase in per capita income
Less than 1.5%	4.4%
1.5—2.4%	2.8%
2.5—3.4%	1.9%
3.5% or more	1.7%

Source: E. G. Stockwell, "Some Observations on the Relationship Between Population
Growth and Economic Development During the 1960's," *Rural Sociology*, 37 (December 1972):628-32.

is our contention that the overwhelming body of evidence
would support the first position stated above. That is, the
high rate of population growth that exists in many if not most
of the underdeveloped countries of the world today represents a major obstacle to their economic development. Some
evidence in support of this position is provided by the data in
Table 3.5 which shows average rates of increase in per capita
annual income during the 1960s for twenty-six underdeveloped countries that have been divided into four groups
on the basis of their annual rate of population growth.

Although it should be noted that a completely adequate
account of the relationship between population growth and
economic development would consider the effect of income
changes on population growth as well as the effect of population growth on the movement of per capita income, the
concern here is solely with the latter effect because it is this
latter effect that is the more relevant issue in the developing
countries today. Assuming that the trend in annual per capita
income can be regarded as a reasonably valid index of the
rate of economic development (see preceding chapter), then
the data for these twenty-six countries clearly reveal the
existence of a marked inverse relationship between the rate
of population growth and the rate of economic development.
For those countries whose population increased by less than
1.5 percent a year during the 1960s, the average annual rate
of increase in per capita income was 4.4 percent, and it
averaged 2.8 percent a year among those countries where

annual population growth rates fell between 1.5 and 2.5 percent. In contrast, the average annual rate of per capita income growth was only 1.9 percent for countries whose annual rate of population growth was between 2.5 and 3.5 percent, and it was only 1.7 percent for those countries that had been growing at a rate in excess of 3.5 percent per year. What we have, then, is clearly a situation wherein the fastest population growth during the 1960s took place in those areas that could least afford it from the point of view of reducing poverty and raising levels of living. Conversely, we have a situation in which the slowest rates of economic progress were associated with the fastest rates of population growth. Furthermore, it can be assumed that the persistence of rapid rates of population growth will continue to exert a depressing effect on the rate of economic development in the low in-come countries.

Some of the specific ways in which population growth might adversely affect economic development programs can be summed up briefly as follows:

1. Where population is growing rapidly a larger propor-tion of national income must be spent on providing basic necessities rather than being used for more productive purposes. In many countries, for exam-ple, potential food surpluses must be used to feed expanding populations rather than being traded on the world market in exchange for needed capital.

2. In many parts of the underdeveloped world con-tinued population growth, by aggravating already existing food shortages, may lead to an increase in malnutrition and the incidence of various deficiency diseases, thereby significantly reducing the produc-tive efficiency of the labor force. Further, such lower productivity due to poor health can jeopardize the quality of the next generation, perpetuating under-development in what can be regarded as a vicious circle of poverty (see Figure 3.4).

3. Population growth increases the need and demand

Figure 3.4 Diagrammatic illustration of the "vicious circle" of poverty and poor health.

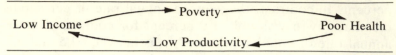

for all manner of public services such as welfare, education, housing, health facilities, etc. Again, capital that is directed to the provision of these services reduces that which might otherwise be available for investment in more productive endeavors.

4. Rapid population growth that hampers social and economic welfare improvements may lead to political turmoil within nations or internecine wars between nations, in both cases causing resources to be diverted away from general development programs.

5. Population growth creates pressures toward unemployment, particularly if it is accompanied by agricultural advances and the associated displacement of farm labor. Paradoxically, because it is the youthful segment of the population that is expanding most rapidly, population growth generates a high ratio of dependent consumers to producers at the same time that is generates pressures toward unemployment. Among other things, this situation could lead to an increase in internal unrest and tension.

6. Rapid population growth also serves to depress wages at the same time that it increases the cost of basic goods and services.

7. In many instances rapid population growth increases the need for foreign aid, thus building up a greater national debt and prolonging a state of financial dependence on the aid-granting nations.

8. Population growth leads to greater demands being placed on the natural resource base, increasing not only the costs but also the rate of resource consumption, thus bringing closer the day when various non-renewable resources may be exhausted.

9. To the extent that continued population growth hampers development efforts in the low income countries it leads to a widening of the gap between rich and poor nations, thereby increasing jealousy and resentment in the poor nations and heightening international tensions.

In short, population growth accentuates virtually every problem that is associated with underdevelopment. Poor health, low education, poverty, low per capita productivity, unemployment, inadequate diets, rapid urbanization, housing shortages, etc.—all become increasingly serious as population continues to expand, and all become increasingly more costly and more difficult to alleviate. And the situation does not look like it is going to improve much in the very near future. With an overall annual growth rate of well over 2 percent in 1976, the number of people living in the underdeveloped areas of the world could be expected to double in about thirty years. Thus, shortly after we enter the twenty-first century there could be twice as many people in these countries who have to be fed, clothed, housed, educated, etc. Since, as we have seen in the preceding chapter, many underdeveloped areas are already seriously deficient in their ability to provide for these basic human needs, the prospect of continued rapid population growth must be regarded as a serious obstacle to their future development. As long as birth rates remain high and population continues to grow rapidly, many of the underdeveloped economies will find themselves in a situation where they will have to run as fast as they can just to stay in the same place—where they will have to achieve very substantial increases in national income just to *maintain* the wide economic gap that already exists between the rich and the poor nations of the world.

The simple facts of the matter are that a disproportionate share of the population growth taking place in the world today is concentrated in the underdeveloped regions that are least able to cope with it. Most of the poor countries are in the midst of major efforts to improve their economic condition, but all too often any potential gains in economic status are being wiped out by rapid and increasing rates of population growth. These increasing rates of population growth are the result of remarkable success in controlling death and the virtual absence of any real fertility control. As long as this situation persists—as long as birth rates do not decline—the rate of population growth in the underdeveloped regions can be expected to remain high, with the unfortunate consequence of prolonging, if not even widening, the absolute gap between the rich and the poor nations of the world.

As long as population growth continues, the only real result of technological gains and so-called economic progress in underdeveloped countries will be an increase in the number of people they are capable of supporting at existing low levels of living. This can hardly be called progress. Continued population growth means only that the years ahead will see more and more people living at marginal levels of subsistence, more and more people leading impoverished lives characterized by the steady erosion of human rights and individual freedom, more and more people with less and less to lose and more and more to gain from the overthrow of the existing order. Not everyone would agree that the population crisis is the most serious problem confronting the world today, but most would agree that the most successful development programs in the coming years will be those that have as one of their major goals the slowing down of population growth through the deliberate reduction of fertility.

Summary

As noted at the beginning of this chapter, the basic demographic situation in the developing countries can be summarized as: (1) a relatively high but declining death rate, in combination with (2) a much higher birth rate, resulting in (3) a rapid rate of population growth, and (4) the emergence of a very young population and a corresponding high ratio of consumers to producers. Furthermore, the rapid rate of population growth, coupled with increasing agricultural efficiency is displacing large segments of the rural population and leading to (5) rapid rates of urbanization. The problems that this demographic situation generates for the overall development problem are equally as serious as the economic problems discussed in the preceding chapter. Bringing about economic development and increasing the levels of living in the poor countries of the world involves both increasing their economic productivity and slowing down their rates of population growth. According to the approach taken in this volume, whether or not these two objectives are attained, or when they are attained, will depend in large part on a wide variety of social and cultural factors that influence both economic productivity and demographic behavior. It is with a consideration of these important sociocultural factors that the remaining chapters are concerned.

4

Culture and Development

The remainder of this text will elaborate the approach taken to the development problem in chapter 1, namely, that a major dimension of the development problem of any society is to be found within the larger sociocultural structure of that society. It is here that one can find such major obstacles to economic and demographic modernization as passive attitudes and value orientations, illiteracy, inheritance laws that lead to fragmented holdings, rigid class structures, and social and psychological pressures to have large families. As has been suggested, it is only when ways are found to overcome or otherwise circumvent these kinds of obstacles that the way will be open for sustained economic development. The discussion in this chapter will focus on the relationship between culture and development, with particular attention being paid to illustrating how various aspects of culture may act to impede economic and demographic modernization. At the outset it must be stressed that traditional culture is not regarded as a necessary obstacle to development in any society; however, any development program that fails to take into consideration the strong influence of traditional culture is doomed to failure from the start. Hence, while we do not insist that cultural change is a prerequisite for development, we do insist that good development planning in any society must be based on a thorough knowledge and understanding of its culture.

What Is Culture?

In the broadest sense, the term "culture" refers to all aspects of human society that are either learned or man-made. Subsumed under the culture of a society would be such things as its family structure, the tools of its technology, its system of social stratification, its stock of capital equipment, its religious beliefs and values, and so forth. In many respects, however, such an all-encompassing definition of culture is inappropriate for the task at hand. Whenever any references are made to the influence of culture on development it would be necessary to specify further what aspect of culture was exerting an influence in a given situation. Hence, a narrower and more specific definition is desirable.

One distinction that is commonly made is that between material and nonmaterial culture. Material culture is the objective dimension of culture and refers to the tangible things that people have invented or built—to the tools of a society, to its technology, and to the things that the tools have built. Homes and factories, automobiles and rickshaws, roads and bridges, sky scrapers and scotch tape, garden rakes and gyroscopes, television satellites and turquoise jewelry, bicycles and bed pans, plastic containers, aluminum foil, hydroelectric power plants, pencils, paper, cloth, medicines and medical equipment—all the things made by people are what comprise the material culture of human society. By contrast, nonmaterial culture, or the subjective dimension of culture, refers to such intangibles as attitudes, beliefs, values, traditions, language, normative standards, and the like. Whereas material culture items exist in concrete form in the real world where they can be seen and touched, nonmaterial culture exists in the minds of people. Nonmaterial culture refers to the underlying "rules and regulations" that govern human conduct—the determinants of human behavior; it is this dimension of culture that we wish to emphasize in relation to economic development. Although it is clearly recognized that the nature of the resource base, the stock of capital equipment, and the prevailing level of technology are extremely important variables in the modernization process, the concern in this chapter will be on nonmaterial culture, or on the subjective aspects of human society that influence the ways in which people behave. A related aspect of nonmaterial culture, social organization or the social structure of society, will be considered in a later chapter.

Culture and Economic Behavior

Economic development, or any kind of economic change, does not occur in isolation, but is part of a much larger and more general cultural transformation. In any society where economic modernization is taking place it will come into contact with numerous other dimensions of culture. Some of these will influence the nature of economic change and the direction that it takes. The strong familistic tradition of classical Japan, for example, has clearly been carried over into the organization of the factory work force in that country—there is a strong reciprocal relationship in which the worker gives his loyalty to a single firm in return for a virtual guarantee of a lifetime job and welfare benefits far in excess of those generally provided by western industrial employers (De Gregori and Pi-Sunyer, 1969:37). Still other aspects of culture may be seriously modified by economic development—as when the end of feudalism in Europe led to a breakdown of the aristocracy and a change in the social class structure of society. In other words, economy and culture are dynamically interrelated; economic development will both influence and be influenced by other aspects of culture. For purposes of this volume concern will be primarily on the influence that culture exerts with respect to economic change. In particular, we shall be concerned with examining those aspects of culture that could potentially function to slow down or otherwise impede national economic and demographic modernization.

As a starting point it may be suggested that economic development has certain minimum prerequisites. It may be assumed, for example, that the economic development of a region or nation implies the presence of some kinds of resources that could be developed or utilized more productively than at present. It may also be assumed that a technology exists that would permit the development of the resources in question. Finally, we would suggest that development requires a sociocultural melieu that will encourage the kinds of behavior that are necessary to achieve more adequate resource development and utilization. To the extent that such behavior is discouraged or not fully encouraged, culture may act as a serious obstacle to economic development.

In terms of the societal approach taken in this volume, which regards economic development as something that can be achieved through a more efficient utilization or exploitation of a given resource base, culture represents a problem to the extent that it either acts passively so that it does not encourage optimal efficiency with respect to resource utilization, or actively encourages inefficiency in resource use. An example of the former would be the other-worldly attitudes in some cultures that put a low premium on material possessions and emphasize the desirability of leading a good life according to traditional standards rather than trying to improve oneself. Such an aescetic orientation is unlikely to produce the aggressive entrepreneurial behavior that many regard as desirable, if not necessary for economic growth (McClelland, 1961). An example of the latter would be the not uncommon fragmented system of land tenure, wherein custom, if not law, requires land holdings to be subdivided equally among all heirs (sons), and which after several generations creates a highly uneconomical situation where a single farmer may have to care for several very small patches of land scattered throughout the community. To cite another illustration concerning the demographic side of the development problem, culture may act passively so as not to encourage fertility decline through a belief that such things as the number of children one has is not something that mere mortals should decide upon or control; such a belief would not likely encourage people to participate in a family planning program. Or again it may contain elements that actively encourage a high level of fertility such as religious values that endorse large families and forbid the use of contraception to limit family size, or attitudes that interpret a large number of children, especially sons, as a visible sign of one's masculinity. Specific government policies that reject family planning as an imperialist plot of the rich nations to keep former colonial peoples under control would be still another illustration of how subjective values can function actively to retard the processes of demographic modernization; to the extent that demographic modernization would facilitate economic development, such pronatalist policies also represent major obstacles to economic modernization. In the following sections we shall consider more fully some of the specific obstacles to economic and demographic modernization that may be rooted in the nonmaterial aspects of culture in the developing world.

Attitudes and Values

The best way to approach this topic is to discuss some specific attitudes that are often found among developing peoples and that contrast sharply with the attitudes with which we are familiar in Western society. Unfortunately, when we seek to make comparisons of this sort (unlike the case with more objective economic or demographic characteristics), it is difficult to find empirical indices of the kinds of differences that exist between developed and underdeveloped countries. Nevertheless, by drawing upon some of the relevant theoretical thinking of the recent past (e.g., Hoselitz, 1960; Spengler, 1955), and by being willing to resort to oversimplification for the sake of illustration, it is possible to dichotomize, in ideal type fashion, a few selected cultural attitudes of developed and underdeveloped areas. Where possible, however, we shall try to illustrate the general ideal type differences with some specific cases to show the nature of the deterrent effect a particular cultural attitude may have on the overall development process.

Economic development entails change of one kind or another, and one area in which there is often a profound difference between developed and underdeveloped peoples concerns attitudes toward change. We in the United States are attracted by slogans that advertise something as "new," "bigger and better," "improved," and so forth; and we tend to look upon certain kinds of change as being basically good and as being synonymous with progress. This attitude, which is generally shared by the other economically advanced nations, is aptly summed up by the mid-twentieth century slogan of one of America's industrial giants: "Progress is our most important product." But this progressive attitude is in marked contrast to the basic conservatism that is characteristic of most preindustrial societies, where anything new and different tends to be regarded with skepticism, if not outright distrust. In these latter societies one often finds a tenacious commitment to the status quo that leads to resisting even the most basic changes. To take a simple illustration, many preindustrial peoples have lived for generations on a bare margin of subsistence, and over the years they have worked out a very delicate balance between their technology and their environment. In such cases the slightest change in the environment can have (and indeed often has had) catastrophic consequences; in such cases it will not be (and has not been) easy to get farmers to abandon centuries old techniques that have proven themselves in favor of some new technology such as hybrid seeds that merely purport to offer a means of increasing their output. In such cases change will come slowly, and only after the new ways have been demonstrated to be clearly better than the old ways.

The extent to which change will be resisted will of course vary from society to society, and from individual to individual within a single society. The point to emphasize, however, is that many Third World peoples are completely unlike Westerners who equate change with progress. (However, not all change is viewed as progress in the Western world; witness the resistance of many Americans to bussing as a means of achieving racial balance in the schools, or the opposition generated by such things as the SST and the proposed construction of nuclear power plants.) Rather, the former often fear change because it represents something new or unknown—they may equate change with disaster such as a flood or an earthquake. More seriously, from the perspective of the development planner, some Third World peoples may regard change as sacrilegious, as a violation of their sacred traditions. In these cases simply demonstrating that a new way, such as the use of hybrid seeds, is a better way and results in greater crop yields will not be sufficient to induce the sought after change.

Another area in which nonwestern cultural values often contrast sharply with those commonly found throughout the developed world concerns attitudes toward adversity and how to react to it. In our western society the Protestant Ethic heritage has taught us that man is an intelligent and rational thinking being who is capable of exercising a great deal of control over his destiny. Through inventiveness and hard work we can meet adversity and overcome the limits imposed by our environment. We in the industrialized nations have proven to ourselves that active mastery over nature and the physical world is possible, and that with effort and perseverance we can be masters of our own destiny. This is precisely what most of us have always striven to achieve. In contrast, people in developing societies are often oriented toward a more passive acceptance of their lot in life; their belief systems often contain explicit references to the inability or inappropriateness of mere mortals to interfere with or otherwise try to change that which fate has decreed. Such a fatalistic acceptance of life and the world can represent a serious deterrent to the adoption of any kind of change— particularly that which some external element might try to impose from without.

On a general level the nature of this attitude can be illustrated by the Spanish expression *"Que será será"* (What will be, will be), or by reference to the Islamic aphorism "Allah wills it." More specifically, the fatalistic outlook often characterizing preindustrial peoples can be illustrated by the belief among some Indian groups in Colombia that whether an infant lives or dies is dependent upon the will of God (Foster, 1962:67); a belief such as this will not actively encourage the adoption of different child caring practices aimed at reducing infant mortality. In short, where people tend to accept their position in life and the nature of the world around them as preordained by fate or some other kind of mystical force, it will be that much more difficult to motivate them to expend extra energy or to adopt new techniques in an attempt either to alter their environment or to enhance their own life chances.

An attitudinal perspective that is related to this fatalism, or passive acceptance of the status quo, is found in the dominant time orientation. Modern industrialized man tends to be future oriented, and he is generally willing to take risks, to experiment, to "save for a rainy day," and so forth. Many traditional societies, on the other hand, are characterized by either a strong past or present time orientation. In the former case one may find economic assets being directed toward such things as the maintenance of ancestral shrines, or to other equally nonproductive uses. Where a present time orientation prevails one commonly finds economic activities being governed by the desire to satisfy immediate needs. The future is too capricious and unpredictable to try and plan for, they say. Or, reflecting the previously noted fatalistic outlook, they may say that the future is predetermined and there is nothing that can be done that will change it.

It is important to stress that the kind of attitude configuration represented by fatalism and a present-time orientation does not mean that the people concerned are ignorant or irrational, nor does it mean that they are satisfied with the way things are. Often these attitudes reflect very rational responses to the realities of the situation. In a world where life has always been hard and precarious, where the unpredictable whims of nature (drought, floods, locust plagues) seem to dominate one's life chances, there is little basis for adopting any other orientation, and such attitudes represent a potential source of resistance to change in many parts of the Third World.

Still another feature that often differentiates the modern Western mentality from that found in Third World cultures would be the attitudes toward work. According to the Protestant Ethic value system characteristic of the Western world, hard work is "good for the soul;" it is a positive end in itself and a means whereby one can achieve material success. In other societies, however, particularly those which are nonacquisitive or which have a present-time orientation, much less of a premium is placed on the value of work. On the one hand, in many preindustrial societies work is synonymous with survival. It is not something one does for moral reasons or in order to get ahead; one either works, and works hard, or one does not survive. On the other hand, some societies tend to place relatively more value on contemplation and other introspective activities such as scholarly pursuits that aim more toward making one a better person from an aescetic rather than from an economic point of view. A specific example of work attitudes different from those commonly found in the Western world would be those of some agricultural groups in Africa who assign major work responsibility to women because "a man was not meant to burrow in the dirt like an animal." Still another example would be the concept of the "limited good" one finds in some peasant societies, and which encourages a person to work only enough to maintain the status quo (see page 121). To the extent that economic development will be enhanced when hard work is valued not only in and of itself but particularly because it will lead to an improvement in one's life chances, then attitudes such as the preceding may act as obstacles in the modernization process.

A somewhat related aspect of work attitudes concerns the daily rhythms of work and leisure. In contrast to the nine-to-five work day with which we in the United States are familiar, it is not uncommon to find different work patterns in many developing societies. In tropical regions, for example, it is common to find the early morning and late afternoon hours being devoted to work while the hours of midday heat are devoted to leisure and relaxation. Development programs which try to adapt to the traditionally established work patterns will stand a much better chance of succeeding than those that try to impose alien and often impractical patterns on the population.

Implicit in several of the preceding paragraphs is the notion that people in developing societies are apt to be nonacquisitive with respect to material possessions and to exhibit a negative attitude toward acquisitive behavior. Again, in contrast to a value of the Western world that accumulated wealth is a sign of one's worth, many people in more traditionally oriented societies would look upon the acquisition of wealth as unseemly or as a mark of selfishness and greed. In our society a man who works hard and amasses a great deal of worldly wealth is, if not held in high esteem, at least respected and envied for his wealth. But, in a different cultural environment, a similar level of respect might be reserved for a penniless priest who has elected to devote his life to the purification of his soul or to the humble scholar who values intellectual pursuits above material gain. Although such altruistic life styles may be respected, these attitudes may not be reflected in everyday behavior. That is, they do not mean that the people in the poor countries do not want to acquire material possessions for themselves, nor that they would not like to enjoy a higher level of living. However, they do mean that different kinds of behavior will be evaluated differently from one cultural setting to another, and failure to understand and appreciate these differences could lead to a serious misinterpretation of people's responses to development programs.

One can easily cite a number of other attitudinal perspectives that frequently serve to differentiate modern Western men from their counterparts in underdeveloped areas— modern man tends to be more nationalistic in his outlook while traditional man's loyalties are often localized, thus retarding the growth of concern with national development goals; modern man tends to value education as an end in itself more so than traditional man; modern man generally evaluates people on the basis of their own merit rather than on the basis of some ascribed characteristics, etc. The point to stress is that the basic attitudes and value systems found in the developing nations of the non-Western world will often differ sharply from those that prevail in modern industrial societies, and these differences may be important determinants of economic behavior. From the perspective of the development planner, they may be crucial in determining how specific economic programs are perceived and evaluated and whether or not they will be adopted.

It must also be pointed out that cultural ethnocentrism, the belief that one's own culture is superior to that of some other society, is found throughout the world. This means that the "West is best" missionary mentality one often encounters in the more highly developed countries is not likely to find much acceptance among developing societies. On the contrary, they will tend to regard their ways as superior to ours, and they will often be disdainful of suggestions that do not fit into their cultural experiences. The implication of this ethnocentrism is that certain features of a development plan may be rejected not so much because they conflict with some fundamental cultural value but simply because they are regarded as inferior. Most vegetarians, for example, will not only refuse to eat meat as a source of protein, they will also tend to regard those who do eat meat as uncultured barbarians.

Attitudes and Values–Summary The major determinants of economic behavior are rooted in deep-seated attitudes and values that will often be extremely resistant to change, especially if the change in question is being imposed from outside the cultural system. It has not been the intent in this section to condemn such cultural attitudes and the value systems of the developing societies. Rather, we have tried to show how some attitudes that are not typically found in the West may inhibit social change in general, and economic development in particular, among some non-Western peoples. Nor do we mean to suggest that people in the developing societies are a bunch of dullards who are so strongly tied to their traditional belief structures and behavior patterns that they will be unable to see the advantages of any new technologies or new ways of behaving to which they may be exposed during the development process. It is fairly safe to assert that most people, particularly poor people, would like to be able to enjoy a higher level of living, and the economic goals of the average man in a developing country are largely limited to achieving a better life for himself and his family. Once the average man can be made to see that national economic development will make it more likely that he will be able to achieve his own personal goals, then many of the attitudes and values that impede economic development will change more readily. Conversely, if the average man can see no advantage to himself to be derived from striving for national development, then he is unlikely to work toward that end and unlikely to alter his traditional attitudes and values. In one sense, then, a major task facing the development planner is to make the average man aware of the advantages that national development will bring to the average citizen. Beyond this, however, the basic point—and one that cannot be emphasized too often or too strongly—is that any development program that fails to take into consideration the prevailing belief system of a people and the possible influence of this belief system on the proposed development plan runs a serious risk of foundering before it gets off the ground.

One final point needs to be stressed with respect to the cultural attitudes and values commonly found in underdeveloped areas: the fact that developing societies may differ sharply from more highly developed areas should not be taken as an indication that cultural homogeneity exists within the former group. On the contrary, one of the often cited problems of development today concerns the vast cultural differences that may exist among the people of any given nation. In Uganda, to cite a single illustration, there are some twenty-five to thirty different tribal groups, each with its own distinctive language and a culture which in at least some respects is different from its neighbors (Goldthorpe, 1975:182). One recent writer has even gone so far as to characterize developing societies in general as "mosaic societies" in which it is often the case that "men are set apart from each other by more than what binds them together" (Wriggins, 1966). The existence of such cultural differences (which refer to such things as language, ethnic group, religion, tribal or regional location, etc.) may act as a formidable barrier to economic growth by fostering petty jealousies that inhibit cooperative efforts. The existence in a single country of many different languages and dialects, for example, may inhibit economic growth not only because of any intergroup jealousies it might create, but also because of difficulties in communicating the various developmental goals and plans to the different language groups. Further, a great diversity of language and dialects can seriously hamper efforts to raise the educational level of the population, one of the most important tasks facing many of the underdeveloped countries.

The Concept of "Limited Good"

It is a fundamental sociological premise that the vast majority of the members of any society share a common understanding, albeit an internalized one, of the way they are normally expected to act in various behavioral settings. To the extent that behavior does not conform to the normative standards of a group, that behavior may be regarded as deviant—and may be labeled by some as irrational. Conversely, "rational" behavior is, by definition, that which conforms to the normative expectations of the group within which it occurs—regardless of whether it might deviate from the standards of some other group, who might regard it as "irrational." The concept of Limited Good, which is derived from anthropology (Foster, 1965), represents an attempt to explain certain patterns of behavior found in traditional or peasant societies that would appear, to the western observer, to be irrational.

According to this concept of Limited Good, peasant behavior is based on an internalized belief that they live in a world in which the supply of all the good things in life (health and wealth, friendship and love, respect and power, security and safety) is fixed and is always in short supply. An analogy can be made with respect to the supply of land in a densely populated area; everybody wants some, but the supply is finite and there is not enough to go around. Such is the situation with respect to *all* the good things in life.

To the extent that Good is seen to exist in a limited and fixed amount, then it follows that the only way one person can improve his position would be at the expense of someone else. In such a setting, any improvement in one man's position with respect to any Good will be viewed as a threat to the entire community. It will indicate that someone in the community is being deprived, and that someone might even be oneself. This would be an unpleasant situation, and it would be very difficult for a group to exist as a cohesive unit for any length of time if some members were constantly gaining something at the expense of others. Accordingly, attitudes and values emerge in peasant societies that encourage behavior designed to maintain the status quo. As one anthropologist has put it:

> If, in fact, peasants see their universe as one in which the good things in life are in limited and unexpandable quantities, and hence personal gain must be at the expense of others, we must assume that social institutions, personal behavior, values, and personality will all display patterns that can be viewed as functions of this cognitive orientation. Preferred behavior, it may be argued, will be that which is seen by the peasant as maximizing this security, by preserving his relative position in the traditional order of things. (Foster, 1965:301)

Although the concept of Limited Good was developed in relation to peasant societies it was clearly intended to apply to all developing societies (Foster, 1972). In fact, some degree of Limited Good was believed to be present in all societies. A kind of continuum was envisaged with the two poles "More Limited" and "Less Limited," and with societies shifting from the "More" to the "Less Limited" pole as their level of development increased.

No claim has ever been made (and we do not make one now) that the cognitive orientation of Limited Good is the only model we have for explaining behavior in the developing societies. However, it is very useful in this respect, and it does much to help us understand why so many developing peoples so often exhibit attitudes and values such as those discussed in the preceding section (a negative attitude toward change, a passive acceptance of the world as it is, nonacquisitiveness, etc.).

Cultural Structure

In addition to traditional attitudes and values, a potential obstacle to economic development can be found in the fact that all of the various parts of a culture are closely interrelated with one another, and together they form a tightly integrated cultural structure. This has at least two specific implications for the general problem of social change and economic development. In the first place, it means that any new addition to the culture must be compatible with the existing structure. If it is not compatible it will be met with resistance, and runs the risk of being rejected entirely. For example, if a society comprised of vegetarians is characterized by widespread protein deficiency it is not going to be of much help to suggest that they eat meat in order to solve their nutritional problem. To cite a couple of other examples, the suggestion that farmers spray their fields with a chemical insecticide in order to kill off particular pests is not likely to be well received if the farmers have a religious belief (as some Buddhists do) that one should not destroy life in any form. Similarly, contraceptive technology is not likely to be readily accepted in a society which believes that children are "gifts of the Gods" and that whether or not one has children, and the number of children one has, is entirely beyond the realm of human control.

In the second place, the fact that culture represents a closely interrelated whole means that a change in one part will be felt throughout the entire structure. An analogy can be made to the circles that spread out over the water when a pebble is tossed into a pond; whenever a change is introduced into any society it will have a similar rippling effect. This means that a particular change or innovation that might make a positive contribution to enhancing the level of economic well being in one respect may have serious negative consequences in some other area of life, and these secondary and tertiary changes can retard overall socioeconomic change. The literature of anthropology is full of anecdotal stories that would support this point (e.g., Foster, 1962:80-85). For example, an attempt to control fish tapeworm among some Eskimo peoples by cooking the fish before eating it had an unforeseen consequence of introducing a vitamin deficiency that had previously been taken care of by eating raw fish. Again, among some preindustrial villagers in Iran the attempt to improve the home environment and reduce the incidence of eye disease by substituting smokeless stoves for open cooking fires was resisted because the heavy smoke from the cooking fires performed the very positive function of helping to control the malaria carrying anopheles mosquito. And among some Andean Indians the use of a raised hearth to facilitate cooking and improve sanitation was seen as dysfunctional because a raised hearth would not heat the floor on which the family slept.

The point that must be kept in mind with regard to the cultural structure of developing societies, as in all societies, is that in every case this structure has been worked out over generations of trial and error experimentation, and the structure that has evolved represents a proven functional adaptation to the natural and physical world around them. What may seem to the western observer to be nonrational behavior will actually be very rational in terms of the prevailing cultural system. We have noted elsewhere (see chapter 2) that in many developing societies massive foreign capital and technical assistance will be required to generate sustained economic growth. In the present context, however, it should be clear that such assistance is not going to be received in a vacuum, but must in each case be fitted into a specific cultural context. Thus, as we have stressed before, a major responsibility of the development planner is to know the culture, and make sure that any proposed innovation does not conflict with basic attitudes and values and that it is compatible with the overall cultural structure.

Some Biophysical Aspects of Culture

One aspect of culture that does not ordinarily occur to most people concerns that significance of certain biophysical differences. Most of us are probably familiar with the fact that persons born and raised at high altitudes develop a greater lung capacity and are thus better adapted to breathing the thinner air than are persons born and raised at lower altitudes. Yet not many of us would associate such differences with the issue of economic development. It is also a fact that in all societies people growing up develop particular bodily motor patterns and styles that make it difficult to adopt positions commonly assumed in other societies. The most obvious example that will have meaning to most of us in the Western world is the posture of sitting. We can sit in a chair for hours without feeling any particular discomfort, but were we to sit cross-legged on the floor for any length of time, or if we try to assume the squatting position commonly used for resting in many non-Western countries, we soon become uncomfortable, shortly develop major muscular aches and cramps, and are forced to change our position. Still another illustration is provided by the practice among many non-Western people of transporting heavy loads balanced on top of their heads. What may not occur to us is that persons used to physical positions such as squatting may find it uncomfortable to sit on a chair for any length of time. This means that development programs that offer new techniques must give some consideration to the physical habits of the recipient population.

Biotechnology is the discipline that is concerned with studying the relationship between man and his technology. The fundamental premise of biotechnology is that "man should be considered, not as an afterthought to be included only when the major elements of equipment design have been completed, but rather as one of the various components which must be fully integrated into the system" (Pierce, 1966:218). A simple example of a good integration between man and his tools would be a carpenter's saw, which is designed to fit the human hand neatly and comfortably.

Since the design of the human component in the man-machine relationship is fixed, the problem faced by the biotechnolgist is one of designing the machine to fit the man. Without going into a long discussion of the premise and basic goals of biotechnology, we simply want to make the additional point that the biophysical characteristics and habits of the population in a developing society are major variables to keep in mind when considering the introduction of some new technology. When the new technology can easily be adapted to traditional physical habits the probability of its acceptance will be greater; conversely, if no attempt is made to accomodate traditional body motor patterns then the chances of its adoption will be greatly diminished. To return to the previously cited squatting example by way of illustration, anthropologists have found that raised hearths or cooking stoves which may be more sanitary but which require one to stand while preparing meals will be a source of physical discomfort and will not be readily acceptable to persons accustomed to squatting (Foster, 1962:89). From our perspective, the implication of the preceding is that those who are involved in planning and implementing various development programs need to consider such things as the physical habits of the people concerned, as well as such things as their traditional attitudes and value systems, as representing a potential source of obstacles to the success of the program.

One other aspect of this topic deserves some mention, and that is the observation that people from different cultures may also display different aptitudes with respect to their ability to understand and cope with modern technology. While it is not likely that any culture will produce persons who are incapable of handling the machinery of modern industrial society, it is possible that a person raised in a preindustrial setting will possess much less technological sophistication than one who was raised in one of the more highly developed western nations (Pierce, 1966). The point here is that some cultures will be able to adapt to the introduction of modern technology much more rapidly than others, and that the development planner has to take into consideration the potential influence of such intellectual differences among people, as well as biophysical differences, on the possibility and rate of cultural diffusion.

Culture and Fertility

According to the approach taken in this volume, the demographic situation constitutes a major dimension of the modernization problem in much of the Third World. As was noted in the preceding chapter, many low income countries are presently experiencing very rapid rates of population growth, and these rapid growth rates are often a serious obstacle to social and economic development. The causes of the rapid growth rates prevailing in so many countries today are to be found in the persistence of traditionally high birth rates in the face of the dramatic declines in mortality that have occurred since the end of World War II. The reason birth rates have remained high in these countries is that the sociocultural melieu is such that it either (1) actively encourages a high level of fertility, or (2) acts passively so as not to encourage a lowering of the birth rate. That is, in spite of a reduction in the traditionally high death rates that once made high birth rates a functional prerequisite for the perpetuation of the society, pressures to maintain a high level of fertility still persist in many parts of the developing world. In this section we shall direct our attention to some of the more specific cultural attitudes and values that may function to encourage the maintenance of a high birth rate in developing societies.

To begin in a general way, it may be noted that many of the attitudes and values discussed above will be reflected in fertility behavior. For example, persons who are oriented toward the future, who are optimistic in their stress upon man's ability to overcome the limits of his environment, and who evaluate others on the basis of their individual achievements will tend to have a relatively low level of fertility (Okediji, 1974). Conversely, attitudes and value orientations that glorify the past, that are fatalistic in their acceptance of the status quo, and that emphasize ascribed status characteristics will tend to be associated with high birth rates.

It has often been asserted that before a man will be motivated to work harder to improve his level of living he must be aware that higher levels of living are possible, and he must have access to realistic means of achieving a higher level. Similarly, the common belief among many westerners that developing peoples could improve their economic situation by utilizing modern methods of birth control to limit family size presupposes a knowledge among such people that such betterment can be attained by reasonable effort. The problem in many parts of the Third World, however, is that a large proportion of the population is illiterate; it has had little if any opportunity to travel much beyond the boundaries of their local community; and it is only dimly aware of different life styles that exist within their own country, let alone in the world at large. This lack of knowledge of viable alternatives is often reinforced by philosophical values that tend to discourage economic competition (the idea of "limited good"), or that tend to associate poverty with a higher level of spiritual development than would be associated with material wealth.

This is not to say that people in underdeveloped areas are content with their poverty. No one likes being poor, but often people become inured to it because they see no realistic alternative. In other words, the mere desire for a higher level of living will not necessarily lead to behavior that results in the achievement of this end. Similarly, the mere desire to postpone a pregnancy or have a smaller family will not be sufficient to ensure that action will be taken to reach this goal. People must not only have small family goals, they must know that it is possible to achieve a small family; the means to achieve the goal must be available and practicable, and they must have the proper motivation and desire to use the means to achieve their goals. As will be seen in this section, however, various aspects of culture represent potential obstacles both to the formation of small family goals and to the use of modern methods of birth control to limit fertility.

To be a little more specific, a major factor influencing the level of fertility in any society will be the importance that is attached to the family as a social unit. One of the primary inducements to the maintenance of high fertility among economically underdeveloped countries today lies in the fact that such societies are characterized by a strong familistic rather than an individualistic orientation. In such societies a great deal of emphasis is placed on promoting the strength and solidarity of the extended kinship group, and one of the most obvious ways this is done is through the positive value placed on having a lot of children. This kind of attitude is particularly prevalent in multiethnic societies where mere numbers have traditionally been highly correlated with military and economic power. In many African nations, for example, it is widely believed that children equal raw power. They are the guarantee that the tribe or ethnic group will have the military strength to hold its own with other potentially competing groups, and the prevailing attitude concerning children is generally one of "the more the better" (Miller, 1971).

All societies that have persisted through the ages have placed a high positive value on having children—otherwise they would not have endured; and in all societies a variety of techniques have been and are employed to encourage the birth of children. In the more highly developed nations of the Western world, where death rates have been low for several generations, the pressures for a lot of children are much weaker than in the past; but among the developing nations today thay are often just as strong as ever. Among the pressures for large families is the prestige structure as it relates to women. Often the only way for a woman to gain prestige and to enhance her economic security is to marry and bear a lot of children—especially sons. Throughout much of the developing world women have few if any viable economic alternatives to marriage—nonfamilial occupations are often not available to women as they are in the industrial societies. An unmarried woman has no status of her own and has to rely on the often grudging support of other male relatives. Within the marital union a woman's status and prestige is largely a function of how many children she has born, and especially of how many sons. Barrenness is one of the worst sins of which a wife can be guilty, and barrenness has traditionally been recognized as one of the few legitimate grounds for divorce—even if the woman is not the one who is sterile. Even when there is no divorce, a middle-aged woman who is childless (especially sonless) is given little or no prestige, but is instead looked upon with contempt or, at best, pity. Not surprisingly, then, most women in the developing world tend to marry early and plan on bearing a large number of children.

The age at which a women enters a sexual union is an especially important determinant of her ultimate fertility, and there is ample evidence to suggest that women in the developing countries tend to marry earlier than their Western counterparts (see chapter 6). In one recent study, for example, it was shown that in contrast to the more highly developed countries where only 23 percent of all brides were under twenty years of age, as many as 33 percent of the brides in the underdeveloped countries were in this youthful age group (Stockwell, 1974:47). Among the poorest or least developed group of countries included in this study fully two-thirds of all women marrying were less than twenty years old at the time of their marriage. There is no assurance, of course, that childbearing will begin as soon as a woman enters a union, as fertility will also be influenced by other factors governing the frequency of intercourse, the use or non-use of contraception, and the success of the pregnancy. However, all else being equal, the younger a woman is when she enters a marital union, the more years she will be exposed to the risk of childbearing and the more likely she is to experience a high level of fertility.

In addition to a generally younger age at marriage, woman in developing societies tend to exhibit higher fertility values than do women in the more highly developed nations. This is illustrated by Table 4.1 which presents some comparative data on the number of children that women say they would ideally like to have. As contrasted with the United States where the ideal family size is 2.9, and where only 9 percent of the women surveyed wanted families having 5 or more persons, preferences with respect to mean ideal family size among the Third World nations ranged from 3.8 in Thailand to 9.4 in Kenya. Similarly, the proportion of women wanting a family consisting of 5 or more varied from roughly one-fourth in both Thailand and Chile to fully one hundred percent in Kenya.

Although the discussion so far has emphasized women, it should be noted that the nature of the prestige structure in many developing countries may also serve to induce men to father many children. On the one hand, some cultures look upon a large number of children (especially many sons) as a visible sign of a man's virility and masculinity. On the other hand, many children constitute security for the family and serve as a guarantee that it will be propagated into the future. Among the Yorubas in Nigeria, for example, children (again, especially male children) have traditionally been regarded as the "pillars" of the house. It is through the children that the family name is perpetuated and the house is preserved after the death of the parents. A typical blessing that one bestows on a new-born baby is "let him (her) attain old age, be healthy and have numerous followers (i.e., brothers and sisters) behind him" (Olusanya, 1969:15).

We may also note in a general way that the religious values

Table 4.1 Ideal family size of women in selected countries.

Country	Date	Mean Ideal Family Size	Percentage Whose Ideal is 5 or More
United States	1972	2.9	9
Thailand (rural)	1964	3.8	26
Chile (urban)	1959	4.0	27
Philippines (urban)	1966	4.5	48
Indonesia (Mojalama)	1969-70	5.0	66
Nigeria	1973	5.7	82
Kenya (Bena)	1967	9.4	100

Source: Helen Ware, "Ideal Family Size." World Fertility Survey Occasional Paper No. 13 (October 1974).

generally prevailing in preindustrial societies tend to act as positive inducements to the maintenance of high birth rates (see following chapter). Over and above the general conservatism of most religious philosophies that tends to resist change, one can find fertility being encouraged by such specific factors as: (a) the stress of filial piety in those societies where ancestor worship is an important part of religious life and where a large number of children (sons) is necessary to ensure that ancestral shrines will be properly cared for; (b) the Judeo-Christian injunction to "be fruitful and multiply"; and (c) various proscriptive attitudes that would mitigate against the practice of birth control such as a belief that children are a gift of God to be sought after and welcomed, or a belief that it is sinful to try and interfere with the normal reproductive process. To cite one specific example of a religious influence on fertility, among some Hindus it is commonly believed that only a man who has fathered a son can go to heaven; in this case the traditional bridal blessing includes the expressed hope that the young girl will be "the mother of eight sons."

Culture and Birth Control

An especially important way in which cultural attitudes and values will influence fertility relates to the extent that they may act as a major barrier to the adoption of birth control. Hence, this topic merits special attention. One factor here will of course be the extent to which members of a society are aware that effective methods of contraception exist, and, though this may be hard for many westerners to grasp, such an awareness is often lacking in preindustrial societies characterized by widespread illiteracy. Furthermore, even when it is known that such methods exist a variety of cultural factors may inhibit their use. To illustrate, a recent survey in Uganda revealed that the vast majority— 95 percent of the men in the sample and 90 percent of the women—did not know of any birth control method other than abstinence (Miller, 1971). Moreover, although all of the persons interviewed in this study lived in an area that had had family planning clinics in operation for twelve years, most had not made any effort to avail themselves of the services offered. The reasons cited by persons who objected to family planning illustrate the cultural influence. Among women, for example, it was felt that children are God's gifts and that either the Pope's orders are not to be disobeyed (among Roman Catholics) or the number of children one bears had to be left in the hands of Allah (among Moslems). Other reasons cited were a misplaced fear that artificial methods of birth control would make one weak and sickly—or fat! And many women indicated they were not interested in birth control because their husband wanted more children or because they feared their husband would suspect them of infidelity if they were to adopt one of the modern methods of birth control.

Among the males included in this survey, similar religious reasons were given for not practicing birth control. And to these religious reasons were added (1) a fear of growing old without having enough children to give him prestige and to carry on his name, and (2) a more general belief that the more children one has the better off the tribe and the people.

Death and Immortality A particularly interesting factor in the case of Uganda lies in the traditional concept of immortality. According to this concept the period after death is divided into two periods—an early period of "death within living memory" and a later period of "death beyond living memory." Following death a person gradually moves from the early period to the later one as fewer and fewer people remember him. As long as a person is remembered by name by his children, his grandchildren, other relatives, or friends he remains in the earlier period, and it is believed that he is not yet completely dead. Such a concept or belief, which would clearly discourage the limitation of fertility, is not unique to Uganda. In fact:

> These are dominant attitudes in many African traditional religions that suggest personal immortality is externalized through procreation.

Children bear the traits of their parents, and in particular, sons are
needed to carry on the memory of the father. The large family is a
symbol of the immortality of the father. The reluctance to engage in
family planning is a logical consequence. (Miller, 1971:11)

Attitudes Toward Women It was noted above that one
of the reasons Ugandan women cited for not practicing birth
control was a fear that their husbands might think they were
being unfaithful. An attitude similar to this was also found
among the Yoruba in Nigeria (Olusanya, 1969) and in fact
exists in many parts of the underdeveloped world. This is an
attitude that is rooted in a belief in male dominance and the
associated belief that women are "pure and chaste" and are
not consciously concerned with matters relating to the process of reproduction. Such an attitude often associates birth
control with prostitutes, thus making birth control
thoroughly unacceptable for one's wife.

On the other hand, women are often regarded as weaklings
who might easily be led astray if they knew about methods of
birth control. Such cultural barriers to the spread of family
planning were clearly illustrated by the various responses
given by Yoruba males to questions concerning whether or
not women should be taught methods of contraception.
Some of the answers given were:

> I am not in favor of teaching women its use for it would be abused.
> I can only teach women with great caution. They are too crafty to
> be taught such methods with complete safety.
> Women should not be taught, for they would be unfaithful to their
> husbands without being caught.

Given such attitudes it was hardly surprising to find that
husbands were often reluctant to sign consent forms for their
wives to receive family planning assistance or that the vast
majority of women are unfavorably disposed to the idea of
family planning.

Summary

In the past, most approaches to the study of economic
development tended to emphasize the three major economic

variables of land (resources), labor and capital. Economic development, or an increase in per capita output, was seen to result from changes in one or more of these input variables. To take a simple illustration, consider the following equation:

$$\text{Land} + \text{Labor} + \text{Capital} = \text{Output}$$

Using this model, an increase in per capita output in agriculture, for example, can be achieved by such things as increasing the amount of land being cultivated while holding labor constant, or by the application of capital improvements (e.g., tractors) that permit a reduction in the labor input. Such models may look good on paper, but for the most part they ignore factors (such as culture) over which the traditional economist had no control. They contain the implicit assumption that economic factors are the only important ones and that everything else can be "held constant." As is apparent from the discussion in this chapter, however, everything else cannot be held constant. Per capita output will be influenced by a number of other important factors, not the least of which is the prevailing cultural system.

The limitations of the pure economic model can perhaps be best illustrated by drawing an analogy with human ecology. The basic ecological approach to the study of human society views it in terms of an ecological complex containing four elements represented by the acronym PEST: Population, Environment, Social organization, and Technology. All human societies consist of a population which possesses a particular culture and social structure governing the behavior of its members, and a particular level of technology with which it wrests a livelihood from its environment. All four elements are dynamically interrelated in the life of any society. However, the traditional economic model can be viewed as ignoring the element of social organization. That is, it incorporates population (labor), environment (land and resources) and technology (capital), but neglects the role of culture and social structure as they relate to economic behavior. More recent post-World War II approaches to the development problem, however, have incorporated the fact that economic behavior is influenced to a great extent by the prevailing culture and social structure, and have put the ecologist's S into the economist's PET.

In this chapter attention has focused on the important influence that cultural attitudes and values will have in the development process. The general conclusion reached asserts that the fundamental cultural attitudes and values found throughout the Third World will often be different from those commonly associated with the more advanced societies, and that these differences represent potential (although not necessary) obstacles to both economic development and demographic modernization. The task of the development planner, then, is to become thoroughly familiar with the prevailing cultural system of particular Third World societies so that development plans and programs can be molded to fit each unique situation. In a later chapter attention will be devoted to the equally important factor of social structure (chaper 6). First, however, chapter 5 will examine the role of religion—the ultimate source of many cultural attitudes and values—as it relates to economic and demographic behavior.

5

Religion

Because religion generally plays a major role in determining people's attitudes and values—many of our most fundamental beliefs and attitudes are rooted in religious philosophy—it is desirable to take a closer look at the relation between religion and development. One of the first things to note is that no matter how lofty their ethical codes, nearly all religions have been serious barriers to human progress. This tends to be so because most religious ideologies are very conservative and lean heavily toward supporting the status quo. Indeed, it may even be argued that religion has to oppose change, particularly if it claims an ultimate truth, for to permit change would be to admit to fallibility and to give up its claim to truth. To cite a few specific instances where religion has acted as an obstacle to change one can note such things as the traditional opposition of Roman Catholicism to "unnatural" methods of birth control, and the retarding influence this position has had on the implementation of family planning programs within the United Nations in general, and within individual Roman Catholic countries (most notably in Latin America) in particular. Another example is the Islamic proscription against usury (lending money for the sake of earning interest), which is not conducive to investing capital for profit. In a similar vein, the heavy emphasis on male sexuality in Islam is not conducive to the ready acceptance of family planning. One can also note that many of the eastern religious philosophies (e.g., Hinduism, Buddhism) are highly aescetic and tend to promote other-worldly attitudes and to place a higher value on spiritual as opposed to material goals. In this section we shall take a closer look at the role of religion as an influence on human activity with respect to both economic behavior and fertility.

Religion and Economic Behavior

It should be noted at the outset that the relationship between religion and economic factors may work both ways; not only can religion influence economic behavior, it can also be influenced by it (Goldthorpe, 1975:237-50). In the latter instance, the economic influence on religion is generally of a kind where economic deprivation leads to increased religious fervor. That is, among people who see themselves as deprived or disadvantaged, and who see no rational means of altering their disadvantaged situation, some solace may be found in religious faith. In a Marxian view, religion becomes the "opiate of the masses." Often this involves the development of a belief in the inevitable overthrow of the existing situation and the establishment of a new order through some kind of supernatural intervention analogous to the chialistic Christian belief in the second coming of Christ and the establishment of the Kingdom of God here on earth. One of the efforts of the Vietnamese to resist French rule in Indochina prior to World War II had such a religious base. A number of sects arose at that time, most notably the Hoa Hoa whose leader preached about the coming of an "Enlightened Sage" who would come to rule the Vietnamese after the French had left. Although this movement gained many adherents and was able to build up a military force during the Japanese occupation of the Second World War, it never really intended to confront the French militarily. Rather, they saw their ultimate triumph as inevitable and they were willing to wait for the will of Heaven to change, at which point they were convinced the French would disappear (Fitzgerald, 1972:79). The growing influence of this sect was cut short in 1947, however, when the Viet Minh assassinated its prophet and caused the sect to be split into several factional groups.

Such deprivation-based religious beliefs, as in the Vietnamese case, are generally oriented toward a passive search for a better world, and they do not generally lead to any overt action aimed at altering the existing economic situation. In some cases, however, they can and do create sufficient fanaticism to generate an open rebellion against the economic oppressor, and occasionally such movements even succeed in achieving their aims—Ghandi's efforts to oust the British from India and the Kikuyu/Mau-Mau uprisings in Kenya are examples of independence movements in the post-World War II years that had their roots at least partially in the religious beliefs of oppressed peoples. Generally, however, the influence that religion exerts on economic behavior is much more indirect than would be represented by any religiously inspired insurrection, and it is this more indirect influence that is most relevant and that most concerns us in this monograph.

In talking about the adverse influence of religion on economic behavior, the one example most likely to occur to westerners concerns the "sacred cow" in India. According to one contemporary Indian scholar (Chandrasekhar, 1965:21-35) the cow does indeed occupy a very special position in India, and the country abounds with cow-worshiping Hindus. Although it can be argued that the sacred cow plays a major functional role in Indian society (it serves as a major draft animal and is the source of dung used for cooking fuel and fertilizer), this situation is economically harmful in a variety of ways. In the first place, the Indian economy is burdened with the need to feed close to two hundred million cattle, as if feeding her vast human population was not enough of a problem! In addition to the fact that they have to be maintained, Chandrasekhar cites at least three other negative aspects of the Indian cattle situation:

1. Because the average Hindu will not eat beef or veal, and in fact generally resents the killing of any cattle, India de-

rives little or no protein from this potential food resource.

2. Paradoxical though it may seem, India derives very little milk from its vast cattle population. Given limited resources, quality can be maintained only at the expense of quantity; yet the proscription on killing cattle means that quality suffers in favor of quantity. The quality of the Indian cow's diet is so poor that they yield the lowest amount of milk of any cattle in the world.

3. Finally, Chandrasekhar notes that the frequent use of cattle as draft animals is an anomaly in the cities, and it can cause all manner of traffic and sanitary problems.

In short, Chandrasekhar concludes that over and above the economic cost of the food they consume, the cattle of India are in a treble sense a useless burden and a painful, sentimental, and expensive luxury.

Somewhat less familiar to most Westerners, but also costly from an economic perspective, is the fact that monkeys too enjoy religious immunity in Hindu society. In many parts of India a lot of food is lost to monkeys ravaging orchards and raiding other food stores. (The religious significance of monkeys in India was called forcefully to our attention in the United States early in 1978 when the Indian government raised a furor over the use of Rhesus monkeys in medical research in this country.) However, such specific cases illustrate only a very small part of the role that religion plays in influencing economic behavior. Our concern here will be on the broader ways in which the general attitudes, values, and behavior patterns of a society may reflect underlying religious ideologies.

The Protestant Ethic

The most famous doctrine concerning the relation between religion and economic development is Max Weber's (1930) classic thesis concerning the association between the emergence of Protestantism (specifically Calvinism) and the rise of the capitalistic economic system of the Western world. Weber was faced with the historical fact that at the end of the sixteenth century the dominant civilizations in the world were located in the East, in India and especially in China. But just two hundred years later, at the beginning of the nineteenth century, European civilization had risen to a level where it clearly surpassed all others. The task Weber set for himself was to explain this reversal—to explain why capitalistic industrial society emerged and flourished in Europe rather than in some other part of the world. On a general level he found the answer in the Protestant Reformation of the sixteenth and seventeenth centuries. Among other things, the reformation challenged many traditional dogmas and put an end to the long established authority of the church over people's minds, thus opening the way for the rise of the rational scientific inquiry that characterized the ensuing "age of enlightenment."

On a more specific level, Weber identified the Calvinist/ Puritan sect as the most significant ideological force behind the rise of modern capitalism. The Calvinists, believing themselves called by divine command, had a strong belief in predestination according to which only a certain number of people are selected for heavenly salvation; Calvinists were motivated to find evidence of their own individual salvation through visible signs of earthly prosperity. However, having achieved material success they were not permitted to enjoy any leisure it might bring, nor were they allowed to use wealth in the pursuit of pleasure. Rather, they were motivated to reinvest their profits continually and to accumulate even more material wealth to demonstrate still further their faithful adherence to the divine call.

Weber clearly did not regard modern capitalism as merely a form of economic organization. Rather, he saw it as the distinct way of life of a whole society that was imbued with what he called "the spirit of capitalism"—a configuration of attitudes and beliefs that had its roots in ascetic Protestantism. Weber went further and identified five major components of this value orientation:

1. A strong inhibition to profit for profit's sake alone.

Profit is a visible sign of one's heavenly as well as earthly success, and it was something to be used productively rather than enjoyed.

2. A drive to achieve active mastery over worldly things and interests, as opposed to any kind of mystical acceptance of the status quo as representing the will of God.

3. An emphasis on rationality and the duty of man to use the reason God had given him to achieve mastery over his world.

4. A universalistic view that regarded all men as children of God who should be judged by the same impersonal and objective standards. Those who were favored would know it by what they themselves were able to achieve, not by what they had given to them.

5. The concept of one's life work as a "calling" and the belief that everyone should accept the task assigned them and do it well.

The combination of these five elements in society created persons who were hard working and thrifty, self-reliant, rationally oriented, and driven by an inner force to achieve economic success. It is to this that Weber attributed the rise of capitalistic industrial society in Europe. Conversely, it is to the absence of such an ethic that he would attribute the failure of capitalism to develop in other areas of the world. In classical China, for example, heavy reliance on superstition and magical beliefs in the philosophies of Confucianism, Taoism, and Buddhism contrasted sharply with the Protestant emphasis on rationality. In India the notion of ethical universalism could not take hold because of the rigid caste system which hindered economic development not only by impeding mobility and making it difficult for members of different castes to work together, but also by creating an intellectual atmosphere that encouraged a passive acceptance of the status quo, in which individual initiative and ambition was severely stifled.

In other words, Max Weber not only attached major importance to the role of Calvinism in the capitalist economic development of the Western world, he also explained the economic retardation of the non-Western world in terms of their traditional religious beliefs and practices. In elaborating how this worked in the case of classical China, one economist (Chiang, 1961) suggests we look at economic behavior as being determined by an "economic mentality" which he defined as the sum total of people's attitudes regarding (1) the acquisition of wealth as a goal in life, (2) the means by which wealth is acquired, and (3) the acceptable ways for disposing of wealth once it is attained. According to the economic mentality of the Calvinist: (1) the acquisition of wealth is a positive sign of one's salvation; (2) wealth is obtained through hard work and thrift; and (3) wealth is to be invested in productive enterprise. But the economic mentality of classical China, with its roots in Confucianism and Buddhism, is very different. The nature of this difference can be illustrated by an examination of some of the traditional folk proverbs of classical China. A few representative proverbs that are significant with respect to the Chinese economic mentality are as follows (Chiang, 1961: 258-259).

1. It is better to understand the classics than to amass riches.
2. Wealth is but dung; benevolence and righteousness are worth thousands of gold.
3. Do not seek for gold, jade, and suchlike valuables; rather desire that each of your descendants be virtuous.
4. Of a myriad virtues filial piety is the first.
5. There are three things which are unfilial, and to have no posterity is the greatest of them.
6. Warn men against covetousness, for wealth thus coveted provokes the wrath of Heaven.
7. Gold and silver are but vain things; after death how can they remain in your hands?
8. Wife, wealth, children, and salary are all predestined.

9. Great possessions depend on fate; small possessions come from diligence.

10. Death and life are predetermined; riches and honors
depend upon heaven.

11. Light your stick of incense at the break of every day;
to Heaven, Earth, Sun, Moon, and Stars devout
thanksgiving pay; pray that in every space crops
may ripen in the sun; wish for every man a long
career of life to run.

12. Kneel once, bow your head thrice, and offer incense
morning and evening.

13. Ancestors however remote must be sincerely sacrificed to.

14. In ordinary life, you must be economical; when you
invite guests you must be lavish in hospitality.

15. Good parents will see that their children marry well;
good children will see that their parents have decent
burials.

Clearly the economic mentality reflected in these proverbs
differs substantially from that of the Calvinistic ethic. This
can be illustrated by relating them to the three attitudinal
configurations cited above as comprising an economic mentality. First, it is clear that proverbs 1 through 5 assign
priority to virtue rather than wealth as a worthwhile goal in
life. Proverb 6 warns that desiring wealth can be dangerous,
while 7 suggests that efforts to acquire wealth are a waste of
time.

Proverbs 8 through 12 relate to the means by which wealth
is acquired. In this case numbers 8, 9, and 10 clearly reveal a
strong belief in fate, whereas 11 and 12 represent a resort to
prayers and incantations as a means of ensuring one's material well-being. In other words, wealth is not something to be
acquired by hard work and thrift; one acquires it either as a
predetermined condition of one's life or by appealing to
some kind of supernatural force.

Since the attainment of material success is so often ascribed to the blessings of fate or of various gods and ancestral

spirits, it is only natural that such gains be used to show one's appreciation to the source. Proverbs 13, 14, and 15 call upon people to spend their wealth in various ceremonial ways in order to show their gratitude to their ancestral spirits, rather than dispose of it in an economically productive way.

In summarizing the interpretation of these proverbs in terms of the Chinese economic mentality Chiang notes that (1) whereas Calvinism encourages the effort to acquire wealth, Chinese religion deemphasizes the value of material gains; (2) where the Calvinist sees wealth as something to be acquired through the pursuit of one's calling, the Chinese relies more on fate and the support of supernatural powers for success in material endeavors; and (3) where Calvinist asceticism results in capital accumulation, the religious obligations of the Chinese lead to the expenditure of capital on nonproductive enterprises.

Although later scholars have clearly and justifiably pointed out several weaknesses in Weber's argument (particularly his claims with respect to the nonrational behavior norms associated with non-Western religions), a number of more recent studies have just as clearly attested to at least the partial validity of his monumental theory. Two specific cases will suffice to illustrate this point (Goldthorpe, 1975:232-34). In the first case we may note that the Moslem Malays of Malaya are generally less economically advanced as a group than other ethnic groups, notably the Chinese and the Indians. This lower level of economic advancement has been explained in a Weberian sense by reference to the fatalism ("Allah wills it") characteristic of the Islamic faith and the resulting resistance to government efforts to make them improve their agricultural practices—since all things come from Allah, and since nothing comes unless Allah wills it, there is little sense in trying to alter one's life situation. This implied retarding effect that Islam exerts on economic development has been challenged, however, largely on the grounds that there is at least one aspect of Islam that tends to encourage the rational accumulation of capital, the *haj*—that is, the need to save money to finance the cost of a pilgrimage to Mecca. This custom gives all Moslems a goal to strive for, and it can lead to extremely rational patterns of work and saving. It can be argued in turn, however, that financing a pilgrimage to Mecca represents a nonproductive use of capital. Hence, from the point of view of economic development, this particular aspect of Islam cannot be regarded as an unqualified plus.

The second case concerns the influence of Buddhism on economic behavior; and here the classical Weberian thesis is that the other-worldly value orientation of Buddhism is an obstacle to rational economic activity. Like Christianity, however, Buddhism is not a single unified faith but consists of many strands. Some of the strands, or subcults, are indeed other-worldly oriented and look upon economic success in a manner opposite to that of the ascetic Calvinist; rather than seeing success as something to work for as a sign of one's salvation, some Buddhists would regard such worldly activity as disproof of one's chances of being saved. Among other strands, however (particularly in Kammatic Buddhism which accounts for the majority of Buddhists) there is a strong incentive to engage in worldly activity, for economic success is one of the ways that will enable a person to "buy" his way into a better position during his next reincarnation in the never ending circle of life. According to the Buddhist faith, life consists of a continuously revolving wheel of birth, death, and rebirth into one of five different realms, or states of being. The five realms into which beings can be reborn are human, animal, wandering ghosts, spirits in hell, and spirits in heaven (Ling, 1969). Of these five realms or states of being, the highest is human, and to enhance the likelihood that one will be reborn into the human realm again one seeks to compile a good *karma* (a good moral balance sheet) that reflects a lot of earned merit. Now, there are many ways for a practicing Buddhist to earn merit, but it is only through economic success that one can acquire the most valuable merit, the merit that comes from extensive giving (*dana*).

Leading a good moral life naturally earns some merit, but one can earn much more by giving; and in order to have surplus wealth to give away the devout Buddhist is motivated to work hard and acquire it through rational economic behavior. The problem here as far as economic development is concerned, however, is that the kind of giving that takes place involves such things as building pagodas and monasteries, spending lavishly on a son's ritual initiation, and making generous contributions to monks. In other words, a good deal of one's surplus wealth is given away in some ceremonial manner rather than invested in more productive economic enterprises.

What we have in both of these cases (with respect to the *haj* and *dana*) is a pattern of behavior that is subject to two interpretations. On the one hand there is a clear incentive among both Moslems and the majority of Buddhists to engage in rational economic action for the purpose of accumulating capital. This is a clear repudiation of the Weberian thesis that non-Western religions encourage non-rational economic behavior. On the other hand, however (and in marked contrasts to Calvinism) both represent cases in which a great deal of one's accumulated capital is put to a personal rather than a productive economic use, and in both cases the rationale for the nonproductive use of capital is rooted firmly in the religious beliefs.

Need Achievement One of the more significant attempts to utilize Weber's Protestant Ethic to explain the process of national economic growth and development is represented by the work of David McClelland (1961; 1963). McClelland has characterized the attitudinal configuration of the Protestant Ethic of western society as a need for achievement. This need for achievement is seen as a strongly felt desire to do well in life, not so much for the sake of social recognition or prestige, but rather to attain an inner feeling of satisfaction at some personal accomplishment. It is an inner psychic state that is implanted in children. Children in all societies are raised on folk tales that convey to them certain values. In our society, for example, the children's stories tend to instill in us a desire to be recognized and appreciated for our own achievements. They also impress upon us the value of effort ("Nothing ventured, nothing gained," and "If at first you don't succeed, try, try again"); and we grow up believing that if we work and try hard enough we will be able to achieve something worth recognizing. Every American child knows, for example, that it was the thrift and hard work of the third "practical little pig" that saved his two wastrel brothers from the clutches of the "big bad wolf." And who among us in the United States is not familiar with the tremendous satisfaction attained through the unswerving efforts of the little engine that thought he could—and did? Children who were raised on stories such as the preceding, rather than stories that stress such things as filial piety and honoring one's ancestors, cooperation rather than competition, and the desirability of earning merit, will be more likely to grow up feeling a need somehow to prove themselves in their society. They will be more concerned with making something of themselves as individuals, rather than preserving family honor, and this need will lead to behavior calculated to achieve some level of recognition.

The kind of behavior that this type of value orientation encourages is labeled entrepreneurial behavior. Entrepreneurs, like those who built the industrial capitalistic society of Europe, are people who work energetically to increase production well above what they need for their own personal consumption. An entrepreneur is one who is driven to continue producing long after his own needs are met. The traditional Marxist interpretation of such men is that they were driven by a profit motive: greed inspired them to organize the resources of production and to exploit the working man so as to maximize personal profit. But as McClelland (1963) points out, such men were not really interested in money for its own sake but for what it represented to them—a symbol of success. For one thing, if they were merely interested in money it is not likely that they would have continued to strive after they had amassed considerable wealth, yet many of them did. For another thing, many of them came from religious sects (e.g., Calvinists and Quakers) that would not condone the use of wealth for personal enjoyment. For the entrepreneur, the value of money lay in the fact that it was an index of how well one was doing—a quantifiable index of how much one had achieved by one's own efforts. That is, while the need for achievement is not directly satisfied by money, monetary profits do serve as a direct and measurable index of how well one is doing in one's job. The greater the profit the better one is doing, and the greater will be the inner satisfaction that one can derive from the sense of a job well done.

One of the most significant defining characteristics of an entrepreneur is that he is a rational risk taker. He is not content to perform a task when he knows in advance what the outcome will be. There is no challenge to such activity, and thus little basis for deriving any inner satisfaction. A person who adds up a column of figures is not an entrepreneur, says McClelland (1963), no matter how efficiently or correctly he adds them up; he is a simple clerk who completes his task by following established rules. On the other hand, a man who decides to add a new line to his business, or to adopt a new production technique, is an entrepreneur because he cannot know in advance what the outcome of his decision will be. That is, he is taking a risk. However, such risk-taking will not be arbitrary. Entrepreneurs are not gamblers who rely heavily on luck or fate in achieving their success. Rather, such risk-taking will be calculated, based on the knowledge and judgement of the entrepreneur. An entrepreneur relies on his own personal skills to reduce the risk inherent in a new venture, and if he proves successful he has more reason to feel a sense of personal achievement for having made the right decision. Thus, an entrepreneur is one who will seek out challenges, who will deviate from traditional patterns, who will innovate and take calculated risks, and who will experiment in search of a better way to accomplish particular tasks; such energetic entrepreneurial behavior is likely to be conducive to economic growth and development.

One of the crucial variables influencing the extent to which a society produces people who have a strong need to achieve and who will engage in energetic entrepreneurial behavior is the extent to which the religion of the family stresses the importance of the individual. The situation as it evolved in Europe in the sixteenth and seventeenth centuries was as follows: Protestantism, with its stress on self-reliance and on the importance of fulfilling one's calling led to strong achievement training in children; this training produced a high need for achievement in the children when they became adults, a need to succeed not for the sake of rewards or prestige but to produce a sense of satisfaction in the results of one's own efforts; this in turn led to the calculated risk-taking characteristic of the entrepreneur, and resulted ultimately in the emergence and growth of industrial capitalism as the dominant economic system of the European world. The problem commonly encountered today with respect to developing areas is that their religions do not place such a heavy emphasis on self-reliance and individual achievement. Hence, the level of need achievement is often markedly less or the proportion of persons in the population characterized by a high need for achievement is much smaller than is commonly the case in modern western nations, and much of their economic behavior is therefore not aimed at the rational pursuit of material success. On the contrary, they often have religious values that actively discourage the kind of behavior that is most likely to promote economic development. Perhaps the beliefs most commonly encountered in this respect are that wealth and success depend more on luck and fate than on hard work and that accumulated capital should be used to maintain ancestral shrines or for other religious purposes such as the Islamic *haj* or the Buddhist *dana*. Another illustration of this is provided by the responsibilities of the head of the traditional Hindu joint family

(Chandrasekhar, 1965). The head of such a family has the major responsibility of preserving the resources of the family to ensure its transmission to future generations. He may not, for example, invest family capital resources in enterprises other than purchasing added land for agriculture. Such a negative attitude toward risk-taking is obviously not conducive to the emergence of the entrepreneurial activity that was associated with the rise of industrial capitalism in the west.

The implication of the preceding for many underdeveloped countries of the Third World is clearly that one of the major obstacles to their economic modernization may be found in their religious value systems and, more specifically, in economic attitudes that the religions support. This is not to imply that these traditional religions are bad or that they must be changed or abandoned as the price of economic development. It does suggest that development plans and programs may want to pay some attention to cultivating the kind of economic mentality that is associated with the rise of western industrial capitalism. As Chiang has suggested:

> If the present underdeveloped lands are interested in the eventual evolution of a system of private capitalism, a class of entrepreneurs will have to be cultivated; and to achieve this, the emergence of a favorable economic mentality is a primary prerequisite. Our definition of "economic mentality" in terms of the three economic attitudes points to the conclusion that it would be necessary to have (a) public encouragement instead of suppression of wealth-seeking, (b) social emphasis on human effort in economic enterprise, along with the eradication of fatalistic resignation, and (c) discouragement of ceremonial and other forms of wasteful expenditures, to facilitate reinvestment of wealth in economic enterprises. (1961:263)

Roman Catholicism and Radicalism in Latin America

Although the preceding discussion has emphasized the negative aspects of religion in many of the Third World nations, there are some striking exceptions—especially in Latin America. Although the Roman Catholic church has a conservative, right-wing orientation, priests within the church, and sometimes members who hold positions of authority, have periodically taken a radical position for social and human rights, often in opposition to their governments. This is not exclusively a twentieth-century phenomenon, but dates back to the days of colonialism, and a brief historical overview is necessary to understand the current situation.

Unlike the settlers of North America, who tended to be just that—people who came with their families to settle permanently and build a new life for themselves—the Europeans who first came to Latin America tended to fall into one of two categories: they were either Roman Catholic missionaries who came to "convert the heathen," or they were explorers who were primarily interested in exploiting the natural wealth of the countries they "discovered." Although the church was primarily in the business of saving souls, it too, through the acquisition of large land holdings, eventually emerged as a powerful economic and political force, and tended to become very conservative. At the same time, however, it periodically became actively involved in various reform movements. In spite of its faults, the church did generally regard the indigenous inhabitants as potential souls and did take the position that they should be educated and treated in a humane fashion.

The role played by the Catholic church in Latin America can perhaps best be appreciated by contrasting it with that of the Protestant churches in North America, particularly with respect to its treatment of black slaves and the indigenous Indian populations. In the United States, for example, the local Indians were systematically robbed, killed, and eventually forced onto small and scattered reservations where to this day they lead lives of considerable deprivation relative to that of the dominant white population. Blacks, on the other hand, were held in bondage where they were treated as less than human beings and generally were denied the opportunity to learn to read and write; in some cases they were even denied the right to marry. Although there were some exceptions, the churches as a whole offered little challenge to these practices. In Latin America, however, the Catholic church actively sought to encourage the humane treatment of the indigenous populations and worked hard to try and educate them. An illustration of its activities in this respect is offered by Peru where in 1917 the church established Catholic University for the purpose of educating the future elites of the country in such a way that they could come to understand and treat the various social problems of the society. Although one may debate the relative success of the church's efforts, the fact remains that at a comparable time in history the church in Latin America was much more actively involved in trying to encourage social change than it was in North America.

Since the 1950s the church has become an even more active source of opposition to many of the conservative military governments and wealthy elites in Latin America and has emerged as a fighting friend of the masses. This more militant activity was given impetus by a conference held in Medina, Colombia in 1968. The bishops who met there came to the decision that the church needed to become more active in its efforts to correct the many social inequities that existed throughout the region. The resulting activism, which involved many high ranking officials of the church, has taken many forms, ranging from relatively peaceful social reform efforts to participation in guerrilla movements, and a number of priests and bishops have been jailed or killed (Longworth and Yates, 1978). On the less militant side, Peru can again be cited to illustrate the positive influence of the Catholic church. In parts of that country the church had by 1956 sold much of its land cheaply to agrarian peasants. Furthermore, with the help of the American Maryknolls it established credit cooperatives for workers in the *sierra* (highlands) to assist them in buying tools and other materials at relatively low prices (Pike, 1967). In addition, the church has also designed a number of radio programs with a practical educational orientation (teaching literacy, new farming techniques, etc.).

The church has been equally as active in a number of other Latin American countries, promoting revolutionary as well as more moderate reformist programs. In one extreme case it has even gone underground and formed a secret organization that advocates violence as the only means of correcting the existing social injustices (Yates, 1978). Because of such activities the radical churchmen have often been labeled as Marxists or Communists. However, such a label is misapplied and is largely a reflection of the fact that many countries in Latin America have governments with a conservative right-wing orientation who are afraid of any militant social reformist activity.

One area where the Catholic church in Latin America has maintained a traditional position, however, is in its opposition to the use of "artificial" methods of birth control; in this respect it continues to represent an obstacle to economic and demographic development. With this exception, however, the Catholic church has generally been a positive force for development in Latin America during the twentieth century.

Religion and Fertility

As was noted at the beginning of this chapter, religion and religious values represent a particularly important aspect of the culture of all peoples. In many cases, especially in preindustrial societies, religion is such an integral part of the culture that it is difficult to separate the religious influence on behavior from the influence of other aspects of culture. Nowhere is this difficulty more apparent than with respect to fertility behavior. The persistence of any society over time has depended on fertility, not only on the fertility of its human members to ensure propagation, but also on the fertility of the soil and/or that of any animals that constituted an important part of the food supply. Accordingly, many aspects of culture, not just religion, tend to be conducive to the maintenance of a high level of fertility. Nevertheless, it is possible to identify certain aspects of culture that are more closely related to religion than others, and it is on these that we will focus attention in this section.

There are two ways in which religious beliefs and values

are relevant to fertility. The first relates to those values concerning the family and the extent to which marriage and childbearing is seen as a religious duty; the second relates to those attitudes concerning the morality of utilizing various methods of contraception to control fertility. That is, religion may enhance fertility in a positive way by encouraging people to marry and have a lot of children, and it may enhance it in a negative way by forbidding the use of effective means of birth control. In the remainder of this chapter we shall focus on some of the ways the major religious ideologies of the world may exert a retarding effect on demographic modernization by contributing to the maintenance of a high birth rate.

Christianity

Christianity, with the injunction of its Judiac heritage to "be fruitful, and multiply, and replenish the earth," evolved as a strongly pronatalist ideology in which the primary end of marriage was seen to be the procreation of children. Although Christianity is comprised of a wide variety of sects, there tends to be a common theme throughout all of them that places a positive value on the sacredness of the nuclear, husband-wife family, rather than on the extended family, and on the idea that a married couple is only the beginning of a family that will not be complete until there are children. Although the husband-wife nuclear family continues to be the basic Christian unit, the years since the Reformation have seen an ever increasing divergence among Christian religious sects in the importance attached to having children. Similarly, there has been an ever increasing divergence with respect to attitudes toward the use of various methods of birth control.

The major difference that exists among Christians today is that which has emerged between Protestantism and the Roman Catholic church. Keeping in mind that there is wide variation among Protestant groups (e.g., some fundamental sects like the Hutterites tolerate no interference in the

natural reproductive process and have fertility levels that
approach the biological maximum), the basic differences
that exist can be summarized as follows:

1. Catholic teaching places a stronger emphasis than
   Protestantism on the importance of having children
   to complete the family.
2. Catholic teaching regards all methods of birth control, other than the rhythm method, as contrary to
   natural law and as illegitimate means of fertility prevention. Protestants, on the other hand, generally
   permit any medically approved method to be used—
   even, under some circumstances, abortion.

With regard to the first difference, Catholic teaching on
this matter dates from the fifth century and the writings of St.
Augustine which stressed that the sole purpose of sexual
intercourse in marriage was the procreation of children. This
is a position that remained virtually unchallenged until 1917
when the Code of Canon Law (Cannon 1013, paragraph 1)
added a secondary purpose—that of "mutual aid and the
quieting of concupiscence." Although the position of the
Catholic church has become increasingly liberal in the twentieth century (e.g., it is now recognized that there may be
valid reasons—medical, eugenical, economic or social—
why some couples may deliberately choose to remain childless), the positive emphasis continues to be on childbearing.
The primary end of sexual intercourse is still seen to be
procreation rather than recreation; and in the absence of
some compelling reason not to have children, a Catholic
couple is expected to have them. Thus, while Roman
Catholics may not be directly encouraged to have many
children, the teachings of the church make it difficult for
fecund couples to prefer—and to have—small families and
still maintain a clear conscience. Among Protestants, on the
other hand, there is little official dogma concerning family
size, and where pronouncements have been made they have
generally stressed the importance of each couple deciding
for themselves within the framework of their own personal,

social, psychological, and economic situation how many children, if any, they would like to have.

Concerning the second difference, the official position of the Catholic church on the use of artificial means of birth control is unequivocal; the only legitimate and acceptable means of limiting the size of one's family is the rhythm method which is based on the natural cycle of alternating periods of fertility and infertility in the human female. This position was most recently reaffirmed in the 1968 papal encyclical *Humanae Vitae* in which Pope Paul VI clearly stated again that the primary end of sexual intercourse in marriage was the procreation of children and that the church vigorously condemned all forms of birth control other than abstinence and rhythm. Among Protestants, however, the prevalent belief today is that any medically approved method of birth control may legitimately be used to control the size of one's family.

Since Protestantism is likely to be, at worst, neutral with respect to family size and the use of birth control (and also because Protestantism is pretty well confined to the more highly developed countries of the Western world), the question of whether Christianity is likely to impede fertility control efforts in underdeveloped societies revolves around the influence of Catholicism. And here the basic question concerns whether, and to what extent, the official position of the church will have a significant effect on behavior at the local level. It is clear that in highly developed societies like the United States, where the overall level of education is high, the behavior of individual Catholics is less likely to be determined by church dogma. For example, the results of one recent survey showed that as of 1970 nearly two-thirds of all white, married Catholic women under age forty-five in the United States were not conforming to the church's teaching on birth control, but were using "the pill" or some other artificial method of birth control (Westoff and Bumpass, 1973). However, in less developed countries having sizable Catholic populations where the church is a real political force (notably in Latin America), it is likely that the church's stand will represent an obstacle to the development and implementation of national family planning programs, particularly if such programs try to encourage the use of so-called artificial methods of birth control. Some evidence of this is provided by the data in Table 5.1 showing some selected opinions that Catholic priests in three different countries have concerning the use of modern methods of contraception. These data clearly indicate that there is a wide range of variation among the Catholic clergy on this issue. For our purpose, however, the significant observation is that the most traditional, conservative position was found in Colombia, the least developed of the three countries sur-

Table 5.1 Selected attitudes of Catholic priests on contraception in three different countries.

Contraceptive Attitude or Opinion	Percent who agree		
	Colombia	United States	Netherlands
1. Family planning is the most effective way to overcome poverty and underdevelopment.	23	35	43
2. It is perfectly all right in marriage to have intercourse just for pleasure.	59	85	72
3. When artifical contraception is used in marriage, the woman becomes a mere instrument of enjoyment.	57	43	7
4. The widespread use of contraception leads to an increase in marital infidelity.	72	51	20
5. Condoms and diaphragms are evil and their use should not be permitted.	80	57	12
6. Use of the pill simply as a contraceptive is evil and should not be permitted.	68	51	5

Source: Burch, T. K., and G. A. Shea, "Catholic Parish Priests and Birth Control: A Comparative Study of Opinion in Colombia, the United States and the Netherlands," *Studies in Family Planning*, 6 (June 1971):121-36.

veyed. In that country the priests were much more likely to support the official positions that: (1) the potential benefits of birth control as a means of relieving some of the problems of poverty and underdevelopment is overrated; (2) the primary end of sexual intercourse (procreation) is more important than the secondary aim of fostering mutual love; (3) and (4) the widespread use of contraception will have harmful consequences for the moral well-being of the society; and (5) and (6) the use of the more effective modern methods of contraception is sinful.

On the basis of the preceding discussion, at least two conclusions are clearly justified. First, among Christian sects the position of the Roman Catholic church with respect to childbearing and the use of contraceptives is much more pronatalist than most Protestant denominations. Second, the extent to which the Catholic leadership endorses the official position of the church is likely to be greatest among the least developed countries. This is not to say that the Catholic church will constitute a major barrier to the development of population control programs throughout the Third World. But it does clearly suggest that in those countries having sizable Catholic populations, the position of the church represents a powerful force that the development planner will have to contend with in trying to establish and implement programs to reduce the birth rate and achieve a state of demographic modernization.

Buddhism

As far as its formal doctrines are concerned, Buddhism can largely be regarded as neutral with respect to fertility and family planning (Ling, 1969). On the one hand, there is nothing in Buddhist teaching comparable to the Judeo-Christian command to "multiply and be fruitful." Neither is there any great emphasis on the religious sanctity of marriage—entrance into married life is not marked by any religious ceremony or blessing—nor, given the values that place a great deal of prestige on being a celibate monk, is there much pressure on men to prove their virility by fathering a lot of children. On the other hand, there is nothing in formal Buddhist doctrine that would argue against the use of contraception. Given such a neutral stance, one might expect Buddhist fertility to be relatively low and unrelated to religious beliefs. Such is not the case, however. In those countries of Southeast Asia where Buddhism is widespread, fertility is as high if not higher than that of other religious groups. Furthermore, at least part of the high fertility among Buddhist populations can be attributed to various aspects of the Buddhist religion.

On the side of positive inducements to fertility, it is not uncommon to hear the argument that the reincarnation aspect of the Buddhist religion would automatically regard the birth of a lot of human beings (and consequent rapid population growth) with strong approval. As was noted earlier, Buddhism defines five different realms, or states of being, into which beings can be reborn: human, animal, wandering ghosts, spirits in hell, and spirits in heaven. In order to be reborn into the highest of these realms, the human realm, one has to have a good moral balance sheet; thus, if the number of human births increases, it signifies an increase in the overall moral well-being of the universe. As Ling has noted:

> If the number of beings in the human realm increases, this must mean that the new entrants must have been, so to speak, upgraded from the realms of animals, or ghosts or spirits in heaven or hell. . . . For an increasing number to be achieving re-birth in the human realm means that their *karma* (or moral balance-sheet) must have improved. An increase in human population is therefore something to be welcomed as a sign of a general improvement in the moral state of the universe. (1969:53-54)

Ling hastens to point out, however, that this kind of interpretation overstates the situation; it is unlikely that the average Buddhist would look upon the current population explosion (if indeed he is even aware of it) as signifying a marked improvement in the state of the world—especially if such a numerical increase is accompanied by an increase in human suffering. Nevertheless, there are other aspects of

Buddhism that would be conducive to a high level of fertility. One of these is the positive value that is placed on childbearing. The birth of a child is regarded as a sign of the Buddha's blessing, particularly if the child is a male. As noted earlier, much of the behavior of devout Buddhists revolves around earning merit, and one of the many ways to earn merit is either to be a priest oneself or to have a son who enters the priesthood. Thus, Buddhist parents want to have at least one son "since a son would be a potential member of the Buddhist monkhood, and he who enters the monkhood earns merit both for himself and for his parents" (Ling, 1969:55).

A much more indirect influence of Buddhism on fertility is found in the extent to which it promotes factors which, although not solely Buddhist, exert a positive influence on the birth rate. In the preceding section, it was noted that the Buddhist concern for earning merit in order to enhance the possibility of a good re-birth results in behavior that is not conducive to economic modernization—*dana*, or the "giving" of money for such nonproductive purposes as building pagodas, repairing monasteries, or providing lavish entertainment for large numbers of people on various Buddhist festivals. To the extent that economic modernization is in fact slowed down by such activities, those characteristics that are associated with low fertility in the highly developed societies (e.g., industrial growth, education of women) will not be able to develop. Thus, despite the fact that its doctrines do not specifically stress the importance of having a lot of children, Buddhism is partially responsible, at least indirectly, for the maintenance of high fertility rates in the Buddhist countries of Southeast Asia.

There is really nothing in official Buddhist teaching with respect to negative sanctions on the use of birth control. In line with the basic reverence for all life forms, however, there is a pronounced disapproval of abortion as a means of population control. This is not to say that there are no conditions under which abortion would be permitted; most Buddhists who would oppose abortion as a means of family planning would approve it in cases where it was necessary to save the mother's life. Nevertheless, abortion is so strongly condemned as a means of birth control that it often leads to the creation of an equally strong opposition to the use of contraception. Here again this opposition may be related to the reincarnation aspect of Buddhism; the prevention of conception may be seen as equivalent to depriving a being of life—equivalent to interfering with the consequences of the *karma* compiled by a being in a previous existence—and such interference and suppression of a potential life should not be permitted.

On a more worldly level, two other beliefs have been found among Buddhists that would mitigate against the use of contraception. On the one hand, there is a fear that the widespread practice of contraception would lead to an increase in premarital and extramarital promiscuity and thus have a harmful moral effect for the society. On the other hand, there is some fear that birth control will lead to a decline in the size of one's own group relative to the size of other competing groups in the society; this could lead to the subsequent domination and persecution of one's own group by some larger and thus more powerful group. As summarized by Ling (1969:59), these three basic objections that Buddhists raise against contraception are: (1) the objection derived from the Buddhist principle that it is wrong to take life, interpreted to include contraception as a deliberate suppression of life and therefore morally wrong; (2) the argument, also found in other cultural situations, that the widespread use of contraceptives will result in sexual promiscuity; and (3) that family planning will operate differentially against the interests of the Buddhist community which practices it, and in favor of some rival group or community which does not.

Thus, while there is nothing specifically stated in the formal teachings of Buddhism that would either positively stress the desirability of having a large family or negate the practice of birth control, there are a number of latent aspects of Buddhist thought and belief that do result in fertility rates being higher than might otherwise be the case. However, with respect to the extent that these latent forces represent serious obstacles to demographic modernization, there would appear to be some basis for optimism. Since they are not deeply rooted in sacred religious teachings, one might expect them to be less resistant to change. In the case of the first objection, for example, the opposition to the use of contraception generally declines as family size increases and as the desire to provide a better life for children already born becomes more important than the desire not to suppress a potential life. Hence, as economic development progresses, creating more varied opportunities for individuals and families, one may expect such a shift in value emphasis. The second objection is largely an appeal to emotions, and is very often expressed not so much for its own merits but as a means of opposing birth control policies because of the kind of fears expressed in the third objection. In this latter case, past experiences of Buddhists with the economic dominance of the Chinese minority in Thailand, for example, and with regard to the Roman Catholic community in other countries of Southeast Asia have done much to create apprehension of becoming subordinate to some other group. This fear represents a major obstacle to the spread of birth control among Buddhist populations—particularly where they may be in a minority, or in real danger of becoming a minority group. In other words, a major factor that the family planner will have to consider in proposing population control policies and programs in particular Buddhist countries will be the relative size of the Buddhist population relative to that of other non-Buddhist groups.

Hinduism

Hinduism does not have as many adherents as the other major world religions. Nevertheless, it is the dominant religion of India, one of the largest of the developing nations (the largest if we exclude Mainland China). Since India is frequently held up to the Western world as having one of the most serious population problems it seems worthwhile to consider briefly the role that religion might have on fertility and family planning in that country.

To begin with we may note that the traditional Hindu religion tends to be implicitly pronatalist in that a male heir is required to carry on the religious functions of the family (Lorimer, 1954:160). According to Hindu belief, the soul of a dead man cannot leave its body in peace until the skull is opened by a son. Thus, a man must have a surviving son to perform the necessary rituals at the time of his death and otherwise to succeed him as heir to the authority and obligations of the family head. Since mortality, especially infant mortality, was high in the past there was a strong incentive to continue childbearing until at least two sons had been born and had survived infancy. In this way the chances that one would survive to perform the required rituals at the death of the father would be enhanced. Of course the more sons one had the better the odds that there would be a survivor to ensure the continuity of the family. Not surprisingly, then, Hindu culture is one in which marriage is not merely a desirable social status but a quasi-religious duty, and in which the traditional blessing often bestowed on the newly married couple was "May you live long and beget eight children" (Franda, 1972:4).

While traditional Hinduism, with its strong emphasis of the importance of a male heir, may be regarded as implicitly pronatalist, there is nothing specific in its teachings that would stress the desirability of a birth for its own sake, or that would forbid the practice of birth control on moral or sacred grounds. Accordingly, there was little negative reaction when India included a population control policy as part of its first five-year plan drawn up in 1951, thus becoming the first major nation in the world to give public recognition to the existence of a population problem and to formulate a policy aimed at doing something about it. However, while there were no specifically religious objections to family planning there was the weight of custom and tradition to contend with, not to mention the apathy and inertia that characterized a peasant population that for centuries had been dominated by the whims of its physical environment. The result was a situation in which population control was official national policy but where not much was done to implement it. After the adverse economic conditions of 1965-66 and the resulting Bihar famine, however, the seriousness of India's population crisis became more evident to the leaders of the country; and when the new government headed by Prime Minister Indira Gandhi came to power in early 1967 "a vigorous, new, antinatalist policy was formulated and an all-out campaign begun to halve the nation's birth rate by 1975-76, if possible" (Chandrasekhar, 1972:269).

While the new policy and the efforts to implement it indicated that India was moving in the direction of achieving demographic modernization, it soon began to encounter resistance. In particular, there emerged a small group of conservative Hindus who were militantly opposed to the government's family planning program. Some of this opposition is based on arguments pertaining both to the religious duty to have a large family and to the immorality that was thought likely to result from the widespread use of contraception. In a fairly recent report on this development (Franda, 1972:4) we are told that one of the leading spokesmen of the Hindu opposition, Sudhir Hendre, has argued that the ideal of India's family planning program (i.e., two or three children per family) is not only "dangerous and irrational" for Hindus, but is also "morally wrong" and will create "a physical and psychological vacuum in the life of the Hindus." Mr. Hendre further asserts that the traditional Hindu marriage blessing to "Live long and beget eight children" is "not merely an empty pious wish of a decaying religion, but a positive directive of an expansionist social order which is confident of supporting an increasing population."

With respect to the argument concerning the immorality of population control Hendre argues that the use of modern contraceptives is "grossly vulgar" and will only lead to social degeneration. In Hendre's own words, as quoted by Franda:

> The temptation of easy sexual intercourse is bound to reduce man's capacity for self-discipline, a sense of social obligation and a higher purpose of life. Men and women will succumb to the life of least resistance, life without moral restraint, a life which guarantees unfettered sexual promiscuity inside and outside marriage. Adultery has been made easier and can go undetected. (1972:4)

Although the religious duty to have children and the potential adverse consequences of contraception for societal morality are frequently cited as arguments against the government's family planning programs, the major factor behind the militant Hindu opposition is largely rooted in economic and political jealousy, as was the case in the previously discussed Buddhist situation. That is, a fear that some other religious group (in this case the Moslems) will displace Hindus as the dominant economic and political force lies behind much of the Hindu opposition to the government's population control policy. Among the several arguments that the opposition has cited to justify this fear is the fact that Moslems have been increasing at a faster rate than Hindus. But, while this is indeed the case, the rate difference has been exceedingly small; from 1951 to 1971 Hindus declined from approximately 85 percent to 83 percent of the population whereas Moslems increased from 9.9 to 11.2 percent (Franda, 1972:3).

The Moslem gains, small though they are, have been attributed directly to such factors as the refusal of Moslems to participate in the family planning programs, and the fact that Moslems are permitted by law to have four wives while Hindus can have only one. Hendre goes so far as to say that among Hindus one male and one female constitute a couple, while among Moslems one man and four wives comprise a child-producing factory. As a result of this situation, so runs the argument, the total population of Hindus is likely to become smaller while that of the Moslems is likely to increase rapidly, thus drastically changing the entire composition and complexion of the Indian nation (Chandrasekhar, 1972:280). Whether such a fear is realistic or not, it has been an important factor behind much of the Hindu opposition to India's national family planning program, and it is an attitude that will have to be dealt with not just in India, but in any country where different religious or other ethnic groups are in competition with one another, if national family planning programs are to be successful.

Islam

When reference is made to the influence of religion on fertility most westerners first thoughts would be of the Roman Catholic Church and its opposition to the use of artificial methods of birth control. In point of fact, however, the most strongly pronatalist of all the major world religions is probably Islam. As Lorimer has pointed out in his very detailed survey of the relation between culture and human fertility:

> Mohammedanism gives strong and unequivocal emphasis to high fertility, and Mohammedan social structures universally support high fertility. (1954:186)

More recently Kirk (1968) has reaffirmed that the level of fertility among Islamic peoples is almost always very high, generally higher than that of other major religious groups, and this very high fertility can be linked directly to Islamic culture and religion. As Kirk stated:

> It would seem that Moslem institutions, more than those of other world religions, favor a generally high natality. Religion and high natality are more closely correlated for Moslems than for any other major religious group. (1968:235)

And further:

> Empirically Islam has been a more effective barrier to the diffusion of family planning than Catholicism. (1968:231)

Islamic scholars would likely hold different views with

regard to whether the Koran expressly encourages people to have children, or whether it forbids the use of birth control methods. For example, the passage in the Koran that says "Do not slay your children for fear of poverty" is generally regarded as an admonition against abortion and, especially, infanticide. However, some scholars would interpret it more broadly to include prospective children that may not have even been conceived yet (Lorimer 1954:187). According to this latter interpretation, deliberate attempts at birth control would clearly be contrary to the teachings of the Koran. Nevertheless, one can identify several aspects of Islamic culture and religion that can account for the generally higher level of fertility found among Moslem populations. Perhaps the clearest discussion of these influences has been presented by Kirk (1968) who cites two sets of factors to explain higher Moslem fertility: general factors favoring high birth rates that are common to all pre-industrial pastoral/agrarian societies; and factors that are specifically characteristic of Islamic societies. With respect to the general factors favoring higher fertility in Moslem countries, Kirk (1968:235) cites three: (a) the level of development, particularly concerning those characteristics that are associated with a low birth rate (e.g., education, industrialization), is generally lower in Moslem countries than among non-Moslem neighbors; (b) a strong pronatalism that derives from such things as a traditionally high infant mortality, a joint family system that relieves the parents of some of the burdens of childbearing, and the need to have sons to provide continuity to the family, agriculture labor, and old age support; and (c) the basic conservatism characteristic of all peasant societies. In the case of Islam, with its long history of having to deal with incursions from the Western World, this conservatism may be more pronounced than might otherwise be the case, thus making it especially difficult to implement any kind of development program. As Kirk notes, Islam has had:

. . . over a millennium of conflict with Christianity and therefore has a conscious resistance to modern (often identified as Christian) influences which threaten the integrity of Islam. A large part of Islam, much the greater part, has within a generation been under the domination of European countries, and many Moslems have found solace and effective resistance in the continuing practice of their faith. . . . Moslem sensitivities have understandably led to a cultural wall against diffusion from Europe despite proximity, political connections, and long-standing trade and communication. (1968:236)

Turning to a consideration of special Moslem characteristics that might be expected to favor a high birth rate, Kirk again cites three: Moslem marriage institutions, the emphasis on sexuality, and the subordination of women.

Moslem Marriage Institutions The first thing to come to mind here is likely to be the fact that Islamic law permits a man to have as many as four wives. As a factor contributing to high fertility, however, polygamy is probably not as important as one might think. For one thing, polygamy is not that widespread among Moslems, most of whom probably have enough trouble supporting one wife. For another, when polygamy does take place it is often because the first wife has failed to produce a child, and even then it is generally limited to persons possessing some wealth. Of even greater significance, it would seem, are the fact that the Koran expressly encourages marriage; the relative infrequency of divorce (although Islamic law makes it fairly easy for a man to divorce his wife, it also required him to return the dowry with the wife and this may act as a restraining force); and the religious precepts that favor early remarriage of the widowed and the divorced.

Emphasis on Sexuality The Christian ideal state of celibacy and the virtues of sexual restraint are not found in Islam. On the contrary Islam teaches that the pleasures of the flesh, especially sexual intercourse, are gifts from Allah and are to be enjoyed. In contrast to some Christian sects, notably Catholicism, neither a celibate clergy nor celibate religious orders are found in Islam. Further, traditional Moslem belief regards permanent celibacy as an abnormal state for a man and as unthinkable for an able-bodied woman.

Subordination of Women Moslem culture has traditionally placed women in a very subordinate position: they are not permitted to participate in the religious ceremonies in the mosque; until recently they were required to wear a veil in public; they were generally not taught to read and write; and within marriage they were clearly under the domination of the male.

Thus, while the Koran may not expressly encourage large families or forbid the use of birth control techniques, the preceding characteristics of Islamic culture combine to produce a situation characterized by: near universal marriage for women, generally at a fairly young age; an almost complete absence of deliberate attempts to control sexual impulses, or the consequences thereof; and reflecting the first and second factors, a very high level of fertility.

Summary

In concluding this chapter it is important to stress that it is not religion per se that is a problem in the developing countries, but rather some of the basic values and beliefs that religion supports. In the Western world our values have their origin in the Greco-Roman and Judeo-Christian traditions in which the emphasis has been on rationality. This has given rise to a value system exemplified by the Protestant Ethic with its emphasis on the use of reason and hard work to attain active mastery over the natural and physical environment. In the non-Western parts of the world, however, especially in Asia and the Middle East, the prevailing value systems have their roots in Islam, Confucianism, Buddhism, and Hinduism, where the emphasis tends to be on the importance of the family rather than the individual and on leading a proper life according to established traditions. Reflecting these different heritages, the cultural value system of the Western world can best be described by words such as rationalism, secularism, materialism, and achievement. The status quo is looked upon as something to be improved. In the developing areas, however, the prevailing value systems can better be described by words such as fatalism, sacred, passiveness, and ascription, and the status quo is often looked upon as something that should be preserved at all costs. In these parts of the world these basic value systems frequently act as major obstacles to social change and development. In noting this, however, it must also be noted that the non-Western religions and the values they support are not necessarily obstacles to development, and our era has witnessed a number of fairly radical changes that indicate some basis for optimism. Japan, for example, a strong familistic society in which childbirth is a major event, relied heavily on legalized abortion to achieve a modern demographic balance. Abortion is also fairly widespread in Latin America—despite the opposition of the Catholic church—and in Mainland China the state has significantly reduced the importance and influence of the traditional family. Such cases clearly indicate that long-standing cultural values can be modified and that what might appear to be serious cultural obstacles to economic development and demographic modernization can be overcome. The important point to stress again, however, is that all socioeconomic and demographic change must take place within a broad cultural context, and those development plans and programs that make a conscious effort to fit into the existing cultural system will meet less resistance and stand a much better chance of succeeding than those that either ignore or that deliberately try to alter traditional attitudes and values.

6

Social Structure and Development

The social structure of a society refers to the fact that social relationships are organized into recurrent patterns of predictable behavior. The recurrent patterns of behavior derive from certain functional needs of a society which must be met. These include the regulation of internal conflict, the adaptability of the social group to its external environment, and the replacement of population through reproduction. In meeting the needs of a society for its continuity, individuals are classified into statuses and roles, the division of labor is elaborated, and surplus resources are allocated on the basis of a system of stratification. Established ways of doing things are so deeply embedded in the life styles of most people at most times and places that there has been a remarkable persistence in the overall qualities of social life from one generation to another.

To elaborate, the social structure of a society can be defined as the sum total of all the patterned relationships that exist among people, and the norms, customs, laws and other rules that govern their behavior in the various structured relationships that comprise a society. These relationships consist of various statuses, the occupants of which have specified roles to perform in order to fulfill a particular functional need of the society. Such relationships are the building blocks of a society; the particular individuals who interact within these relationships are born and then die, coming and going generation after generation, but the basic patterns persist. To take an example, every society has some kind of family unit that performs particular functions such as procreation and training of the young which contribute toward the perpetuation of the society. In this family unit each member occupies a particular status (husband, mother, eldest son, sister) and has particular roles to perform according to the established norms and customs governing behavior. Each status is interrelated with all others (husband-wife, parent-child), and there are established rules governing behavior in these interrelationships. The particular individuals comprising a given family are constantly changing as new members are born, old members die, some leave to form their own family, and others join through marriage. But the basic structure of the family, the basic patterned relationships among the several statuses, persists from one generation to the next.

Numerous other examples of such patterned social relationships could be cited. All societies have some sort of stratification system, for example, according to which the members of the society are assigned particular social positions based either on certain ascribed characteristics (sex, family of birth, caste membership) or on achieved characteristics (educational attainment, earned wealth). There is a collection of specific norms and customs governing the behavior of persons occupying particular statuses, both toward persons within the same status group and toward persons occupying other status positions. Similarly, every society has some kind of division of labor comprised of statuses and associated roles pertaining to the performance of particular economic tasks—farmer, toolmaker, soldier, doctor, teacher, factory worker. Every society has some more or less formalized system of education for the young. Every society has some kind of hierarchial authority structure, or government, in which individuals at the top exercise varying degrees of power and control over those below them. All of these patterned relationships, these collections of statuses and roles that perform specified functions, have one element in common. They all exist over and above the specific individuals who occupy given positions at particular times, and they persist beyond the lives of the particular individuals. It is the interrelationship among these and other patterned relationships among men that constitutes the social structure or social organization of a society. This chapter will be concerned with the relevance of social structure for the twin problems of economic growth and demographic modernization in the developing countries today. We shall begin by first considering the general question "Is any one type of social structure likely to be more helpful or more harmful for the overall development process than any other type?" Following this we shall examine more closely several of the more important features of social structure that may be related to both economic productivity and demographic behavior.

Social Structure and Economic Development

The most overriding concern of sociologists who have studied the problem of economic development has been the relationship between social structure and economic behavior. Much of the earlier literature on this topic has recently been subjected to widespread criticism, particularly by Third World scholars, but the basic issues at stake are far from being resolved. In this section we shall review some of the controversies and then describe some of the ways in which certain features of social structure may be related to economic behavior and the process of economic growth in the underdeveloped countries.

The most well known attempt to define the components of a structural framework for the comparative study of economic behavior is represented by the pattern variable scheme of Talcott Parsons. This is a scheme that identifies five dimensions (pattern variables) which govern how people will choose between pairs of alternatives in various behavioral situations. Although Parsons intended to provide a framework for the comparative study of all aspects of different societies or social systems, it can easily be adapted to focus only on those activities which concern economic behavior, or behavior related to the production of goods and services (Hoselitz, 1960). According to Hoselitz, three of these pattern variables are particularly relevant to the discussion of economic development. They are:

1. Alternatives pertaining to the basis for allocating status and economic rewards (achievement versus ascription). The choice an individual has to make in this situation is whether to orient his behavior to another person on the basis of the latter's performance in some behavior situation (achievement) or on the basis of some specific attribute the latter possesses, such as age, sex, race, kinship, etc. (ascription).

2. Alternatives pertaining to the criteria for evaluating other persons (universalism versus particularism). The choice an individual is faced with here concerns whether to treat another person on the basis of some universally defined value or in terms of some particular relationship one has to the other person. For example, if one is in a position to hire people for a specific job does one select employees from among those who have passed some universally accepted test of one's level of competence such as a civil service examination or from those who bear some particular relation to him, such as a son or other relative, or a member of the same clan or tribe?

3. Alternatives for defining ones activities and scope of interest in relation to other persons (specificity versus diffuseness). In this case the choice is based on whether the behavior of an individual in a given situation is limited to some specific obligation, or whether it involves a wide range of expectations, rights or duties. For example, if a person

borrows money from a bank he or she will sign a contract containing specific obligations for repaying the loan within a given period of time at some predetermined rate of interest (specificity). However, if a person borrows money from a friend or other family member, the debt incurred may extend far beyond an obligation to repay the loan to include expectations of some kind of reciprocal aid or mutual assistance to the lender, perhaps even to the lender's family, at some future date (diffuseness).

Hoselitz (1960) has applied this scheme to the topic of economic growth, and his analysis suggests the following generalized or ideal type observations:

1. Underdeveloped societies tend to allocate rewards on the basis of ascribed status charactertistics (sex, kinship, caste membership), whereas the more developed societies rely more heavily on individual achievement as the means of acquiring economic goods. In the former, the nature of the economic activity in which one engages is generally predetermined by various ascribed characteristics (men hunt while women farm, the members of one caste are bankers and moneylenders while the members of another are street cleaners, etc.). In the latter, however, economic activity and the rewards derived from it depend largely on what individuals are able to achieve for themselves, and such societies usually have well-developed systems of education for imparting the specialized skills needed for the performance of particular economic tasks.

2. In developing societies, economically relevant tasks are distributed on the basis of particularistic criteria (who one is), whereas universalistic criteria (the skills or talents one possesses) predominate the task assignment process in the more developed societies. In the latter type of society a person will be hired for a job because he possesses certain qualifications such as education, training or experience that are required for the performance of the job. In a society where particularism prevails, however, a person's job will de-

pend upon his particular clan, caste, or immediate family.

3. Finally, in developing societies, where the division of labor is not well developed and where the level of productivity is generally low, economically relevant tasks are typically diffuse—a man will be a hunter, a farmer, a warrior, a house builder and a tool maker. Further, such societies are generally characterized by diffuse obligations for mutual support among a wide range of family, clan or tribe members. In more advanced societies, by contrast, social and economic roles are functionally specific. The increasing complexity of postindustrial society requires an ever more specialized division of labor in which each person will have a specific job for which he or she has received some level of special education or training (doctor, nurse, lawyer, stenographer, college professor, electrician, or retail sales), and the obligations for support are generally limited to a narrowly defined group of people.such as the members of one's immediate family.

In contrasting economically developed and underdeveloped societies in this way, Hoselitz notes that the three pattern variables must be seen in combination and as closely interrelated with one another. In a society where economic roles are very specific, for example, one also finds a correspondingly greater emphasis on universalism (the possession of specific skills) and on achievement (the recognition for having acquired special skills). Conversely, where economic roles are diffuse one finds more reliance on particularistic criteria of evaluation and a greater importance attached to ascribed status characteristics. Operating within this framework, economic development would be a process whereby a society undergoes a basic structural transformation from a type characterized by diffuseness/particularism/ascription to one characterized by specificity/universalism/achievement. That is, to paraphrase Hoselitz (1960:35), as a society undergoes economic development there is an increase in the division of labor—an increase in the specificity of productive tasks. As the number and variety of functionally specific tasks increases, there is a greater need to have them performed by persons possessing specific knowledge or skills; accordingly, there is an increasing reliance on universalistic criteria in the assignment of productive tasks, and ideally competition for particular tasks becomes open to all those who possess the necessary qualifications rather than only to those who occupy particular status positions in the society. Finally, the process of filling specific roles on the basis of objective qualifications rather than on the basis of traditional social rankings leads to an increasing importance being attached to the possession of the necessary skills and an increasing regulation of economic behavior on the basis of achievement rather than ascription.

This approach to the analysis of economic behavior and economic development has been severely criticized in the literature, most notably by Andre Gunder Frank (1969:24-39). Frank has challenged this scheme on several grounds, first on the basis of its empirical validity. For example, some developed countries (e.g., Japan) are more characterized by particularism than universalism, whereas the rise of strong nationalistic movements in many developing countries indicates the widespread presence of indigenous universalism. Similarly, although reward within roles is indeed based heavily on achievement in the United States, there are many elements of ascription such as sex, skin color, and ethnicity that are deeply imbeded in the American stratification system and that strongly influence the roles one occupies in our society.

Second, Frank attacks this general scheme in terms of its theoretical adequacy, charging that it is a wholly abstract model that ignores the reality of past historical causes as well as the nature of the present international economic situation and implies that underdevelopment can be eliminated simply by changing particular structural features of the poor countries. Furthermore, he argues, by regarding such structural change as an integral part of the development process, it implies that the existing structure in developing societies is inherently bad. However, such things as rewards based on

ascription are not necessarily in themselves evil or conservative in consequence. In many of the developing countries
where a son may indeed be recruited into a top management
position in his father's business, he will most often have to
undergo a rigorous period of education and training prior to
such recruitment. Moreover, as Gusfield (1973) has pointed
out, some traditional elements may very well be conducive
to economic development; for example, the extended family
in India and some Middle Eastern countries has proven
highly beneficial to the growth of certain business enterprises.

Finally, Frank criticizes the pattern variable approach
from the point of view of its policy effectiveness. In this
respect he notes that the pattern variables of development—specificity, universalism, and achievement—are associated primarily with the middle class, leading to the notion that development will be enhanced only through the
promotion and rise of the middle class. However, the internal structure of many developing societies is such that when
the middle class does grow it does so not at the expense of the
rich but at the expense of the large masses of the poor, thus
leading to even greater underdevelopment for the masses.

In another more recent critique, Stokes and Harris (1978)
have also questioned the validity of the pattern variables,
especially the universalism-particularism dichotomy. Their
basic objections are made on the grounds that economic
development or industrialization are traditionally supposed
to remove particularistic criteria. The general objections are
that this may be an inaccurate distinction even for western
nations, and to try to apply it to the developing nations may
compound the error. Second, industrialization is not as dependent on certain fixed prerequisites as many authorities in
the field (e.g., Rostow, 1960) would have us believe. The
experience of South Africa, for example, illustrates how
particularistic variables may be perpetuated by industrialization. A more specific objection to the utilization of the pattern variables is that many of the developing nations are

modernizing from the center, unlike the western nations which modernized from the periphery (Stokes and Harris, 1978:269). The elite—the center—is the force for moderniza-tion in the developing countries, for it holds the economic and political power. Therefore, even if modernization or development takes place, particularistic criteria are still utilized, and help to perpetuate the old social order. Stokes and Harris claim that the South African case is also generalizable to other developing nations which are develop-ing from the center, or as others have put it, "from above" (Palmer, 1973; Pitt, 1976; Laidlaw, 1976).

While it is easy to accept the validity of such critiques, one has to be careful not to throw the baby away with the bath water. It can be suggested, for example, that much of the criticism rests on too literal an interpretation of the pattern variables as distinguishing sharply between developed and developing societies. Admittedly they do not; but neither are they intended to. Rather, they are intended to be used as ideal types, and as such they do have value as a starting point in the analysis of the relationship between social structure and economic development. That is, adhering to the original Weberian conception, distinctions such as those provided by the pattern variables may be and should be viewed as ideal type constructs that never exist in reality, but are useful for comparative studies simply because they emphasize similarities and differences of typical modes of conduct. Furthermore, they allow the development of hypotheses which explore the events that brought the phenomenon to light or that seek to explain present day economic behavior. One of the definitions of an ideal type is that it is to be utilized to study parts of social life which can be found at any time independent of historical events (e.g., the family). It may also refer to a phenomenon that has a particular historical basis such as the Protestant Ethic discussed in chapter 5. There-fore, while the ideal type is limited for many purposes, it does retain some analytical usefulness, particularly for our purposes in this chapter. In the remainder of this section we have singled out particular aspects of social structure which are discussed in terms of the possible negative or positive effects each may exert on the many facets of the overall development process, as well as in terms of how the development process may effect them.

Personality

One aspect of any society that is intimately related to its characteristic social structure is the dominant personality mode. In this section attention will be focused on the way in which personality may be related to social change and economic development. In it we will examine some of the studies that focus on the development of certain personality traits, or on the attitudinal configurations and behavior patterns that either adversely or positively affect development.

Innovative and Authoritarian Personalities (E. E. Hagen) One of the most thorough analyses of the relationship between personality type and economic development is contained in E. E. Hagen's book, *On the Theory of Social Change* (1962). Hagen's essential thesis is that there are two fundamental personality types—innovative and authoritarian. The former is characterized by such things as a creative imagination, a high degree of self-confidence, achievement orientation, etc., and is seen to be conducive to economic development. The authoritarian personality, on the other hand, is defined as the polar opposite of the innovational—as characterized by a lack of creativity, low self-confidence, and the lack of a strong achievement drive; and this type is generally regarded as an obstacle to economic development. The bases for making the distinction between these two polar ideal types are cognition, needs, and values.

Cognition refers here to the way in which a person perceives the world around him. The basic distinction is whether the world is perceived as bewildering, arbitrary and threatening, or whether it is perceived as orderly and understandable and capable of manipulation.

Needs refer to the various inner drives that guide the way in which a person reacts to the world around him. Hagen (1962:105-11) identifies four classes of such needs: manipulative, aggressive, passive and succorant-nurturant needs. Manipulative needs reflect a view of the world as an orderly system that can be understood and dealt with in a rational manner. They include: need achievement, the need to attain satisfaction for achieving some goal (solving problems) by the successful exercise of one's own judgement and abilities; need autonomy, the need to be independent of the control of others and to make one's own decisions; and need order, the need to have order in one's life, to have everything arranged in a logical and systematic manner. Aggressive needs are associated with a view of the world as threatening and in which the proper course of action is fighting back rather than trying to understand and manipulate it. These include: need submission, or the need to escape the necessity of decision making by receiving and following direction from others; and need dominance, or the need to oppose and attack that which appears threatening and to overcome opposition by force. Passive needs are: need dependence, or the need to receive guidance from others to avoid the risk of failure or frustration from making decisions oneself; and need affiliation, or the need to be near and enjoy the reciprocal affections of others like oneself. Finally, succorant-nurturant needs are: need succorance, the need to have one's needs gratified by a sympathetic other—to be supported, protected, loved, consoled, etc.; need nurturance, or the converse need to give succorance, to provide support, protection, love, consolation, etc.

Values are the standards which determine the way in which a person will give vent to his needs. There are two basic sets of values: moral values that relate to the individual's sense of what is good or bad, right or wrong; and manipulative values that determine where an individual will choose to exercise his initiative and capabilities.

It is the interaction and integration of these three basic

elements in a person that determines his dominant personality type. The two distinct polar types under discussion here can best be summarized by quoting directly from Hagen. The person with an innovational personality

. . . views the phenomena of the world, at least in an area which he values highly, as forming systems whose operation is orderly and amenable to logical analysis. . . . He also views the world as valuing him, though his perception may be a qualified one which creates anxiety in him: he may see the world as valuing him only provided that he achieve effectively. His high need succorance, need to receive assurances of being valued, then drives him to achieve and is the source of that deep religious sense of duty to achieve that is so often present in innovational personality. He is also high in need autonomy, achievement, and order; and since he conceives all phenomena, no matter how disorderly superficially, as capable of being understood, these needs cause him ever to be alert to new disorderly phenomena within his field of interest in order that he may have the pleasure of autonomously achieving discovery of the order that governs them. Moreover, because he understands himself and hence has empathy with the needs of others, he is high in need nurturance. Perhaps it is because of this need nurturance that the scope of an innovational individuals moral values is broad. He is apt to regard the welfare of individuals and groups over a wide area of his society and perhaps other societies as (almost) equal in importance to his own. The degree of his regard declines only slightly with respect to groups farther and farther removed from him. (1962:119)

By contrast, the authoritarian personality

. . . perceives the phenomena of the world as forming a system whose operation is not orderly and not capable of analysis. Hence he is high in need dependence. He also perceives the world as not valuing him highly, and sees power as residing in position rather than resulting from accomplishment. Because of the rage and the need to curb it which these perceptions generate in him, he is high in need submission-dominance and low in need succorance-nurturance. He is low in need autonomy and achievement and probably low also in need order, though he may be conceived as high in need order but driven to satisfy it by evading recognition of inconsistencies or discrepancies in his perception of phenomena. He regards the welfare of very few if any individuals as (almost) equal in importance to his own, and outside of that limited group the degree of his regard for the welfare of others declines rapidly. (1962:119)

The significance of these two polar personality types lies in the fact that the process of economic growth requires a high degree of creativity and innovation (Hagen, 1962:34-35); thus social change and development will be much more likely to occur in societies where the innovative personality type predominates. The problem, however, lies in the assertion that the social structure of traditional (developing) societies gives rise to and perpetuates the authoritarian personality. Traditional societies are seen as static societies in which the lines of stratification and authority are rigidly drawn. The external world has proven to be arbitrary and unpredictable—delayed rains create drought conditions, floods wash away crops, babies die at a high rate, etc.—and it is easy to come to regard one's life as governed by unseen forces over which one has no control. Children are taught their place in the authoritarian hierarchy of human relationships and to find solace and protection within their small social units and in dependence on those individuals who are above them in the hierarchy. They are taught not to express curiosity or to explore their environment; rage and frustration are to be repressed; and they learn that accomodation to the status quo, rather than creativity and innovation, is the best way to avoid the pitfalls and dangers inherent in a world that is controlled by the arbitrary action of unseen powers. The end product of this socialization process is an adult who is highly authoritarian, who is unable to tolerate dissent or deviance among those who are below him in the social structure, and who relies heavily on the judgment and authority of others who are above him in the stratification system.

The interrelationship between social structure and personality is so pervasive that the necessary conclusion is that social change or development will not occur unless there is a change in personality (Hagen, 1962:86). Hagen's hypothesis is that this occurs as a response to an "invasion." There is a change in the social structure that leads to a withdrawal of status respect for the lower elites, a status loss which alters child rearing practices and leads mothers to push their sons into entrepreneurial activities. Individuals experience anxiety over the situation and develop feelings of ineffectiveness as old attitudes and behavior no longer suffice to meet their needs, Gradually the evolution of the innovative personality takes place. The innovative person continues to exhibit anxiety, but now the anxiety is accompanied by a need to achieve, to succeed, and he is able to channel his anxiety into productive efforts. Thus, the key to social change and development is seen to be a breakdown in the traditional social structure and a corresponding change in child rearing practices that leads to a shift in the dominant personality mode from authoritarian to innovative, and the emergence of behavior patterns more conducive to economic development.

Although Hagen's analysis of the relationship between social structure and personality is extremely insightful, his emphasis on the importance of personality change for economic development has been challenged on several grounds. Not the least of these is that it has an inherent western bias that essentially "blames the victim" for being underdeveloped while ignoring the importance of such things as the structure of the international economic system. It also rests on the assumption that the child internalizes and remembers all his childhood experiences and subconsciously acts upon them throughout the rest of his life. More recent studies, however (e.g., McClelland and Winter, 1969) have suggested that personality traits conducive to economic development, such as need achievement, can be effectively taught to adults; still others (Inkeles and Smith, 1974; Kunkel, 1970) see important personality changes as being generated by exposure to various aspects of modern life that one may encounter throughout one's lifetime. It can also be suggested that such personality changes may actually not be necessary and that the authoritarian personality may in fact be useful in promoting development—witness the economic expansion of Nazi Germany during the 1930s, that of Japan following their defeat in World War II, and the progress made by Taiwan during the 1950s and 1960s. That is, there may be some basis for arguing that a society where the authoritarian personality type is the dominant one will be more likely to accept the strong leadership and direction that many today see as essential for economic growth in the Third World (see chapter 8).

Hagen's theory can also be criticized on the same grounds that most personality theories are challenged. That is, they assume that the basic attributes of personality are laid down in early childhood and remain relatively fixed for the life of the individual. Thus, a generation or more must pass before there can be any significant changes in the modal personality of a society. If this assumption is correct, and if there is any basis to the assertion that social change and development require a change in personality, then the outlook for any noticeable economic progress in the developing world in the near future must remain bleak. However, as will be seen below, there is some basis for rejecting this assumption and for concluding that basic personality transformations can occur after persons have reached adulthood.

The Modernization of Man (Inkeles and Smith) A somewhat similar approach, though one that would be more optimistic than Hagen's personality theory of social change, is represented by the "modern man" concept of Alex Inkeles and David Smith (1974). Like Hagen, the latter authors would argue that societal development is intricately related to the presence of a particular personality configuration, and that economic development "requires a transformation in the very nature of man" (Inkeles and Smith, 1974:289). The basic transformation is characterized by the emergence of what they define as a "modern man" who, in many respects, closely resembles Hagen's innovational personality. Specifically, a modern man is defined as

. . . an informed participant citizen; he has a marked sense of personal efficacy; he is highly independent and autonomous in his relations to traditional sources of influence, especially when he is making basic decisions about how to conduct his personal affairs; and he is ready for new experiences and ideas, that is, he is relatively open-minded and cognitively flexible. (Inkeles and Smith, 1974:290)

And further,

> The modern man is quicker to adopt technical innovation, and more ready to implement birth-control measures; he urges his son to go as far as he can in school, and, if it pays better, encourages him to accept industrial work rather than to follow the more traditional penchant for office jobs; he informs himself about the goods produced in the more modern sector of the economy, and makes an effort to acquire them; and he permits his wife and daughter to leave the home for more active participation in economic life. In these and a host of other ways, . . . the man who is more modern in attitude and value acts to support modern institutions and to facilitate the general modernization of society. (Inkeles and Smith, 1974:313)

The basic point at which Inkeles and Smith depart from Hagen is with the process, and especially the length of time required, for an individual to undergo the transition from "traditional man" to "modern man." Based on an extensive study carried out in several different countries possessing different cultural heritages, Inkeles and Smith tested their basic theoretical premise that men become modern not as a result of childhood training, but through the particular life experiences they undergo; they were able to demonstrate empirically that the basic characteristics of the modern man can be acquired in adulthood in the space of just a few years. They went further and identified the specific modern institutions, contact with which leads to the modernization of man. These were the school, the mass media, and the factory. In all of the countries they studied it was found that as the level of education increased there was a corresponding increase in the proportion of men exhibiting the basic characteristics of modernity. Persons who went to school learned much more than reading, writing, and arithmetic. They also learned new values, attitudes, and ways of behaving. They acquired a different sense of time and a stronger sense of personal and social efficacy; they participated more actively in communal affairs; and they were more open to new ideas, new experiences, and new people. They interacted differently with other people, showing more concern for minorities and those below them in the social structure. They placed a higher value on science and rationality and accepted change more readily; they were more willing to consider limiting the number of children they would have. ''In short, by virtue of having had more formal schooling, their personal character was decidedly more modern''(Inkeles and Smith, 1974:143).

In the same way they found that as contact with the mass media increased, it was associated with an increase in modern attitudes. The mass media bring people new information, suggest new ideas, demonstrate new ways of doing things, stimulate higher aspirations, etc.—all of which serve to induce greater modernity in persons exposed to them. (See chapter 7.)

Perhaps the overriding conclusion of the Inkeles and Smith study, however, concerned the major role of employment in a factory as a source of modernity. It made no difference whether the factory was large or small, labor intensive or capital intensive; it was found everywhere that industrial work was a major factor in making men modern. The authors were able to conclude that

> . . . the factory is unmistakably a school in modernity. In its own right, the organizational experience it provides serves consistently to change men in ways which qualify them as more modern in attitudes, value, and behavior. (Inkeles and Smith, 1974:174)

The important conclusion to be drawn from this study is that while it may indeed be true that certain personality traits and characteristics may be associated with economic development, these traits can be learned through a process of exposure to modern institutions. That is, personality is not something that becomes fixed by a certain age in childhood, but is instead something that can and does change through a continuous process of adult socialization. Further, this study casts doubt on the widespread assumption that economic development can only be achieved at a great cost to the psychic well-being of the peoples in the Third World, which suggests that the process of modernization may be far less disruptive of the developing societies than has been supposed.

Behavior Modification (John H. Kunkel) A somewhat different though related approach to this topic is represented by the behavioral model for social change suggested by John Kunkel (1970). Kunkel begins by rejecting as inappropriate what he calls the "psychodynamic model" of human behavior, or the model that would explain behavior in terms of various components of man's internal state such as attitudes, values, and need dispositions. Instead, he offers a "behavioral model" which, similar to the preceding modernization of man thesis, looks at an individual's behavior as being shaped by the activities in which he engages. More specifically, he asserts that

> . . . the great majority of behavior patterns are established and maintained by means of the differential reinforcement of activities after they have been performed. That is, not all possible activities, but only those deemed "desirable" by a group or society are rewarded, others are not, and still others may be punished. When an activity is rewarded after it has been performed, the probability of repetition in similar circumstances is increased and eventually approaches certainty. Conversely, when an activity is punished or not rewarded, the probability of repetition under similar conditions declines and eventually approaches zero. (Kunkel, 1970:27-28)

In other words, human behavior can be altered and social change initiated or accelerated through a process of altering those aspects of the social environment that constitute rewarding or punishing consequences for specific activities, rather than by trying to change inner psychic states. In terms of its relevance for developing areas, there are two aspects to altering human behavior: using punishment tactics to eliminate kinds of behavior that are inimical to economic development, such as the practice of hoarding wealth, or high levels of fertility; and using rewards to encourage kinds of behavior that would be beneficial to economic development, such as saving and investing, or low levels of fertility.

In one sense, Kunkel is agreeing with scholars like Inkeles and Smith who assert that exposure to modern institutions (e.g., schools) can shape new behavior patterns, but he goes one step further by adding that such new behavior patterns will not emerge unless there is something to be gained by them:

> Education programs, extension services, training institutes, and similar limited efforts to change men's actions will not be very effective as long as there are few opportunities and rewards for the expression of the new behavior patterns that are introduced. Widespread behavior modification is not likely until significant changes occur in the social context of individuals. This does not necessarily mean that wholesale and fundamental changes are always required. Rather, it means that the specific aspects of a person's environment which affect the new behavior patterns—for example job opportunities and pay scales for engineering graduates—must be changed so as to reinforce the new patterns of activity. (Kunkel, 1970:101)

Kunkel reinforces his argument by citing various cases, such as the now fairly well-known Vicos Project organized in Peru by the anthropologist Allan Holmberg of Cornell University. In this project, a large *hacienda* in the Andean valley about two hundred fifty miles northeast of Lima was leased for five years beginning in 1949, and the traditional feudal-type relations between the *patron* and the local Indians were abolished (that is, they did away with the obligation for each household to provide the *patron,* or landlord, the labor of one adult member for three days a week, as well as the use of animals and other services such as periodic work as cooks, watchmen, and general servants). Instead, the Indians began to be paid for their labor, and a system of credit was established to enable them to buy seeds, fertilizer and insecticide. Repayment for the credit was to be a prearranged set amount rather.than an amount determined by the size of the crop, thus permitting the Indians to keep or sell a larger share of what they grew. The result was an increase in individual autonomy, the emergence of new patterns of leadership, and a sizeable increase in crop yields! In other words, when the external conditions were changed so that the Indians could realize something concrete for their increased labor, they worked harder. "New behavior patterns and hard work, in other words, were strongly reinforced" (Kunkel, 1970:145).

While Kunkel's approach has much to recommend it, the successes he tells about have been limited to relatively small scale projects, and one has to wonder about the feasibility of radically altering the economic structure of a larger social unit in order to bring about the desired changes in behavior unless, of course, one is willing to accept a rigidly controlled society, such as that of Communist China (see chapter 8). Nevertheless, it does represent another challenge to traditional theories that see a relatively drawn-out change in personality traits as a prerequisite to social change and development, thus reinforcing the conclusion noted with respect to the "modern man" theory. That is, attitudes and behaviors (which are simply the external manifestation of attitudes anyway) can be changed in a relatively short period of time, and such changes are likely to be far less disruptive to the psychic well-being of those involved than has often been assumed.

Summary A number of other scholars would side with Kunkel and with Inkeles and Smith in their assertion that the various attitudes, personality traits, and behavior patterns that are conducive to economic development can be learned. McClelland and Winter (1969), for example, have been able to show that need achievement can be instilled in adults irrespective of their cultural origins, and they have suggested that development programs in the various Third World countries include training programs in order to instill such a need. The disagreement does not seem to be so much with a recognition of the interrelationship between personality and economic growth, or with the idea that certain personality traits will be more conducive to economic development than others. Although there is some recent evidence to suggest that the importance of psychological modernity as a determinant of modern behavior has been overrated (Armer and Isaac, 1978), the main source of disagreement seems to concern the amount of time required to change personality, and the most appropriate mechanisms of promoting either personality change or change in overt behavior patterns.

The Family

The family is without doubt the most important and fundamental institution in human society. It is the basic social group in which people are born, nurtured and socialized to the proscribed norms, values and behavior patterns of the society. It is the group in which most people live out the greater part of their lives, and no other social group has as much influence on one's behavior as the family to which one belongs. This is not to suggest that the nature of the family in any given society determines all human behavior, but the influence it exerts is extremely pervasive. At the same time that the family is singled out as being such a vitally important social group, it can also be noted that there is perhaps no other institution that has exhibited historically, and exhibits today, as much diversity in structure and function among human societies as the family. In the present context, concern is with the ways in which some of these differences may act to promote or inhibit the process of economic growth in the developing societies.

The basic distinction commonly made with respect to family and society is that the small nuclear family, consisting of a married couple and their dependent children, is characteristic of modern industrial society, whereas the large extended family, whose members comprise several generations as well as extend outward to include cousins, uncles and aunts, nephews, etc., is characteristic of traditional or developing societies. Further, it is generally accepted that this extended family type represents a major obstacle to social change and development. In the remainder of this section we will describe these two polar types in greater detail, with particular reference to the influence they may exert on economic behavior.

The nuclear family, which is characteristic of modern urban industrial societies, is commonly defined as consisting of a married couple and their immediate unmarried or dependent children. Family relationships are focused on a relatively small number of persons, generally limited to those between husband-wife, parent-child, and sibling-sibling. Marriage is monogamous, with choice of spouse being largely left up to the individuals concerned; kinship is bilateral, that is, descent is traced equally on the father's side and mother's side. The nuclear family is characterized by an absence of strong clan or lineage ties, and it generally maintains its own separate household away from those of other relatives. The basic functions performed by this type of family are reproduction (procreation) and the socialization of the young. The family head works on his own behalf and has sole responsibility for the support of his wife and children. There is no pooling of income with that of other relatives and no obligation to share the fruits of its labor with other households, although relatives do, of course, call upon and assist each other in times of emergency. The nuclear family represents, in effect, a more or less autonomous, economically independent unit.

By contrast, the extended family which is found in varying forms throughout many of the now developing societies, is generally comprised of a number of nuclear families covering several generations. Family relationships are typically diffuse and involve a much larger number of people—including grandparents, uncles, aunts, cousins, and in-laws—than in the isolated nuclear family. Marriage may be either monogamous or polygamous, and parents exercise a great deal of control or influence over the selection of spouses for their children, as well as over many other important aspects of their lives such as the education they receive, and the work they do. Kinship is generally unilateral with descent being traced mainly through either the male or female line, most commonly the male line. In addition to procreation and childhood socialization, the extended family performs a number of other important functions in traditional societies, including educational, religious, recreational, status giving, and protection functions that are normally performed by other more specialized institutions in the more advanced societies. One of the key differences in this respect relates to the family's economic function, which is much broader in traditional than in modern societies. In the former, the several nuclear families comprising an extended family often share a common household presided over by the family patriarch; in contrast to the relative autonomy and independence of the isolated nuclear family, the extended family is characterized by strong kinship ties, shared responsibilities, and a high degree of mutual obligation for the support and maintenance of all family members.

In the present context, the key question is whether one of these two family types is more or less beneficial than the other during the process of development. Traditionally the view has been that the nuclear family type is more adaptable to a changing society. Because of its smaller size, weaker kinship ties, and economic independence, the nuclear family is more mobile. Further, because of its relative autonomy as an economic and social unit, it puts a greater premium on preparing the individual to take care of himself; it places a higher value on individual achievement; and it allows for a greater emphasis on universalistic standards of performance. The extended family, on the other hand, is seen to have many features that may serve to inhibit the modernization process. To take a specific illustration, Chandrasekhar (1965) has cited several aspects of the Hindu extended family in India that tend to limit economic behavior:

1. Because of its strong kinship ties and responsibilities, it serves to retard both the geographic and occupational mobility that are a major characteristic of a developing society.

2. Because of the mutual obligations to care for all family members, the extended family weakens initiative and undermines any spirit of adventure. Dependents who remain at home know they will be taken care of and well looked after by the family head, so there is less incentive to leave or to engage in any daring or risk-taking enterprises.

3. Although the total resources available to the large

extended family may be considerably more than those of a single nuclear family, the need to maintain and preserve family resources in trust for the future mitigates against investing capital in productive enterprises that might entail a risk. The family head is seen as a caretaker rather than a risktaker, and resources tend to be invested in such non-productive things as land, or gold and jewelry—things that can be retained for transmission to future generations.

4. Chandrasekhar notes that even though Hindu law permits a man to enjoy the fruits of any wealth he may accumulate during his lifetime, the incentive to accumulate such wealth is negated by the injunction that, on a man's death, all his wealth and property automatically goes to the extended family rather than to his immediate progeny.

While it is explicitly recognized that the extended family does serve a number of important functions in Hindu society—it provides a kind of social security in the event of illness or unemployment, as well as the guarantee of being cared for in one's old age—Chandrasekhar concluded that the extended family in India has been a strong force against innovation, experimentation, and capital accumulation—all of which are the mark of a developing society. In other words, the nature of the Hindu extended family has had an inhibiting effect on modernization in India.

Although Chandrasekhar is referring to the specific case of India, many of the characteristics he cites are applicable to the extended family in other areas of the Third World. Perhaps the most outstanding of these are the traditional welfare functions of the extended family and the heavy emphasis on mutual obligations for support. Mutual obligations within the framework of an extended family tend to be anti-individualistic, and numerous illustrations can be cited to show how they may inhibit the development process. In addition to discouraging initiative because of the security they provide (as in the preceding Hindu illustration), mutual obligations can have the more direct negative effect of encouraging the rejection of economic assistance. In Peru, for example, fishermen who were offered assistance by a development agency—improved net equipment, motors for boats, etc., all of which would have contributed to a larger catch—resisted on the grounds that the increase in their wealth resulting from the larger catch would only mean that more relatives would move in with them and look to them for support. Similarly, Maori industrial workers in New Zealand refused to participate in an improved housing program for fear all their relatives would move into their new house with them (Foster, 1962:90-93). In both of these illustrations, the proposed increase in the living levels of the individuals involved would have forced them to face the dilemma of either disregarding the family obligations that their cultures expected of them or of having to support an increasing number of idle relatives with little or no profit to themselves; in both cases the dilemma was avoided by resisting the innovative programs being suggested from above.

A cautionary note is in order before one jumps to the conclusion that the extended family is a necessary obstacle to economic development—particularly when one views the case of Japan where the traditional family structure played a major role in facilitating the modernization process. Studies of the extended family in a number of other still developing countries such as Nigeria (Nafziger, 1969) and Lebanon (Khalaf and Shwayri, 1966) have clearly shown that the extended family need not have a negative effect on entrepreneurial activity, and that many of the traditional family norms may actually exert a supportive influence on industrial growth. The rule of nepotism common in family-run firms, for example, will not be economically dysfunctional when those family members who are given positions of responsibility have been educated and thoroughly trained for their positions. The centralization of authority in the hands of an autocratic patriarch will not be bad if the patriarch is well-informed about market conditions, and if he makes his decisions in a rational and calculated manner. And the oft cited conservatism of the family head as caretaker rather than risktaker, as one who is constantly playing it safe in order to maintain the family's position, has been found to be more of a western-based myth than a reality in many parts of the developing world. Such evidence clearly calls for a reevaluation of the traditional view that the extended family will be a major obstacle to modernization in the Third World; it may be in some specific cases, but the relationship is obviously not a necessary one. Similarly, it indicates the need to modify the traditional theses of "fit" and "convergence" according to which there is seen to be a good "fit" between the nuclear family type and the modern industrial system, and that one can therefore expect a "convergence" of family patterns toward this nuclear type as societies undergo modernization (Goode, 1963). The evidence from countries like Nigeria and Lebanon would clearly suggest that such a convergence is not a necessary corollary of the development process.

As a step toward clarifying the relationship between family type and modernization, Straus (1972) has recently suggested a theoretical typology based on two dimensions: problem solving ability and the number of societal functions performed by the family. The first dimension, problem solving ability, is offered as a substitute for the more common "traditional" versus "modern" categorization of society and is defined as the ability to cope with situations and circumstances that require some sort of group (family) effort—most particularly for new situations, such as might arise during a transitional period, for which there is no traditional response to fall back on. The second dimension, the number of functions performed by the family, is suggested as a substitute for the traditional "nuclear" (few functions) and "extended" (many functions) dichotomy. Based on whether a society ranks high or low on these two dimensions, Straus identifies four types of family organization that are likely to make different contributions to the modernization process (see Figure 6.1). These types may be summarized briefly as follows:

Figure 6.1 A taxonomy of families in relation to modernization contribution.

Span of functions of extended kin group			
High		Low	
Problem solving ability		Problem solving ability	
Low	High	Low	High
(A)	(B)	(C)	(D)
Maximal	Maximal	Moderate	Moderate
Deterrent	Contribution	Deterrent	Contribution

Source: Adapted from M. A. Straus, "Family Organization and Problem Solving Ability in Relation to Societal Modernization," *Journal of Comparative Family Studies*, 3 (January 1972): 75.

Type A is high on the number of functions performed by the family; low on problem solving ability. This is the classical extended family described earlier in which fixed forms of behavior have evolved that may be well suited to a relatively static premodern social order, but which lack the flexibility needed to adapt to the changes of a modernizing society. Lacking flexibility and adaptability, this type will tend to resist change and will exert a maximal deterrent effect on modernization.

Type B is high on the number of functions performed; high on problem solving ability. This type corresponds to the extended family as found in Japan and Lebanon in which the family performs many functions and exerts considerable influence over family members, but in which, for varying reasons, "a substantial part of this influence has been channeled in directions which promote modernization and adaptation to the demands of a modern society" (Straus, 1972:76). It is suggested that this type of family will make a maximal contribution to modernization.

Type C and Type D correspond to the more familiar nuclear family type (low on number of societal functions performed), and it is suggested that each will exert a moderate effect on modernization. Type C will act as a moderate deterrent (although low in problem solving, the influence of the extended family is sufficiently weakened so as to reduce the negative influence on development); Type D will exert a moderate *contributing* effect (although high in problem solving, the influence of the extended family is sufficiently weakened to reduce the positive influence on development).

In an oversimplified way, what Straus is proposing essentially is two ideal type family structures (extended versus nuclear) that can behave or function according to either traditional or modern norms. In this sense, then, what one would have would be a typology like that in Figure 6.2.

While the Straus typology, as well as our interpretation of it, is debatable on theoretical grounds (some would argue that Type D, representative of the isolated nuclear family in contemporary industrial societies, ought to be assigned a stronger positive influence), it does have value in providing a broader perspective for looking at the relationship between family structure and the development process. Specifically, it provides a start on a new theoretical framework that gets away from the traditional stereotypes that the nuclear family is good for development whereas the extended family is an obstacle to societal change and modernization, and it provides a basis for analyzing both nuclear and extended family types in terms of both the functional and the dysfunctional influences each may exert during the modernization process.

Figure 6.2 Modified taxonomy of family type in relation to modernization contribution.

Straus Family Type	Characteristics	Effect on Development
A	Extended structure, traditional behavior	Strongly negative
B	Extended structure, modern behavior	Strongly positive
C	Nuclear structure, traditional behavior	Slightly negative
D	Nuclear structure, modern behavior	Slightly positive

Role and Status of Women

One of the most sorely neglected topics in discussions of Third World development concerns the role and status of women in society. On the one hand, relatively little attention has been given to the possible economic contribution that women in developing countries could make in the overall developmental process, thus virtually ignoring a vast potential resource. On the other hand, even less attention has been devoted to studying the effects of development on the roles and statuses of women in these emerging nations. Very often the changes associated with development have had a very disruptive effect on the lives of women (more so than on men); this is a problem that is in need of a great deal more research. Research in this area has been increasing in recent years, however, and this brief section will touch on a few of the more salient issues that have been raised. The point to keep in mind is that the entire process of development and the problems associated with it involve both men and women, and that many of the characteristics of developing areas noted elsewhere in this volume, such as high rates of illiteracy, lack of educational opportunities, and absence of political participation, apply to women as much as to men—in many cases even more so. Over and above these general problems, however, there are some aspects of the development process as it relates to women that merit special consideration.

Underutilization of Female Labor In many of the presently developing societies women have traditionally been relegated to second class citizenship, and in others where they previously enjoyed more equal status they have lost it. Sometimes legally, sometimes merely by custom, women have been relegated to a position vastly inferior to men in many parts of the Third World. Women generally have only limited political and legal rights and very few economic opportunities, and in these countries they have become largely dependent on some man (father, husband, son) for whatever they have in life. The limited educational opportunities that are available, for example, tend to be restricted largely to males so that illiteracy and the lack of related economic skills are much more widespread among women. To the extent that women as mothers and child-rearers are major culture bearers, this situation tends to be perpetuated in the values of the society. It represents another of the many obstacles to development that are found throughout the Third World.

An especially important corollary of the inferior status of women in the developing countries is the economic waste that comes from excluding women from the nonagricultural labor force. This has been noted especially with respect to India, one of the world's largest developing countries. In that nation, according to Chandrasekhar (1965:21ff.), the result of the inferior status accorded women has been an enormous economic waste. Even though Hindu law regards men and women as equal in the eyes of God, the actual situation that has evolved over the centuries is one in which the status of women has been reduced to that of chattel; daughters live under the domination of their fathers, wives are subjugated to their husbands, and widows live under the direction and rule of their sons. This position of women's subjugation to men has been perpetuated by a number of aspects of Hindu culture: there is a social ban against widows' remarrying; there are laws that prevent women from inheriting property; and women do not have equal access to educational and employment opportunities. An especially serious factor in this respect has been the *purdah* system which has kept the women of a family in virtual isolation from the outside world. Women at the extreme ends of the social scale were less likely to have their lives governed by these customs; economic pressures often made it impossible for women in poor families to conform to traditional roles and forced them into the labor force, whereas women from wealthy families, where Western values have often penetrated, have been able to acquire some education and become relatively emancipated from the traditional restrictions. However, the large majority of women continue to lead traditional lives. For the vast majority of women between the two extreme social groups, traditional beliefs and customs still govern behavior, with the result that a very sizable segment of the population is effectively excluded from gainful employment. Thus, in India and in many other developing countries as well, a large proportion of the population represents nothing less than a colossal waste of human resources.

Another process, which has been labeled "sanskritization," may also be applied to the situation of women in India and in other developing countries as well (Tinker, 1976b). As economic conditions improve for men, they become less willing to have their wives perform any kind of menial task, such as agricultural labor or work outside the home, even when the economic contribution of the wife could be of value to the family. Even when the men in these families are earning just enough to put them near or slightly above the poverty level, the fact of having a wife who does not work is a source of prestige for the male—and, of course, women in the developing societies may themselves welcome this withdrawal from the labor force as it represents a status symbol derived from modeling themselves after upper-class women. In this situation about the only important function remaining to women is to marry and produce children, but this is really not what countries that are trying to lower their birth rate need.

There are, of course, striking differences within the developing world in the extent to which women participate in the labor force. In Latin America, for example, close to 40 percent of the adult female population is employed in nonagricultural occupations, and approximately one-third of the nonagricultural labor force is comprised of women, although most are employed in the tertiary sector, primarily as servants. In the Muslim countries of the Middle East and North Africa, however, only about 5 percent of the adult women are employed in the nonagricultural sector, and barely one-tenth of the nonagricultural labor force is comprised of women (Youseff, 1972; 1976).

According to Youseff (1972), these variations in the utilization of women in the labor force can largely be attributed to differences in family and kinship organization between Middle Eastern and Latin American societies. Both are characterized by traditions of strong familism, patriarchialism and male supremacy, and by religions (Islam in the one case, Catholicism in the other) which reinforce the family and women's role within it. However, unique historical experiences have created vastly different situations with respect to the relative freedom of women in the society. In the Muslim Middle East, where traditional cultural patterns have been little altered by contact with Westerners—indeed, many of their customs have been strengthened in order to protect the societies from becoming Westernized or "Christianized"—the institutional structure depends entirely on the family and kinship as the basis of social organization. The structure of the larger family unit provides that there is always a male member (father, brother, cousin, or uncle) who is economically, legally, and morally responsible for all female members. Women are kept in seclusion, and tight control is maintained over their behavior in order to protect the honor of the family. This seclusion and control is maintained by explicit provisions that guarantee economic support for all female members at all times regardless of their marital status. This has the effect of preventing them from participating in any kind of public activity that involves contact with the opposite sex and leads to a situation in which female involvement in the labor force is extremely low.

In Latin America, on the other hand, Youseff (1972) identifies two distinctive historical experiences that have challenged the role of the kinship unit and the power of its control over women. The first is the nature of the Spanish conquest which was characterized by, among other things, widespread miscegenation among the Spanish conquerors and Indian women. Marriage was not part of the arrangement, however, and this interbreeding provided little or no support or protection for the Indian woman and her offspring. This led to a considerable amount of social displacement within the Indian family unit; specifically, the male elders who were the presupposed guardians of family honor lost their claim as protectors (often through enslavement), thus depriving the family unit of considerable authority and prestige. The lower classes in particular have been unable to outgrow the Spanish legacy of female concubinage, and the males have been unable to regain the power to exercise control over their womenfolk. The result has been widespread sexual freedom for women, marital instability, and high illegitimacy rates. Women are frequently in a position where they have only themselves to rely on for economic support.

The second experience can be found in the activities of the Catholic church. In an effort to form links with the society in order to propagate the faith, the church concentrated on women, particularly as mothers, as the agent for the transmission of religious doctrines. Women had to be prepared for this function, so the church provided schools and universities for their education and trained them to perform-nonfamilial functions such as religious instruction; it also provided them with opportunities to participate in various church-sponsored activities such as the distribution of charity. Although women's liberation was not the intended consequence of this strategy, it had the effect of providing women with nonfamilial alternatives and an identity outside of the family. In Latin America, then, in contrast to the Middle Eastern situation, both economic necessity and the existence of nonfamilial alternatives have resulted in a far greater participation of women in the labor force.

Deterioration of Women's Status To the fact that they are frequently underutilized as a source of potential labor can be added the claim that the process of development has itself had a negative impact on the status of women. In fact, it is very likely that the two are closely interrelated; development has contributed to a loss of status for women because it has taken away many of their traditional roles without replacing them with meaningful alternatives. Youseff (1976) has suggested that the lessening of economic independence for women as their traditional labor force roles are undercut by new methods and new technology leads to an increasing differentiation of sex roles that maximize the status of men at the expense of women. This is a question that requires further investigation. Unfortunately, most of the studies that have dealt with women in the less developed countries have focused almost exclusively on factors such as education and labor force participation in so far as they are related to fertility behavior, and on the relationship of fertility levels to economic development (e.g., Heer and Turner, 1965; Stycos and Weller, 1967; Weller, 1968). That is, they have focused largely on women in terms of their fertility and how it may effect development. The focus has been on "welfare" functions rather than on women as an important part of the developmental process (Zeidenstein, 1978). What has been neglected is the other side of the relationship, or the effect that development might have on women—particularly on how it might effect the role and status of women in society. This in part reflects the fact that those who have been involved in the study of development have been either Westerners, or Western trained, and they have carried the Western stereotypes of women as mother and homemaker over into their development studies and programs (Boserup, 1970; Burke, 1978; George, 1978; Tinker and Bramsen, 1976). One illustration of this is found in the sphere of agriculture. Traditionally, especially in Asia and Africa, women were responsible for the production and marketing of agricultural food crops (Zeidenstein, 1978). However, when the European colonialists arrived they were shocked by what appeared to them to be women doing the work that was supposed to be done by able-bodied men. Their efforts to remedy this situation, efforts that have continued to this day, seriously eroded the economic status and prestige of women. The Europeans changed the order of things by establishing a commercial agriculture for the production of export crops, and by bringing men into the agricultural labor force as wage earners. Women of course continued with some agricultural work, generally at a minimal subsistence level, but their status as major economic contributors to their families was lost. Men were educated while women were not, as women's place was believed to be in the home, and it was the men who were trained in the more efficient methods of modern agricultural technology. It was believed that women were not interested in that sort of thing; in addition to which they were thought not capable of utilizing the new technology, especially in regards to machinery (Boserup, 1970; Burke, 1978; Mead, 1976). The resulting loss of status for women also contributed to a great waste of potential labor and associated losses with respect to agricultural output (Zeidenstein, 1978).

Summary Enough has been said to warrant the conclusion that western influence and the beginnings of development have had a marked negative effect with respect to the role and status of women. As Tinker (1976a) has described the situation, development has had a negative effect for women in at least three ways: by omission, or failure to utilize women in their traditional productive roles; by reinforcement of values which relegate women to the home; and by addition, or by the imposition of various western values pertaining to what is and what is not appropriate women's work.

In view of the preceding it can be suggested that the overall development process will be enhanced to the extent that the role and status of women in the developing world is improved. Specifically, one recent study has identified *six myths* about women and development that need to be eradicated (Blumberg, 1976:12-19). These may be noted briefly as follows:

1. The notion that women are "parasites" on the nation's economy who have little to contribute in the way of productivity.

2. The belief that the process of development naturally and inevitably leads to an improvement in women's lives.
3. The lower class poor in urban areas are trapped in a life of poverty that reflects disorganized female-centered family patterns.
4. Women are basically baby machines whose primary function is to bear and care for children.
5. Fertility patterns are irrational and cannot be explained logically.
6. There is no relationship between the economic position of women, their status, and fertility rates.

For the most part these points are well taken, particularly numbers 1 and 2. In the first place, as we have noted, women do in fact, have much to contribute to the development process, if only development planners would recognize this and make an effort to include women in development plans and programs. Secondly, the evidence that is available does not reveal much improvement in the lives of women as development has gotten underway in the Third World. Rather, development generally has had a positive effect only on the lives of men; for women it has generally meant a loss of economic functions, an accompanying loss in status, and (for many) a deterioration in living levels. In India, for example, the situation of women has deteriorated so badly that it has led to an increase in the mortality of females relative to that of males (Zeidenstein, 1978). India is unfortunately not an isolated case. Throughout the Third World, development programs have omitted women as productive participants, and the consequences are disheartening, to say the least.

One of the more positive steps recently taken by the United States to promote development efforts is the "Percy Amendment" (Section 13 of the Foreign Assistance Act) which requires that bilateral development "give particular attention to those programs, projects, and activities which tend to integrate women into the national economies of foreign countries, thus improving their status and assisting the total development effort" (quoted in George, 1978:2). The Agency for International Development has set up an office to monitor such efforts, and there has been an increasing focus on women's economic roles, illiteracy programs, and especially the role women play in nutrition (George, 1978; Schick, 1978). Up to this point, however, the projects have been on a relatively small scale. Projects need to be initiated on a wider scale, for as Sullerot (1971:248) has pointed out, the participation of women is essential to the solution of all the great social and political problems confronting the less developed nations today: "Overpopulation, starvation, underdevelopment, illiteracy—all of these issues can only be solved with the assistance of women." It is obviously difficult to imagine population control programs succeeding without the cooperation of women, but it is equally as important to involve them in economic programs. It is not only the policies of governments in the low income countries that must change, but also the attitudes of outsiders who tend to be a major force behind research and development projects (Pala, 1977).

Along with increased education, an expansion of civil rights, and greater economic rights and opportunities, there needs to be greater participation of women in the political process. Although there have been several remarkable women in the developing world who have risen to positions as heads of state (most notably Indira Ghandi in India), they are the exceptions—as is also true in the more developed countries for that matter. The enhancement of the position of women in all areas of society will, we believe, contribute a great deal to the progress of economic development and demographic modernization.

Crime and Development

Another topic that has been seriously neglected in the study of developing areas is crime. This is somewhat surprising in view of the vast amount of literature devoted to this subject in the more advanced countries, particularly in the

United States, but there are many factors that may explain this relative lack of interest (Clinard and Abbott, 1973). On the one hand, criminologists in the developed countries may simply not be interested in Third World crime, or they may be operating under an ethnocentric assumption that the theories and models developed in the western nations are more or less generalizable to the non-Western world. On the other hand, problems in the developing countries themselves may inhibit the study of crime and criminal behavior. High rates of illiteracy, for example, may hamper the administration of questionnaires; various customs and taboos may prohibit the asking of relevant questions; many countries, for reasons of national pride, may not want to admit to having a crime problem; and still others may regard crime in the same light as the demographic problem—as something that will be reduced as a natural accompaniment of the overall development process. The latter is obviously not likely to be the case, as is attested to by the widespread prevalence of crime in some more highly developed societies. The facts of the matter are that crime has been increasing in the Third World, and that a good part of this increase is likely due to structural changes and dislocations brought about by the beginnings of urban-industrial development in these societies (Clinard and Abbott, 1973; Lopez-Rey, 1970; 1971; Potholm, 1969).

One of the most comprehensive cross-cultural studies of crime that has been undertaken indicates that some similarities do exist between the developed and developing countries with respect to crime (Clinard and Abbott, 1973). Based on research carried out in Uganda, these authors found that crime, as in the developed countries, is heavily concentrated among the younger segment of the population, and that much of it could be explained in terms of classical "differential association" theory. Young people migrating to the urban centers in search of economic opportunities often find themselves isolated from family and kinship ties, and they find support through banding together in gangs where they often learn criminal behavior as a means of livelihood.

The types of crimes engaged in within the developing countries also exhibit some similarities to the more advanced nations. Among men, the more common criminal activities involve theft, armed robbery, black marketeering, gambling, bootlegging, etc. Among women, crime most commonly manifests itself in the form of prostitution or theft by domestic servants (two "occupations" which are most readily open to women in developing countries). There is one aspect of crime, however, that is generally more prevalent in the Third World than in the industrialized nations, and that is political crime—most notably terrorism and political corruption. The former reflects the political instability that so often accompanies rapid social change, whereas the latter (discussed more fully in chapter 8) is often built into the traditional forms of doing business. Both kinds of activities can have serious detrimental effects on the overall process of economic development.

Part of the crime problem in the developing countries reflects inadequacies in the criminal justice system, particularly the police and the courts. On the one hand, as is also true in the more advanced countries, the police force is often understaffed, overworked, and underpaid. The ratio of police to population is 1 per 430 inhabitants in the United States as compared to 1 per 1,330 in Mali and 1 per 2,500 in Nigeria (Potholm, 1969:151). Further, the police in many developing areas, particularly in Africa, often have to perform tasks commonly undertaken by the military in other parts of the world. For example, in many countries the police force is larger than the military establishment (e.g., Ghana, Liberia, Niger, Upper Volta); and in addition to its law enforcement duties it is also often the mainstay of national defense and the force keeping a particular government in power. Finally, on the more positive side, it can be noted that, like the military, the police may function as a modernizing agent by being a source of political socialization, by contributing to national integration, and by serving as an avenue of upward social mobility (Potholm, 1969). The role of the military as a modernizing agent is discussed more fully in chapter 9.

The judiciary system is often based on previous colonial models and is often antiquated and ill-suited to the situation in the developing countries (Potholm, 1969; Lopez-Rey, 1971). There are often long delays in trials and marked inequities in sentencing. Part of this problem may be a reflection of the wide socioeconomic inequalities that exist in the developing countries where crime and criminal behavior is defined and justice dispensed by elite groups, thus leading to an uneven administration of justice under which the poor suffer most. Though, of course, the same is also true in more advanced societies where the probability that a given criminal act will lead to arrest, conviction and punishment increases as economic status decreases.

Although recent years have witnessed an increase in scholarly interest in the problems associated with crime and the criminal justice system in the Third World, this remains a relatively unexplored area in which a great deal more research is badly needed. Furthermore, this need can be expected to increase as the development process continues to produce major structural changes and dislocations within the developing societies.

The Stratification System

Every society has some system according to which its members are divided into social groups and ranked in some kind of hierarchial fashion. The criteria used as the basis for ranking people may vary—some societies rank people on the basis of achieved characteristics such as educational attainment or occupational skills, whereas others will base status rankings on such ascribed characteristics as ethnicity or family membership—and such systems will differ in the extent to which it is possible for a person to move from one status position to another. However, the fact of some form of status differentiation within societies is nearly universal, and the nature of the existing stratification system represents another important aspect of social structure that needs to be considered in relation to the overall topic of social change and development in the Third World.

Like all aspects of social structure, the influence of the stratification systems on national development will vary according to their particular forms and content. In general, however, it can be said that the more open and flexible the system of stratification—the more one's status is determined by one's own achievements, and the greater the opportunities for interclass mobility—the more likely it is to have a positive influence on development. Conversely, where the stratification system is relatively closed and rigid—where one's status is predetermined by some ascribed characteristic or where there is little opportunity for social mobility—it is more likely to exert an inhibiting effect on societal development. People will obviously be more likely to work harder if there is a realistic chance that the added effort may lead to an improvement in social status and/or levels of living; but where one's position in the class structure is relatively fixed and unchangeable it will tend to weaken initiative, discourage innovation, and reduce the incentive to work harder and save in an attempt to get ahead.

Still another inhibiting effect of a closed stratification system is that fact that the elites or privileged classes are likely to be more concerned with maintaining the status quo than with promoting national development. A good example of this in recent times is afforded by the ill-fated Allende regime in Chile. Although Allende's fall can partly be traced to outside interference in Chilean affairs (notably by the United States), it also reflects the fact that the commercial and business elites in that country represented a potent force against many of the changes Allende's Marxist government was trying to promote. Somewhat similar was the fate of the agrarian reform programs that the reformist government of Fernando Belaunde tried to implement in Peru during the late 1960s. In this case, part of the failure can be attributed to a reluctance to push hard for land expropriation and redistribution in order not to offend those political elites who were the landowners of the large coastal estates that accounted for a large share of Peruvian export revenues (Laidlaw, 1976:65-66).

One modification to the preceding generalization may be in order. If the stratification system remains too rigid, particularly as the modernization transition proceeds and expectations rise, it may become a cause for violent action. Persons who are on the outside or at the bottom of the system may come increasingly to resent the inferior status enforced on them by the society, and such persons will be more apt to be attracted to revolutionary movements that call for a radical restructuring of the economy and society. The communist revolutions in China and Cuba illustrate this point, as do some of the more recent independence movements in other Third World countries. With this exception, however, it is reasonable to conclude that the more rigid the stratification system in a society, the more likely it is to exert an inhibiting effect on national economic development. As one contemporary Indian scholar has aptly noted, any society that permits the stratification of its members on no more rational lines than on the basis of membership in some particular group sooner or later discovers that it has indulged in an expensive luxury (Chandrasekhar, 1965).

India, of course, is the example par excellence of a country where the presence of a rigid stratification system has acted as a serious impediment to economic development. The traditional caste system in India, which is reinforced by the land tenure patterns and inheritance laws under which land is largely owned and passed on within the high caste families, restricts mobility and inhibits the dissemination of new ideas (Shea, 1964). The masses of the people in India are locked into fixed status positions with very few avenues of escape, and this has a number of deleterious economic consequences. For one thing, it tends to enforce a division of labor based on caste membership rather than on aptitude or ability, thus preventing the most productive use of potential occupational skills (Chandrasekhar, 1965). This situation is further aggravated by the intense subdivision of the main castes and their proliferation into hundreds of subcastes, each of which is associated with a very specific and often minute occupational role such as street sweeping, whitewashing walls, cleaning drains, etc. Not only does caste membership limit occupational choice, it also largely determines where one is permitted to live. Thus, the Indian caste system restricts horizontal spatial mobility at the same time that it prevents vertical social mobility—both of which are generally seen as a necessary corollary to economic growth.

In the case of India, a particularly serious problem is represented by the casteless persons, or those who were formerly known as the "untouchables." These people, numbering over fifty million, are the real marginal people of the country. Despite laws to the contrary, untouchability is still a severe mark against a person, and custom continues to force millions of people to lead a degraded subhuman life, at the same time that it deprives the nation of the potential economic contribution of a large segment of its population. If Indian society is a closed one with respect to caste, it is virtually a frozen society as far as the casteless are concerned, and the discriminatory attitudes existing in India toward this group (as well as toward other lower castes) has represented a major obstacle to economic progress in that country.

India is of course not the only Third World country with a rigid system of stratification. Although they do not reach the extremes of the Indian caste structure, many of the countries in Latin America also have relatively rigid stratification systems. In the case of these latter countries, however, the class structure can perhaps be best understood in terms of its relations to the international stratification system; Latin American elites in particular tend to be more closely tied, economically and culturally, to the more highly developed countries than they are to their fellow countrymen. This situation can best be illustrated by reference to the international business community. Many of the major corporations in Latin America are foreign-owned multinational corporations. Although they employ many nationals of the particular countries in which they are located, these nationals tend to transfer their loyalties to the company, very often to the detriment of the nation. Such loyalty transfers likely reflect a desire to advance oneself economically, rather than a conscious rejection of their country, but the effect is still the same; they tend to act in the best interests of the employing company rather than in the interests of their country.

Other important elements of the stratification system in Latin America (which represent problems in other Third World areas as well) include a caste-like element that leads to a denigration of and discrimination against Indians and other dark skinned peoples, despite the commonly heard claim that racial division and discrimination do not exist in Latin America. It is possible for persons of Indian descent or "color" to move upwards in the social strata and to become "lighter" as they accumulate money; but it is a very difficult process. One illustration of this situation is provided by the national political systems, in which very few people with Indian features have risen to positions of prominence.

Somewhat similar to the situation in India, there is also a notion that certain people are better suited for particular types of work than others. While it is fairly common throughout the world to denigrate menial work, the situation is more acute in the developing countries, especially in Latin America; manual labor is for the lower classes, whereas white collar and professional occupations are the proper pursuits for the upper classes. Although agricultural and other technical specialists are badly needed throughout the Third World, relatively few people choose to follow these professions. Instead they enter law, architecture, or medicine. There are far too many lawyers in Latin America and far too few agronomists. A "gentleman" simply does not work with his hands, and this tends to inhibit development in many important sectors of the economy.

The importance of the stratification system and the role elites play in Latin America has recently been illustrated by Walton's (1977) study of elite groups in Colombia and Mexico. He found, briefly, that where the system was relatively open—where there was equalitarianism, local control over economic programs, and more opportunities for social mobility—economic development was enhanced. On the other hand, where the class structure was relatively closed and where dependence on the central government was high, elites tended to be uncooperative, capacity for decision making was low, and economic development was hindered. Walton's findings also lend some support to Frank's (1969) earlier noted historical dependency thesis. Those cities that historically had the closest ties with the colonial powers (i.e., the metropolis) tended to be characterized by the most closed stratification systems and by the least development. Conversely, those cities that were relatively isolated from the metropolis, and that had started to develop more recently, tended to have more open and fluid class systems, and were characterized by a greater degree of economic development.

In summary, then, the more open the stratification system, the more likely development is to occur. Although this is an easy generalization to make, it does not do much to tell us how to go about modifying the relatively closed systems that exist throughout much of the Third World. As the preceding discussion has shown, national stratification systems tend to be rooted firmly in the unique history of the particular regions, countries, and cities. They are not going to be changed overnight—witness the case of India where the detrimental influences of the caste system persist despite contrary legislation. Nevertheless, this is one area where change must occur if efforts to achieve economic development are to be successful. Furthermore, since fertility is generally much higher among the lower exploited classes, a loosening up of the stratification system will also facilitate the attainment of a modern demographic balance between low birth and death rates. The relationship between fertility and social structure will be discussed more fully in the following section.

Social Structure and Fertility

The best-known attempt to understand the relation between social structure and fertility is represented by the analytical framework for the comparative study of fertility proposed by Davis and Blake (1956). According to this framework, the social structure of a society influences levels of fertility in so far as it effects behavior relating to one or more of the three basic steps in human reproduction. These steps are sexual intercourse, conception, and gestation and birth. The social structure of any society will be related to fertility to the extent that it influences the frequency of intercourse, the use or nonuse of various methods of birth control, and the outcome of conception. The specific aspects of culture and social structure which effect fertility through their influence on these three steps are called the "intermediate variables," and they may be conveniently summarized as follows (Davis and Blake, 1956:212):

I. Factors Affecting Exposure to Sexual Intercourse (Intercourse Variables).
   A. Factors governing the formation and dissolution of marital (sexual) unions during the reproductive period.
      1. Age at marriage.
      2. Permanent celibacy (proportion of women never marrying).
      3. Amount of reproductive period spent after or between unions that are dissolved by death, divorce, separation, or desertion.
   B. Factors governing exposure to intercourse within unions.
      4. Voluntary abstinence.

5. Involuntary abstinence (due to impotence, ill health, or temporary separation of spouses).
6. Frequency of intercourse (excluding periods of abstinence).

II. Factors Affecting Exposure to Conception (Conception Variables).

7. Fecundity or infecundity, as affected by involuntary causes.
8. Use or nonuse of contraception.
9. Fecundity or infecundity, as affected by voluntary causes (e.g., sterilization).

III. Factors Affecting Gestation and Successful Live Birth (Gestation Variables).

10. Foetal mortality from involuntary causes (miscarriage).
11. Foetal mortality from voluntary causes (abortion).

Each of the eleven variables cited above may have either a positive or a negative effect on fertility. For example, all else being equal, a young age at marriage, by increasing the length of time a woman spends in a sexual union where she is exposed to the risk of becoming pregnant, will have a positive effect on fertility. Conversely, an older age at marriage will tend to exert a negative influence on fertility. The problem in the present context is that the traditional social structures characterizing developing societies tend, more often than not, to place a positive value on the various intermediate variables, thus encouraging a higher level of fertility. Resorting to oversimplification for the sake of illustration, the developing countries of the Third World may be contrasted with the more advanced industrialized nations with respect to these eleven variables as follows:

1. The average age at which a woman enters a sexual union tends to be much lower in the less developed societies (positive effect on fertility) than in the more advanced societies. As noted in chapter 4, the proportion of women marrying in the late 1960s before age twenty ranged from only 23 percent among the most advanced countries to approximately two thirds among the least developed countries.

2. Nonmarriage (permanent celibacy) is generally much more prevalent in the more industrialized societies than in the underdeveloped countries. To illustrate, data for 1970-71 reveal that the proportion of women in the age range twenty to forty-four years (the main childbearing ages) who are married lies between 85 and 90 percent in such developing countries as Liberia, Morocco, Pakistan and Turkey, and is as high as 95 percent in Nepal. By contrast, only about 70 percent of the "eligible" childbearing age women in Finland and Switzerland were married (United Nations, 1974: Table 26).

3. In general, the rate of marital dissolution through separation or divorce is higher in the more developed countries, but remarriage is also fairly common. In the less developed countries, on the other hand, the traditional social structure tends to promote greater stability of marriage, thus giving this variable a positive effect on fertility. At the same time, however, there is a considerable range of patterns with respect to remarriage when a union is dissolved through divorce or death of a husband. In some countries in Latin America, remarriage takes place fairly rapidly (positive effect), while in others (e.g., India) it may be actively discouraged (negative effect). Accordingly, depending upon the particular society, this variable may exert either a positive or negative influence on fertility.

4. Voluntary abstinence due to taboos on intercourse such as the fairly common practice of requiring that couples abstain from having intercourse for varying lengths of time after the birth of a child or during periods of particular religious significance is fairly common among many developing societies but relatively rare in the industrialized countries.

5. Involuntary abstinence due to factors such as poor health is likely more common in the less developed countries. On the other hand, involuntary abstinence due to mobility and separation of spouses probably occurs with greater frequency in the more highly developed industrialized countries. It is thus difficult to contrast the two broad groups of

countries in terms of which ranks higher (more positive) or lower than the other with respect to this variable.

6. Similarly, although it may be suggested that the frequency of intercourse may favor fertility more in the developing than in the developed nations, there is really no reliable evidence to show that the average frequency of intercourse among comparable age groups varies significantly from one society to another; hence this variable is also assigned an indeterminate value with respect to its influence on fertility in both types of societies.

7. Involuntary sterility appears to be most prevalent among the underdeveloped countries. Although Davis and Blake (1956:234) would assign an indeterminate value to this variable, more recent evidence indicating that fertility often increases as a consequence of improvements in nutrition and general health status as societies start to develop suggests that this variable can be assigned a negative value for the less developed countries and a positive value for the more highly developed countries.

8. There is ample evidence throughout the demographic literature to justify the generalization that the practice of birth control, particularly the use of the more effective modern methods for preventing conception, is much more pronounced among the industrialized countries than in the less developed societies.

9. Similarly, although it is on the increase in some developing societies, resorting to surgical sterilization as a means of putting an end to childbearing is still much more common in the industrialized countries.

10. Involuntary foetal mortality, again reflecting poorer nutrition and generally lower levels of heatlh, is more common among the less developed countries.

11. Voluntary foetal mortality, which may include infanticide as well as abortion, was historically a fairly common means of population control. Today, however, deliberate infanticide is rare, so that this variable largely refers to the use of abortion. A number of industrialized countries (nota-

bly Japan and a number of East European nations) have relied heavily on legalized abortion as a means of reducing fertility levels, and abortions can generally be obtained with relative ease in most other advanced nations today. Among the developing countries, however, the evidence is less conclusive. To illustrate, as of 1975 a number of countries (e.g., Argentina, Ecuador, El Salvador, Hong Kong, India, Zambia) provided relatively easy access to abortion, whereas others (e.g., Bolivia, Colombia, Indonesia, Liberia, Philippines, Zaire) had legislation banning abortions (Tietze and Murstein, 1975). Depending on the particular developing country, then, this variable could have either a positive or negative influence on fertility.

Figure 6.3 Positive and negative fertility values assigned to the "intermediate variables" in more developed and less developed societies.

Intermediate Variables	More developed societies	Less developed societies
Intercourse Variables		
1. Age at marriage	−	+
2. Permanent celibacy	−	+
3. Time spent outside unions	+/−	+/−
4. Voluntary abstinence	+	−
5. Involuntary abstinence	?	?
6. Frequency of intercourse	?	?
Conception Variables		
7. Involuntary sterility	+	−
8. Use/nonuse of contraception	−	+
9. Voluntary sterility	−	+
Gestation Variables		
10. Involuntary foetal mortality	+	−
11. Voluntary foetal mortality	−	+/−

Figure 6.3 presents an overall view of the positive/negative values assigned to the several intermediate variables in terms of their most likely general effect on fertility in the more developed and less developed countries. Clearly, the positive or high fertility values are more characteristic of the latter, particularly with regard to those variables relating to the early stages of the reproductive process (age at marriage and the proportion married), and to the use of modern

methods of birth control. It is also clear that the lower fertility levels characteristic of the more advanced countries have been achieved not by the attainment of low (negative) fertility values for all the intermediate variables, but only for a few crucial ones: age at marriage, extent of nonmarriage, and the use of modern methods of birth control. The major question now, of course, concerns what features of the social structure in traditional societies encourage high (positive) fertility values on these key variables, and how they came to be modified during the historical development experience of the industrialized nations of the Western world. This is a question that will have to be answered separately for each individual society; and the answer will entail an examination or consideration of such things as (1) exogenous environmental factors (nature of the resource base, climate and topography, size and age composition of the population, mobility and population distribution, levels of infant mortality, etc.); (2) the social and economic structure of the society (the religious belief system, role and status of women, the nature of the economy and the organization of economic activity, the structure and functions of the basic family unit, etc.); (3) prevailing norms pertaining to ideal family size; and (4) norms pertaining to the specific intermediate variables (the age at which women are expected to marry and begin childbearing, the extent to which marriage and childbearing is seen as the most desirable or proper "occupation" for women, whether or not the various birth control techniques are regarded as legitimate or acceptable means of preventing conception or childbirth, etc.) (Freedman, 1975). A recent useful suggestion for drawing these factors together in a more concrete form is represented by the societal model for understanding fertility behavior offered by Demerath (1976). This model is described more fully in chapter 8.

Although an adequate understanding of fertility behavior necessarily entails a consideration of all the factors cited above, it would be fairly safe to generalize and say that the major source of the different fertility values of industrialized and developing societies lies in the previously noted differences between them with respect to the structure and functions of the family. As was pointed out earlier in this chapter, the importance of the family as a social and economic institution is far greater in the developing countries than in the more advanced nations. Given this crucial dominating importance of the family, it naturally follows that the larger it is the better (Deyrup, 1962). Accordingly, as already discussed briefly in chapter 3, the organization of the family in the less developed countries tends to promote high fertility through such practices as the encouragement of early marriage, defining household activities as the only important and honorable field of activity for women, guaranteeing economic support for all members of the family, and allocating status and prestige to women on the basis of the number of children (especially sons) they bear. In such societies it is safe to say that for many women the best that life can offer is marriage to a prominent man and rearing a large number of healthy children to solidify her position in the family and in the society.

Since the traditional extended family puts such a heavy emphasis on early marriage and large numbers of children it is not surprising to find resistance to the use of modern methods of birth control. It would follow from this that the widespread acceptance of small family goals and the means to achieve small families (i.e., contraception) will be enhanced as the importance of the traditional family declines. This is not to say that the governments of the less developed countries have to launch an all-out attack on the structure of the family in order to reduce levels of fertility and slow down rates of population growth, although the experience of the People's Republic of China discussed in chapter 8 shows that such an attack would not be without precedent. However, it does mean that the success of fertility control programs will be facilitated to the extent that the influence of the traditional family can be lessened. For example, if job opportunities for men are expanded so that they will not be so closely dependent on family ties for support, if women are offered economic alternatives to marriage and motherhood, and if national systems for providing unemployment compensation as well as some kind of social security for support in one's old age are established—all could weaken the economic position of the family in society and thereby enhance the emergence of low fertility values. Essentially this is saying that as the process of economic development proceeds it will be accompanied by a decline in the social and economic importance of the traditional extended family, and that some of the byproducts of this will be the emergence of low fertility values, a decline in the birth rate, and a slowing down in the rate of population growth. In other words, demographic modernization is seen to be a byproduct of socioeconomic development. The point, however, is that the governments of the developing countries can take active steps to encourage those structural changes, particularly with respect to the family, that will facilitate demographic modernization. This topic will be discussed more fully in chapter 8.

Summary

This chapter has dealt with the basic question ''Are some forms of social structure likely to be more conducive or more harmful to economic development and demographic modernization than others?'' For the most part, this question can be answered affirmatively; but it is a qualified yes that does not provide us with many generalizations.

In coming to grips with this question we focused first on the broad structural characteristics that are commonly associated with countries at the high and low ends of the development continuum, and second on a few specific aspects of social structure (personality, family, status of women, and stratification). The aim of the discussion has not been to arrive at some definitive conclusion pertaining to the role of social structure in development; rather, the intent has been to illustrate a few ways in which various aspects of

social structure may influence either economic or demographic behavior in some societies. The general conclusion
to be drawn from the discussion is that while both economic
and demographic behavior are clearly influenced by social
structure, the relationship is not a fixed one. For example,
women in developing countries generally occupy a status
well below that of men; but the relationship of this inferior
status to economic behavior can vary from societies where
women are kept hidden away from the rest of the world to
societies where they are expected to participate actively in
the labor force and to make a major contribution to the
economic support of the family. Similarly, one can find
examples where the traditional extended family has been an
obstacle to social change, and other examples where it has
been a positive force for development. Also, although an
authoritarian personality type is more likely to resist change,
there are cases where such a personality configuration may
have facilitated economic development. In other words, the
relationship between social structure and development is
there, but one cannot make a single generalization that
would describe the nature of the relationship.

The classical diffusionist approach would regard changes
in social structure as part of the general preconditions for
national economic development. However, it should be
clear from the discussion in this chapter that there is no basis
for regarding such change as uniformly necessary. There
may indeed be many instances where a particular country
may want to adopt policies aimed at deliberately modifying
some aspect of its traditional social structure in order to
enhance development—for example, to expand educational
and employment opportunities for women in order to derive
greater benefit from their labor potential, as well as facilitate
a decline in fertility. In other cases, however, it may be
possible and even preferable to fit new forms of behavior into
the traditional structural context and let change in social
structure come about, if it occurs at all, as a gradual response
to overall economic development. Japan, for example, was

able to achieve a modern demographic balance through the heavy reliance on legalized abortion without altering the basic structure of the traditional Japanese family.

One other important point to come out of the discussion in this chapter is that the overall development process will not only be influenced by social structure but will also have a reciprocal influence on it—oftentimes an adverse influence. Specific cases in point here would be the frequent deterioration in the well-being of the female population as development gets underway, and the increase in crime that often occurs as family and kinship ties become looser. Thus, while it may be true that changes in some aspects of social structure may be desirable to enhance development efforts in many parts of the Third World, it must be kept in mind that such changes may have negative as well as positive consequences for the societies in which they occur.

In concluding this chapter the important point to emphasize is that the overall social structure of any developing country will often differ quite markedly from the ideal type model we generally associate with a developed country. Further, economic and demographic behavior patterns, as well as the nature of people's responses to various development programs, will be greatly influenced by social structure. As in the case of culture, then, a thorough knowledge of the prevailing social structure becomes a major requirement for anyone seeking to plan for or otherwise understand the process and problems of development in any specific country.

Education and the

Mass Media

7

Perhaps the most outstanding fact pertaining to the developing nations today is that they need to do so many things to achieve the sought-after transition to a modern state. They need to improve agricultural efficiency; they need to expand the industrial and manufacturing sector; they need to develop improved means of transportation and communication; they need to reduce rates of population growth; they need to invest in public health and sanitation services; and they need to provide the necessary facilities for raising the educational level of their people. There are often so many needs in competition for the scarce capital resources that they cannot all be met at once, and this raises a crucial question of priorities. Where should scarce resources be allocated in order to derive maximum benefit for the society as a whole? The specific answer to this question will of course vary from country to country and will depend upon the particular combination of circumstances outlining the special nature of the development problem in each. While noting this, however, it can also be asserted that education is one area to which most developing countries should (and do) give high priority.

If there is one article of faith that is almost universally shared in developing countries, it is that education must be expanded and must be expanded rapidly. Governments emphasize the need to eliminate illiteracy, to provide universal and free primary education, and to produce enough manpower with technical and academic skills to meet the requirements of development plans. Villagers simply have the conviction that, although they did not go to school themselves, their children are going to do so, and government has a duty to provide schools for them. (Jones, 1971:315)

The reasons behind the demand for more education are varied; people tend to regard education as a means to the attainment of a better life, whereas governments want it in order to respond positively to some of the demands of the people, and also because they see a more literate population as a source of national pride. Beyond this, however, they clearly see the need to create a literate and technically skilled population as one of the major prerequisites for national economic growth and development. With respect to the demographic dimension of the development problem, education will contribute to fertility reduction because it tends to raise the age at which people marry; educated women generally have smaller families than women with little or no education; the costs of education to parents lead to smaller desired family size; and the general social and economic development resulting from increased educational levels creates conditions favorable to a decline in fertility (National Academy of Sciences, 1971:53-54). This chapter will be concerned with the general topic of education in developing societies, with particular attention being focused on the role of education in development, some of the problems developing countries face with respect to the development of adequate educational facilities and services, and the special role of the mass media as an agent of education and development.

The Role of Education in Development

On its simplest level, education means literacy, and the importance of a certain threshold level of literacy for economic development has long been recognized. In one of the earlier studies of this topic (Golden, 1955) it was noted that literacy is not only a useful index of the level of modernization in a country, but is also a necessary precondition for socioeconomic development. There are so many complex tasks within an urban-industrial setting that require an ability to read and write for their adequate performance that it seems a truism to say that a literate labor force is indispensable for the transition from the state of underdevelopment to one of development. Moreover, there are some who would take this conclusion a step further by suggesting that literacy (generally defined in terms of some minimal ability to read and write) is far from sufficient, and that the most successful development programs will be those that invest in education beyond the primary level. David McClelland, for example, who has suggested that a high achievement orientation in a society is significantly related to economic growth (see chapter 5) has noted that this relationship becomes stronger as the overall level of education in a society increases:

> . . . high achievement motivation predicts economic growth; more knowledge (as represented by more education) predicts economic growth, but motivation plus knowledge predicts growth better than either motivation or knowledge alone. . . . All the achievement motivation in the world, without knowledge (as in some preliterate societies), should have little effect on economic growth, and vice versa: It should take more than a highly educated populace to produce rapid economic growth. (McClelland, 1966:268-69)

In assessing the educational status of a population at least two sets of measurements are needed—one pertaining to the present level of educational attainment, and the other pertaining to what progress is being made to raise the level of educational attainment (e.g., measures of school enrollment, amount of money being invested in education). Examination of the available data pertaining to these two kinds of measures clearly reveals the magnitude of the problem facing the developing countries with respect to education. On the one hand, the data presented in Table 7.1 for the 1970 period indicate that nearly half of the adult population in Asia is illiterate, whereas in Africa only about one adult in four can read and write. The problem is less acute in Latin America, but even in that region nearly one-fourth of the adults are illiterate. On the other hand, the dimensions of the problem are further illustrated by the fact that per capita expenditures on education are smaller in the developing than in the developed countries (Population Reference Bureau, 1976a:12), and also by the fact that a large proportion of the school age population throughout the developing world is not enrolled in school. According to one recent study, for example, only about half of the primary school age children in the less developed countries were actually enrolled in school, and at the secondary level only about one out of every five eligible children was in school (Stockwell, 1974).

Table 7.1 Estimates of adult illiteracy, by region: 1970.

Region	Percent illiterate
Developed Regions	
North America	1.5
Europe and USSR	3.6
Oceania	10.3
Underdeveloped Regions	
Latin America	23.6
Asia	46.8
Africa	73.7

Source: Population Reference Bureau, "Literacy and World Population," *Population Bulletin*, 30, No. 2 (1976).

The Functions of Education

In general, it may be said that education derives its importance in part from the enrichment it brings to the lives of the individuals exposed to it, and in part from their increased earning power associated with the acquisition of particular skills. This latter function is especially important for economic development, because it is one of the principle means of expanding the productivity of the economy. More specifically, it can be noted that the formal educational institutions in any society perform a wide variety of important functions. They perform a socialization function of passing on the culture and social roles of a society to its youth, so they will be able to behave appropriately and perform the roles expected of them; they perform the standard teaching function of transmitting the knowledge and skills required for specific occupations; they perform a cultural preservation function wherein children learn what the sacred beliefs, values and goals of the society are; they perform a political indoctrination function that strives to create a national identity and a sense of pride in being a member of a particular society; and in some countries they perform an important elite selection function through a gradual process of singling out, generally through a series of competitive examinations, those who will be further educated and trained eventually to assume leadership roles in the society.

Of these several functions, two are perhaps especially significant for economic development. The first is the teaching function. No nation has achieved economic development without also having a high percentage of the population that was literate. Hence, the primary function of the educational institutions of a society is to teach the basic skills of reading, writing, and arithmetic in order to raise the overall literacy status of the population. Beyond reducing illiteracy, the teaching function also entails transmitting particular skills, both intellectual (the ability to reason logically and to interpret cause and effect in a scientific manner) and technological (modern methods of agriculture, the use of machines) that will equip the educated adult to serve the society in a more economically productive manner.

The second major function of the educational system of a society is its socialization function. Schools do much more than turn out people possessing particular kinds of knowledge and skills. They also turn out people with particular attitudes and values, and in this way schools can be a major vehicle for breaking the "cake of custom" in traditional societies and instilling new attitudes, new expectations, new ways of behaving, etc. As one observer has noted:

General education in the elementary schools is perhaps the best way for breaking the fetters of the traditional way of thinking just as it is for teaching people to read, write, and count. . . . The elementary school is the place where one could succeed in destroying superstitions, where first of all one could stimulate ordered thinking and where one could impart knowledge of a new and better life. (Peaslee, 1969:299)

As education increases, the grip of custom and superstition is lessened, horizons are broadened, people's minds are opened to new ideas and they become more receptive to change. They become more empathetic, that is they develop a greater capacity to see themselves in another person's situation, and they thus become less rigid in their outlook; they become more innovative with respect to the adoption of new ideas and new ways of behaving. Education will bring greater confidence in one's own ability, and achievement motivation will be increased as people are taught to value recognition for their individual accomplishments. To the extent that successful modernization will depend at least in part on the emergence of such modern attitudes and values to displace more traditionalistic orientations, the educational institutions of a society are in a position to exert a very positive effect on the overall development process.

Education and Employment One other function of education in developing societies is what may be called the employment function (Harbison and Myers, 1964), by which is meant simply that education creates opportunities for employment; in societies where agricultural development is releasing a lot of workers from farm occupations and where there is widespread unemployment or underemployment, this can be an especially important function.

This employment function operates in two general ways. On the one hand, the educational sector is itself a source of employment. Compared to other industries, education is very labor intensive. It is one of the principal employing sectors in many developing countries, providing a variety of teaching and administrative jobs at all levels. Moreover, at least as far as teachers are concerned, the educational sector is one that becomes even more labor intensive as it develops. In contrast to both agriculture and manufacturing industries, which tend to become more capital intensive as they progress and as machines take over the work of men, student-teacher ratios generally become lower as one progresses to higher levels of education. First of all, then, educational institutions represent a major source for employment in many developing countries, and the growth and development of educational institutions will generally be accompanied by an expansion of associated employment opportunities.

On the other hand, the employment function of education is also seen in the multiplier effect it has in creating jobs in other sectors. As the educational level of a population rises, new tastes and interests will emerge, and there will be a growing demand for new goods and services. Educated people want more and better consumer goods; they want more sources of information (books, newspapers, radio); they want more medical and health services; they want more opportunities for entertainment and recreation; and they also want more and better educational opportunities for their children—all of which stimulate growth and enhance employment in these other sectors of the economy. In the second place, then, the expansion of education generally leads to the expansion of employment opportunities in a variety of related sectors as well as in the educational sector itself.

No one is naive enough to suggest that the solution to the problem of developing areas, particularly to the problems of unemployment-underemployment, lies solely in the growth and expansion of the educational sector. However, it is suggested that investment in and the development of the educational institutions of a society will have a positive effect on economic growth and modernization—not only by raising the educational attainment level of the population and turning out people with more modern skills, attitudes, and value orientations, but also by contributing to an increase in employment opportunities in a number of different sectors of the economy.

Education and Fertility

Two major points can be made with respect to the fertility correlates of education. First, there is an obvious and fairly strong inverse relationship between education (particularly the education of women) and levels of fertility. Societies in which a higher proportion of adult women are literate tend to have lower birth rates, and within any given society women with a higher level of educational attainment tend to have smaller families.

The second major point is that the countries that have attacked the illiteracy problem most vigorously and have invested most heavily in programs to raise the overall educational status of the population have experienced the most significant declines in fertility—particularly when the expansion of education facilities has been accompanied by a breakdown in traditional sex role structures and a corresponding increase in the social status of women. Cuba and the People's Republic of China are two cases in point. In the former case, although many anti-Castro, pro-Western critics may be reluctant to accept it, Cuba is today regarded by its Caribbean neighbors as a tropical success story in development. One important aspect of its success may be the heavy emphasis that the Castro government put on education. Government expenditures on education increased ten-fold from the end of the revolution to the mid-1970s, and education, once limited largely to the rich and privileged classes, is now free to all through the college level. An indication of the success of this revolution in education is seen in the fact that the illiteracy rate, which was approximately 25 percent in the 1950s, has reportedly been cut to about 4 percent today. Associated with this low rate of illiteracy is the fact that Cuba today has one of the lowest birth rates (21 per 1,000 in 1975-76), and one of the lowest rates of population growth (1.5 percent per year) of any country in Latin America (Population Reference Bureau, 1978a). In China, a similar vigorous campaign of socioeconomic development that included both improving the status of women and raising the educational level of all groups has been accompanied by some major fertility reductions (see chapter 8).

In general it can be said that the earlier discussed association between literacy and other facets of modernization— empathy (or the ability to see oneself in the role of others), a stronger achievement orientation, broader horizons and increased knowledge, a greater inclination toward innovativeness—are all very relevant for the attainment of a greater degree of control over levels of fertility and the rate of population growth. Thus, it can be concluded that investment in education may have a double payoff for many Third World countries; on the one hand it may act as a major stimulant to economic growth; on the other hand it may act as a major depressant on the rate of population growth. The potential positive effect of education on economic growth and the parallel negative effect on fertility and population growth combine to make education one of the most promising areas of investment in many developing nations.

Problems of Education in Developing Societies

There are many problems associated with the role of education in the developing countries, not the least of which is the sheer magnitude of the task. In many such countries there is a dearth of schools and other educational facilities; teachers are often poorly trained and in short supply; and many basic essentials such as desks, books, and laboratory equipment are lacking. Such shortages are compounded by the fact that the number of illiterates requiring basic education is already far greater than can be absorbed into existing facilities, and their number is growing rapidly. Moreover, even if it is assumed that the logistics of this situation can be worked out, there are still a number of other problems that relate to the role of education in development. One of the major ones concerns the type of educational system that emerges and the major functions it is seen as performing. Although the preceding section stressed the positive role that education can play in promoting economic development as well as a decline in fertility, this should not lead one to neglect the possibility that education may also have a negative impact on the modernization process. Writing in the *Comparative Education Review* several years ago, Curle (1964) suggested that the educational system of a particular country could be classified into one of three types depending on its major function:

> . . . *traditional,* which implies an emphasis on maintaining the traditional values of a static society; *economic,* which implies particular emphasis on technical education and various techniques of gearing the output of the educational system to the needs of the economy for skilled personnel; *political,* which implies the use of the school system to implant a political ideology in the young. (Curle, 1964:233)

All educational systems will of course focus on each of these functions to some degree, but the key issue concerns the amount of emphasis given to each. From the point of view of development it is the economic function that is most important, and to the extent that too much emphasis on either the political or the traditional function (particularly the latter) interfers with its economic function, then the educational system could represent an obstacle to modernization. Too much emphasis on the political function of ideological indoctrination, for example, could stifle the emergence of some of the characteristics of an educated person cited above as potentially beneficial for the modernization process. If the effort to implant a particular political ideology is so strong that it rules out consideration of any alternatives, it is likely to produce persons with narrower outlooks, less empathetic abilities, and less inclination to think in innovative ways. However, whether or not such political emphasis will be bad for economic growth and development is far from clear. Most underdeveloped countries that have emphasized the political function in their schools have also been very strongly oriented toward achieving national economic growth (e.g., the People's Republic of China), and the heavy reliance on schools to implant a political ideology has been accompanied by an equally heavy emphasis on the need to reduce illiteracy and create a more knowledgeable and more skilled population. Thus, while too much emphasis on the political function may have a stifling effect on the intellectual development of a people, it need not adversely affect the rate at which they acquire the particular knowledge and skills needed for development. In fact, it may well be that imparting basic economic skills within the context of national political indoctrination could actually facilitate the modernization process. Whether it does or not will likely depend on the amount of control the government exercises over the economy, and on the extent to which the government is actively motivated to achieve national economic growth (see chapter 8).

The situation will be different in a country that emphasizes the traditional function of education. If the educational system is geared toward the maintenance of the status quo, promoting traditional values and behavior, or preserving traditional class or caste barriers while serving the interests of a small group of governing elites, then it will tend to perpetuate the educational inequalities that presently exist rather than having the economically desirable effect of increasing the overall educational level of the masses of the people. Schools in which this function is stressed tend to place heavy emphasis on the kinds of traditionalistic attitudes and values that have been cited earlier as potential obstacles to modernization (see chapter 4) such as: the value of large families; the importance of filial piety or paying homage to one's ancestors; the racist ideology of South Africa and similar attitudes pertaining to the elite status of certain favored classes (as in many Latin American countries), or castes, as in India (the position of the Indian government with respect to caste today is an enlightened one, and the caste system is officially outlawed, yet the traditional caste barriers are still fairly rigid). The major problem associated with such educational systems, however, is that they do not provide any real educational opportunities to the bulk of the population. They are generally limited to a very small segment of the population—the children of the wealthy elite—while the masses are kept in ignorance and poverty. As one authority has noted:

> Those in the ruling group are not prepared to accord to those they rule full political rights or social opportunities for educational betterment. (Curle, 1964:239-40)

Considering the remaining economic function, if the educational system is most strongly oriented toward reducing the widespread illiteracy characterizing many countries in the Third World and imparting a variety of basic technical skills, then it will be most likely to have the positive impact on the modernization process described in the preceding section. Thus, it can be concluded that while the development of the educational institutions of a society do indeed have a strong potential for being a positive force in the modernization process, the relationship is not a necessary one. Rather, it will all depend on the extent to which the economic function is emphasized over, or at least closely integrated with, the political and traditional functions.

Education and Unemployment

In the preceding section some attention was given to the employment function of education, or to the fact that the development of the educational institutions in a society can have the positive effect of generating employment opportunities not only in the educational sector itself but also, through its multiplier effect, in a variety of other sectors such as consumer goods manufacturing, communications, and entertainment. It must be noted at this point, however, that education may have the opposite effect; by turning out too many educated adults too fast (faster than they can be absorbed into the economy), or by turning out people with the wrong kinds of skills (lawyers rather than engineers), education may actually contribute to higher levels of unemployment (Harbison and Myers, 1964). At the primary level, for example, people who acquire some ability to read and write will often not be content to follow their traditional occupations, especially if they are in agriculture. Such persons will tend to migrate to the already overcrowded urban areas in search of better economic opportunities, and this can lead to shortages in the rural farm labor force at the same time that it adds to the ranks of the urban unemployed.

At higher levels of education the problem could be even more serious. The jobs that are available for secondary school and university graduates are few in number in many of the less developed countries, and too rapid a development of the institutions of higher learning could lead to the creation of a large number of unemployed intellectuals. In many Third World countries, a secondary school diploma or a university degree are often regarded as a ticket out of the traditional life style and an entry permit into an elite class that is not supposed to engage in manual labor. Further, people in the developing societies who are trained in the arts, the law, and the humanities are educationally maladjusted in a society that needs agricultural scientists, engineers, doctors, and nurses. Often, the kind of work that may be available to them as primary and secondary school teachers is, because of low status and low pay, regarded as inferior and generally undesirable—particularly if, as is often the case, the jobs are located in the rural hinterland miles away from major urban centers. One response to this situation may be the emigration of large numbers of educated adults to other countries where there is a greater demand for their skills, thus contributing to what has become a serious "brain drain" problem for many of the poorer countries. On the other hand, an increase in the number of unemployed intellectuals may lead to an increase in social unrest; rising educational levels create rising expectations, and if expectations are not met rising education could lead to increased frustration and serve as a potent incentive for social revolution.

Related to this latter point is the fact that too rapid an expansion of education in a country can create a serious gap between the older, less educated generations and the rising generation of more highly educated persons. This widening gap can become a source of serious conflict and misunderstanding between the educated youth and their uneducated elders. Younger generations have always come into conflict with their elders, and if this conflict is exacerbated by widespread unemployment among the youthful educated classes it can contribute even more to a rupture in the stability of a society. Thus, although the development of national education systems may indeed have a positive influence on employment, it will do so only to the extent that educational expansion is carefully planned to produce the kinds of persons that are most needed to fit into a particular country's overall program for social and economic development. Countries where illiteracy rates are high need to give major emphasis to the development of their primary education system rather than to universities, whereas countries where literacy is on the rise are more likely to need to shift emphasis to the secondary or higher levels to sustain the drive toward maturity. Some students of this topic have gone so far as to suggest various formulas to determine such things as the level of primary school enrollment that should be attained before a productive expansion of secondary school facilities can take place (Peaslee, 1969); but the main point is that each country must achieve some kind of balance between the needs of its economy and the aims of its educational institutions. This will entail very careful planning on the part of the governments of the present developing societies. Otherwise education could have a negative rather than the positive effect on employment described in the preceding section. As Harbison and Myers noted several years ago:

A country which fails to achieve such a balance may produce the wrong kind of high-level manpower; it may invest in the wrong kind of education at various levels; it may allow the perpetuation of the wrong kind of incentives; and it may emphasize the wrong kind of training. The net result, undoubtedly, may thus be to aggravate rather than to alleviate unemployment. (1964:8)

Linguistic Diversity

It was noted in chapter 4 that most developing societies are characterized by a great deal of cultural heterogeneity. For example, they are often comprised of many different tribal, ethnic, or religious groups, and (of particular relevance to the present chapter) such countries frequently lack a common indigenous language but instead have several different languages or dialects that may be in competition with one another for official recognition as the national language of the country. The establishment of some sort of official national language is of course highly desirable in order to enhance the modernization process, not only because there has to be some common ground for communicating within a country to establish some degree of national identity, but also as a means of conducting day-to-day business activities within the world and national economic systems. Thus, the governments of many Third World countries are confronted with the dual task of establishing an educational system that will teach people to read and write a language that will be useful to them and at the same time preserving the integrity of its diverse ethnic and linguistic groups. As was noted in one recent survey of the world literacy problem:

> . . . a permanent dilemma confronts those responsible for literacy campaigns: to teach the minority group how to write their rich spoken language, respecting their logical patterns and their oral lexical patrimony, thereby giving them a written code that they will rarely be called upon to utilize—or to teach them a useful "lingua franca," which is not spoken by the group, and the teaching of which will create many technical and didactic complications. (Population Reference Bureau, 1976a:13-16)

What this often means, in effect, is that the people in many developing societies have to become bilingual—they grow up learning the indigenous language of their particular ethnic group and then have to learn to speak, read and write in an entirely new language when they go to school.

In no country, perhaps, is this problem of linguistic diversity more dramatically illustrated than in India. India not only has a variety of spoken languages, it also has a number of traditional scripts or written languages, and "each of these scripts, and the language and culture associated with it, is not unnaturally regarded as a priceless heritage and jealousy defended" (Goldthorpe, 1975:190). This represents one more problem that the Indian government has had to contend with in its modernization efforts. The situation is further complicated by the fact that under British colonial rule English was established as the official language, and it was the language that was adopted by the Indian upper classes. One effect of this was to create a wide communications gap between the English-speaking elite and the masses of the population. After independence the Indian government sought to close this gap and bring the government closer to the people by establishing Hindi and the Devanagri script as the official language and script of the country. However, this decision was objected to by many of the non-Hindi-speaking people of India who felt that they and their languages and cultures were being discriminated against; when the law making Hindi the official national language took effect in 1965 a number of riots broke out in various parts of the country. In response to this opposition the government re-treated to a concilliatory position that continued to recognize English as an alternative official language for the non-Hindi-speaking segments of the population. India is thus in the position of having two official languages over and above the several indigenous languages of the diverse cultural groups. In other words, although many countries have to deal with the problem of bilingual education, the educated people of India "have to be not bilingual but tri-lingual, and (to coin a term) they have to be tri-scriptal as well; for they have to learn first the language of the state, with its traditional script, then Hindi in Devanagri script, and then English in Roman script" (Goldthorpe, 1975:191). The need to spend time learning to read and write in more than one language obviously takes its toll in reducing the amount of time that can be devoted to other subjects such as mathematics, the sciences and history, and this in turn can have a deleterious effect on the overall quality of the education received.

While the problem in India may be more dramatic than in most countries it is far from being unique. The problem of linguistic diversity is least serious in Latin America where most countries share a common Spanish heritage, but in Africa and parts of Asia it is fairly widespread. In Sri Lanka, for example, there are three major languages with their own distinctive script; in Pakistan the largest spoken language group is Punjabi, the script of which is different from that used for the official language of Urdu; in many of the Islamic countries where English or French are major languages of communication, the Arabic language and script also constitute important means of communication and unity; and in sub-Saharan Africa only a small handful of the new states are based on a single language and culture. An extreme illustration of the latter is provided by Uganda where there are twenty five to thirty different cultural groups, each with its own distinctive language (Goldthorpe, 1975:188-191). The presence of such a variety of dialects and language groups in a single country must be taken into consideration as still another problem to aggravate the task of establishing a national education system and of reducing illiteracy.

Demographic Problems

At the beginning of this section it was noted that the sheer number of illiterates throughout the Third World represents one of the major dimensions of the education problem. Moreover, it is a dimension that is being made more serious by continued rapid population growth. A clear illustration of this is provided by the fact that although the developing countries have recently made impressive progress in reducing the proportion of the population that is illiterate, the absolute number of illiterates in the world has increased, and will likely continue to increase during the coming decade. One reason for this is that very large numbers of children drop out of school each year before they have sufficiently mastered basic reading and writing skills. The magnitude of this drop-out problem is difficult to measure, because it is an embarrassing situation that many countries may be reluctant to acknowledge; nevertheless, recent estimates prepared by the World Bank indicate that the majority of children between the ages of five and fourteen years in the developing countries are not enrolled in school, and that this situation is likely to persist well into the 1980s (Population Reference Bureau, 1976a). However, the major reason for the steady rise in the number of illiterates is to be found in the rapid increases that have taken place in the size of the child population. This problem is so serious in the developing countries it has been estimated that they will have to double the number of places available in primary schools every thirty years or so just to maintain the current level of school enrollment (Jones, 1971:317). This means doubling the number of classrooms, the number of desks and books, the number of teachers, etc.—all of which means a substantial increase in the amount of money countries need to invest in education simply to maintain the status quo.

The rapid and substantial increase in the school age segment of the population can of course be traced to the basic demographic situation characterizing most developing countries today (see chapter 3). Specifically, it lies in the persistence of traditional high levels of fertility in conjunction with fairly pronounced declines in mortality, especially in infant mortality. Accordingly, an increasing proportion of the babies that are born survive to put more and more pressure on the adequacy of existing educational facilities, and seriously threaten the quality of the education that is received.

Enhanced infant survival while birth rates have remained high has also significantly altered the overall age structure of the Third World population: as the number and proportion of youth has risen it has been accompanied by a corresponding decline in the proportion of the population that is in the adult working ages. That is, the group whose taxes must be used to finance education programs has grown progressively smaller in relation to the size of the dependent school age population it must support. In summary, then, it can be concluded that the current demographic trend of rapidly increasing numbers of young people represents a serious obstacle to the emergence of a literate, educated population in the developing countries in two basic ways: first by stretching out the time period during which educational targets can be reached, and second by increasing the costs of reaching particular targets. As was noted in chapter 3 above, rapid population growth frequently means that potential development capital has to be diverted to basic maintenance activities, and no where is this more apparent than in the educational sector.

The Role of the Mass Media in Development

A number of contemporary scholars regard the development of the mass media (newspapers, films, radio, and television) as a major factor that will facilitate social change and development in the poor countries of the Third World. As one authority has noted:

> When new roads, newspapers, radio, television, movies, or books come into a society, powerful effects can usually be observed over time. Changes follow in the way people think and in the things they value. . . . All over the world, it has been found that those individuals and villages that have access to the printed page or radio have more modern attitudes, are more progressive, and move into modern roles faster than those who do not. (de Sola Pool, 1966:98-99)

In other words, economic development has been enhanced by the development of mass means of communication. The data presented in Table 7.2, which depict a clear and very pronounced direct association between economic status and mass media development, dramatically illustrate the extent to which mass means of communications are lacking among the poor countries of the Third World. Closing this communications gap should have high priority in the national development plans of these countries.

The mass media are, in effect, a major adjunct of the general educational institutions of a society—a major means

Table 7.2 Indices of mass media development in rich and poor countries: circa 1970.*

Annual per capita income (U.S. dollars)	Newspaper circulation: copies per 1,000 inhabitants	Radios: number of receivers per 1,000 inhabitants
$1,500 or more	354 (15)	421 (15)
$500—$1,499	195 (21)	234 (22)
Under $500	*36 (75)*	*78 (94)*
$300-$499	95 (14)	156 (17)
$100-$299	34 (38)	91 (44)
Less than $100	5 (23)	22 (33)

*Indices are averages for the countries in each income group. Numbers in parentheses indicate the number of countries on which averages are based.

Source: E. G. Stockwell, ''The Dimensions of Development: An Empirical Analysis,'' *Population Review*, 18 (1974):35-51.

of imparting knowledge and information, and of influencing the development of particular attitudes and values. In general it can be said that the most effective medium of mass communication is likely to be radio (Goldthorpe, 1975:206-9). Newspapers, books and magazines are a major medium of communication in the more advanced countries, but their effectiveness in any society obviously depends on the level of literacy, and most of the developing countries are characterized by a relatively high level of illiteracy. Films and television may be useful for disseminating propoganda, but these are generally regarded as entertainment media rather than as teaching devices, and the production of films and television programs also requires the services of a large number of highly trained and skilled technicians, as well as some fairly extensive outlays of scarce capital. Radio, on the other hand, is particularly well suited to the communications needs of the developing societies—it is a much cheaper medium of communication than either films or television; the availability of battery-powered transistorized radio sets means that radios can be moved around fairly easily and are not dependent on the establishment of a network of electrical power; and radio breaks through the barrier of illiteracy more decisively than any other medium of communication. In addition, radio has the advantage of being able to reach a mass audience at a single moment in time, and it is able to transmit important news events within minutes of their occurrence.

The potential uses of radio (and of other media of mass communication where they are applicable) in promoting national development are many and varied (Schramm, 1964). Radio can be used to help develop a sense of national identity by teaching a people about its history and cultural heritage; it can be used to inform the populace of national development policies and goals; it can be used as a vehicle of general education to pass on information or to acquaint people with such things as new agricultural techniques and practices, new public health programs, the availability and location of various employment opportunities, etc. In the area of fertility and population growth it can be a very useful means of informing people about national family planning goals, promoting the desirability and advantages of smaller families, and publicizing the existence and nature of various family planning services and facilities. In this latter regard it has been noted that one of the important outcomes of the use of mass media in family planning campaigns is that, through repeated discussions of the subject, it has contributed to a weakening of some of the traditional taboos and embarrassment attached to sexual behavior (Population Reference Bureau, 1976a). In this way the mass media have contributed toward the emergence of an atmosphere within which such things as birth control knowledge, attitudes and practices can be more openly discussed, thus exerting a potentially positive influence on the success of national family planning programs.

Beyond these obvious uses of radio and other mass media as a means of imparting information or propaganda, the development of modern systems of communication has the more subtle effect of modifying the ways in which people think. In noting this, however, it must be stressed that the mass media will have relatively little influence in changing those traditional attitudes and values that are very strongly held (e.g., religious beliefs), especially if the traditional values are continually reinforced in day-to-day interactions with one's friends and relatives. Nevertheless, proper use of the mass media can effect less strongly held beliefs, can encourage the emergence of new norms of behavior, and can contribute to the development of new tastes and aspirations.

The significance of new aspirations for the development process can best be appreciated by reference to a simple formula devised by the philosopher William James:

$$\text{Satisfaction} = \frac{\textbf{Aspiration}}{\textbf{Achievement}}$$

This formula translates simply into the fact that people will be satisfied to the extent that their achievements live up to their aspirations, that is, to the extent that they get what they want (Lerner, 1963). When there is a serious imbalance in this "want:get ratio," when people aspire to much more than they have achieved, it will create frustrations and generate behavior aimed at restoring the balance. On the other hand, if people are satisfied and are getting most of what they want, they are less likely to be interested in trying to change the situation. Indeed they may actively resist change as representing a potential threat to the balance that has been established between their aspirations and achievements. In any event, with this model in mind it may be suggested that one of the development functions the mass media could perform would be to unbalance the want:get ratio by creating higher aspirations, thus encouraging people to work a little harder or plan a little more rationally in order to raise their level of achievement. That is, by exposing the people of the developing countries to the nature and magnitude of the vast economic differences that exist between the rich and the poor nations, and by playing up the possibility of closing this gap, the mass media can further the revolution of rising expectations taking place throughout the Third World and thereby (ideally) mobilize greater popular support for national development programs.

The preceding is certainly not meant to imply that simply

broadcasting a lot of propaganda to increase peoples aspirations is the answer to the development problem, particularly if the people's wants are increased at a faster rate than they can be met. In this case, in fact, the impact of the mass media on national development plans could be negative; aspirations that are encouraged but unmet will lead to increased frustration, could cause modernization efforts to flounder, and might even be an incentive for revolution. However, a well-balanced media campaign that identifies realistically attainable goals (such as the higher per capita family income that could come with smaller size families) has the potential of playing a positive role in the overall development process.

Not everyone, it must be noted, shares this favorable view of the mass media as a modernizing agent. In the more highly developed countries, for example, the intellectual community frequently criticizes the mass media "for trivializing, for inaccuracy, for lack of balance, and for irresponsibility both in the selection of the news, the manner in which they present it, and the intrusions which their agents (reporters, cameramen) make into private lives and public ceremonials" (Goldthorpe, 1975:213). The mass media are further accused of oversimplifying complex issues and problems, of manipulating public opinion to the advantage of the "power elite" who control them, and of catering to the lowest common denominator of public intelligence. In the less developed countries, on the other hand, where the government often maintains very strict control over its content, the mass media often function largely as sources of propaganda—playing up those aspects of the national situation that show the government in good light while ignoring other aspects (e.g., not reporting crop failures, underestimating the volume of unemployment, overstating the success of various development programs). For the most part, such criticisms are justified, but their validity does not detract from the fact that the mass media has the potential to be used in a definitely positive way to promote the overall process of modernization.

Summary

This chapter has focused on some of the effects that the expansion of educational institutions and mass media development can have in the Third World countries of Africa, Asia, and Latin America, not only by contributing to economic growth but also by encouraging the emergence of low fertility values and a corresponding decline in the birth rate. Although there are numerous problems and limitations associated with this aspect of a development problem, and although there are potentially negative effects that need to be considered, the overall conclusion is that an increase in educational levels will have a beneficial effect for the developing countries. It is clear that a strong potential for a positive influence is present. A key factor in determining whether or not this potential is realized is likely to be the policies and actions of the ruling authorities, and the amount and type of control the governments of the developing countries exercise over their educational institutions. In many respects, in fact, it can be concluded that one of the most important factors that will determine the success or failure of many Third World development programs is likely to be the role played by the central government. It is this all-important role that is the subject of the next chapter.

8

The Role of
the State

The formidable pressures and problems of modernization are such that most scholars clearly agree that the state or government will need to assume a much more direct role than in the past in the planning and implementation of development programs in all areas of society. Although it was once common for western scholars to equate centralization and economic planning with totalitarianism, socialism, and communism, and although our ideological commitment still encourages us to argue that participatory democracy is the most desirable form of government, the inhabitants of the Third World, as well as many professional students of social change, would today argue instead that democracy might be equated with anarchy and economic inefficiency. Ideological preferences aside, the fact of the matter is that many of the developing countries have rejected both the Western democratic/capitalist model and the authoritarian/socialist model of the eastern bloc nations. Rather, they have often adopted a compromise model that is felt to be better suited to their own particular situation. In Africa, for example, many of the governments that have emerged have followed a policy of "African socialism" (Goldthorpe, 1975:258-59) which rejects both capitalism and Soviet-style economic development with a centrally planned economy. A major aim of the new African states is the "Africanization" of their economies through increasing their control over foreign-run businesses. This African socialism has taken different forms—in Tanzania private businesses have been nationalized and socialist policies implemented within the framework of traditional kinship and community units; whereas in Kenya there has been little nationalization, and "Africanization" has been sought by encouraging foreign-run firms to hire and train Africans for managerial positions. The main point, however, lies in their rejection of both Western capitalism and Soviet communism, and in an attempt to disengage themselves from the rivalries and conflicts between the two. Rather than seeing the major split in the world to be between capitalism and communism, they see it as being between the rich industrialized nations and the poor countries of the Third World, and they have chosen to draw on elements of both capitalism and communism as they are relevant to their own unique situations.

A somewhat different model has emerged in some Latin American countries. This is the model of the corporate state which is regarded by Wiarda (1973) as unique to that region—he refers to it as the "Fourth World" to differentiate it from the less developed and slower developing African and Asian Third World countries. His basic contention is that many Latin American governments have been modeled on the Iberian (Spanish) tradition, a somewhat authoritarian tradition that bends to change gradually rather than seeking a radical transformation of society. The governments in Latin America have blended an authoritarian structure with a commitment to many basic democratic ideals; they have not been unyielding, though change has occurred sometimes, though not always, in response to violence. For the most part, reflecting the basic paternalistic structure of the society, changes have been imposed gradually from above, and there has been considerable progress in many Latin American countries as compared to the other less developed regions of the world. Part of the explanation for this is of course the fact that many of the African and Asian nations have not been independent as long as most Latin American countries. Wiarda points out that it is often difficult for North American social scientists to comprehend this type of change because it does not fit with our Protestant Ethic orientation with its emphasis on rationalism, secularism, and individual achievement; he asserts that we are unwilling or unable to understand and appreciate the kind of paternalistic approach characteristic of predominantly Spanish Catholic societies (Wiarda, 1973:210).

The basic point that needs to be emphasized is that there is a clear need to re-examine traditional concepts of the role of the state in economic development and to realize that different forms of government will continue to evolve in the developing nations of the Third World. The crucial question relates not so much to the particular form governments assume as it does to the role they take in their efforts to promote national development. The one thing that most people agree on today, however, is that the governments of the Third World nations will have to play a much more active role in planning their economies than was the case in the historical experience of the west. This point will be elaborated more fully in the following section.

The Need for Government Planning

There are a number of specific reasons that can be cited in support of the case for strong government leadership in virtually all areas of public life in the developing areas of the Third World. First, even in the western democracies that emphasize private enterprise and pay lip service to a laissez-faire role for the state in economic activities, some form of state planning has always been present; and today the importance of sound government planning is generally recognized and accepted. In the United States, for example, there are a number of major government regulatory agencies (e.g., Interstate Commerce Commission, Federal Communications Commission, Environmental Protection Agency) as well as a number of laws for the regulation of private industries and the protection of the consumer. That is, even though our ideological commitment is one that encompasses a laissez-faire role for the state, our society is one in which the national government continues to assume an increasing role in regulating private behavior.

Second, for most of the underdeveloped countries, a strong central government will be necessary ⹁ ⹁ provide some degree of stability to the society. In citing this reason it is important to stress that stability does not mean stagnation; we are not arguing in favor of a conservative or repressive state whose primary concern is the maintenance of the status quo and the suppression of civil and human rights. Rather, we are arguing that stability in the form of some measure of order in a society is generally accepted as a precondition for social and economic development. Where the internal economic situation is unstable, as when there is widespread banditry, runaway inflation, a fluctuating tax structure, or deepseated social unrest that could spark a revolution, it will have a depressing effect on the volume of capital investment. Where there is no order or direction in a society, where there is no basis for predicting with reasonable confidence what the outcome of a given act will be, there is less chance that capital will be committed. One of the major functions of the state, then, is to provide the order and direction necessary to maintain a level of societal stability that will, at the very least, not discourage investment in productive economic activities.

Third, the diversity and magnitude of the problems facing most developing nations is such that solutions are far beyond the reach of private enterprise. There needs to be some control over the use and exploitation of whatever natural resources exist in a country, for example, and in many cases this means that government must rigidly regulate the activities of private enterprise. In many cases this will entail such drastic measures as the nationalization, either complete or partial, of privately owned industries and particularly of the multinational corporations whose control lies outside of the developing countries. These countries need to develop manufacturing, to increase agricultural productivity, to build social and economic infrastructures such as roads and highways, power dams, communication facilities, and public utilities, and to provide a wide variety of social services, such as schools, water purification facilities, hospitals, and welfare programs for the aged and infirm. They also need to develop a greater sense of national identity and national unity, and all of these need to be provided while trying to overcome such formidable obstacles as the presence of competing interests groups reflecting such things as ethnic pluralism or great disparities with respect to the distribution of income and wealth; rapid population growth; high rates of illiteracy and the associated lack of technical and administrative personnel; traditionalistic attitudes and values that are opposed to change; and rapid rates of urbanization and associated high levels of unemployment. In addition to these there are a number of external factors such as trade arrangements with other countries, the existence of foreign controlled multinational corporations, and problems of defense and national security that need to be reckoned with. These are only a few examples of the many and diverse problems that face most developing countries today, and they should serve as a persuasive argument in support of the need for a strong government actively involved in planning and implementing national development programs. Furthermore, the kinds of problems identified cannot effectively be dealt with on a piecemeal basis, or by several sectors operating independently within the same system. The problem of population growth will not be solved by a few urban hospitals providing family planning facilities; needed land reform programs are not likely to be implemented by those who presently own the land; the manufacturing concern that builds a road to move its products from factory to market is not going to be concerned with the development of a national transportation network; and the industry that builds a hydroelectric dam to generate its own power is unlikely to be concerned with providing energy to the larger society. Indeed, many manufacturing and industrial establishments will be reluctant to set up business unless and until such services are provided. What is needed is some kind of centralized authority with the power to mobilize resources, to raise capital through taxation or through foreign loans, to establish priorities, and to direct the allocation of resources in accordance with the established priorities.

To cite still another problem, the large majority of underdeveloped countries in the world today are countries that at some time in their past experienced colonial rule. The economic development of European society during the past three hundred to four hundred years has been accompanied and facilitated by the physical spreading out of Europeans to settle, colonize, and otherwise dominate the native peoples of Asia, Africa, and Latin America. Thus, another argument in support of the need for a strong central government in the presently underdeveloped nations lies in the necessity to deal with both the historical and current vestiges of colonialism and neocolonialism. One of the biggest single resources that the former European powers left to those Third World nations that are successor states to one-time colonial regimes is a governmental structure—a legitimate organization for the exercise of authority and control over a specifically defined area, along with the associated bureaucratic apparatus for administration, law enforcement, taxation, and so forth (Goldthorpe, 1975:253-55). One of the problems with this legacy, however, is that while the administrative structure may be there, the personnel needed to staff it are often insufficient in number or inadequately trained. That is, the former colonial masters created a bureaucratic structure for governing, but they generally did not educate and train a sufficient number of the indigenous population to function as administrators, particularly top-level administrators. On the one hand, this may be explained as a deliberate policy based on the fear that an educated people would be more difficult to control. On the other hand, it may be the result of an ethnocentric attitude that the native population was basically inferior and uneducated in Western ways. In either case the result is a scarcity of educated personnel among the local populace.

A somewhat different problem exists with respect to the small minority that has been educated in the western tradition. One of the most salient features of a colonial society is that most, if not all, of the institutions of a modern society were first established and controlled by foreigners, particularly by Europeans (Goldthorpe, 1975:45). One consequence of this was that those members of the indigenous population who were given any training were trained in the European manner—frequently being sent back to the colonizing country to receive their education. Very often, in this case, their training and subsequent entry into the government bureaucracy has resulted in a more or less complete break with their native culture. That is, to become Westernized often meant that one had to reject one's own culture and identify with that of the particular colonial power, whether with the Dutch in Indonesia, the French in Indo-China, the Americans in the Philippines, or the British in Burma and India, etc. A particularly angry description of this process was expressed by Jean-Paul Sartre in his preface to Frantz Fanon's book, *The Wretched of the Earth* (1963:7):

> The European elite undertook to manufacture a native elite. They picked out promising adolescents; they branded them, as with a red-hot iron, with the principles of western culture; they stuffed their mouths full with high-sounding phrases, grand glutinous words that stuck to their teeth. After a short stay in the mother country they were sent home, whitewashed.

Reflecting this past experience, many of the newly independent nations have an administrative apparatus that is staffed by persons who think of themselves as independent of and superior to both their own native society and the popular political leaders that have emerged since independence. Sometimes this has led to migration of the educated elite to the country of the former colonial masters, but at other times it has resulted in jealousy and conflict between the rising political elite and the members of the established bureaucracy as to who has the authority to do what. On the one hand, such jealousy, suspicion and confusion often results in competing interest groups making different decisions and formulating conflicting policies (this conflict becomes especially apparent between civilian and military matters, and conflict between civilian and military leaders is a major source of political instability in many Third World countries today). On the other hand, where there is confusion over the lines of authority it may result in important decisions not being made, either because no one knows who is responsible for making particular decisions, or because the various competing groups are reluctant to commit themselves to a course of action that may turn out to be the wrong one.

This problem of factional rivalries is especially acute in many developing societies—especially in Africa with its multitude of diverse tribal and ethnic cultures—and such factionalism can be a major impediment to national development programs. They may be especially detrimental to fertility control programs which some factions may view as a genocidal attempt to reduce their influence by reducing their numbers. The Katanga separatist movement in the Congo; the internal strife that led to the division of Pakistan; the Nigerian civil war; the militant Hindu opposition to India's family planning program discussed in chapter 5; the more recent rebel movements in Angola, Ethiopia, and Zaire; and the guerilla opposition to the white-to-black power transfer in Rhodesia—all illustrate the problems that factionalism can create in the underdeveloped countries. Further, they represent one more argument in support of the need for a strong government in these countries—a government which can form, assume power, stay in control, and unite and lead a nation; in today's world this often implies a relatively small, even autocratic group to provide the needed strong leadership.

Still another problem is represented by the existence of

widespread corruption in many Third World countries
(Goldthorpe, 1975:265-66). Where government control is
weak or where authority is not exercised, lower level administrators have the opportunity to strike private bargains
with respect to the enforcement of particular laws and
policies. Often it is easier and more profitable for businesses,
especially the large multinational corporations, to bribe local
officials or inspectors to get preferential nonenforcement of
laws than it is to try and cope with formal requirements. At
the local level, the factionalism noted above contributes to
such corruption; the success of an out-group may depend
more on politics than on hard work and initiative, and
whether or not a person is permitted to stay in business may
depend on the payment of some kind of tribute. Such practices may benefit individual businessmen or corporations,
but they cannot be regarded as being in the best interests of
national development.

So far the discussion of the need for a strong national
government has focused on the internal problems that
emerging nations must deal with in order to raise their level
of economic development. Another aspect of the situation,
however, concerns the relations between the poor countries
and the rich countries, and the need for the former to assert and
maintain a degree of economic independence from the latter.
As was pointed out in the earlier discussion of dependency
theory, at least part of the cause of underdevelopment in the
Third World today can be traced to the causes of the development of the modern Western nations (Frank, 1969;
Wallerstein, 1974). According to this view the poor countries
of the world are economically underdeveloped today as a
direct result of the economic exploitation they have suffered
in the past and still suffer. Historically, when many of these
Third World countries were colonized by one or more of the
presently highly developed countries, the nature of the colonial relationship was largely one in which the satellite country provided industrial raw materials and other natural resources to the mother country. That is, many of today's

underdeveloped countries were encouraged to develop export economies that contributed to the industrial growth of the western nations while at the same time ensuring their own economic stagnation. In many of these same countries today the emphasis on the production of food and raw materials for export is one of the major factors underlying their present low economic status. One of the most glaring examples of this situation in recent years is provided by the famine conditions that existed in the Sahel countries of West Africa during the early 1970s. In part, the food shortages experienced in these countries can be traced to the fact that during the period in which they came under French domination they developed an agriculture based on the production of one or two specialized cash crops for export rather than a diversified agriculture for the production of food resources (Amin, 1971).

Reflecting the way in which their economies have been organized by past colonial masters, there is today throughout the underdeveloped world a paradoxical situation wherein many countries that are basically agrarian in structure are forced to import much of their food stuffs. Furthermore, and this is perhaps the most serious problem with respect to economic development, the cash income that the poor countries receive for their exports and the cash they have to pay out for their food imports is determined largely by prices that are set in a world market over which they have no control. Often this has meant paying out relatively more for food imports and receiving relatively less for raw material exports than would have been the case if they had more equitable access to world markets and greater control over the pricing structure. In other words, what were once more or less self-sufficient peasants have today become highly dependent on the landowners, the merchant class, or the government for the sources of their livelihood, and the quality of that livelihood in a particular developing nation is heavily determined by fluctuations in the international market prices of its major export crops.

One notable exception to the kind of situation just described that has developed in recent years is represented by the emergence of OPEC (Organization of Petroleum Exporting Countries) and the assumption of direct control over the world price of crude oil by the countries that produce and export it. Another, although so far less successful exception, is represented by Brazil's effort to raise the price of coffee. Such action obviously requires a strong central government, not only to assume control over the indigenous resource base but also to establish the international agreements with other nations that will be necessary to enhance their successful development—one of the reasons that Brazil's efforts met with only limited success was that not all the coffee exporting countries cooperated in the price-fixing venture.

In summary, then, the need for strong central governments in the poor countries today is supported both by the nature and magnitude of the internal development problems that they face, and by the nature of a world economic system in which the underdeveloped countries have historically been (and in many cases still are) the exploited suppliers of the resources and raw materials that have enabled the industrial growth of the more highly developed nations. It must be stressed, however, that while a strong government may be necessary to ensure long-run national economic growth, it will not be sufficient by itself to guarantee such growth. Uganda under Idi Amin clearly had a strong central government, but many of Amin's policies were clearly detrimental to the overall economic well-being of that country. His expulsion of the Asians, for example, had a seriously crippling effect on local commercial life, and the excesses of his regime resulted not only in a costly loss of human life but also caused a serious "brain drain" in which a large number of the more highly educated Ugandans fled their country (Kyemba, 1977). Any government that is interested primarily in its own self-aggrandizement, or that seeks to meet the immediate or short-run interests of a small group of economic and political elites, is likely to do more harm than good. What is needed, then, is not merely a strong government, but a properly motivated government—one that is concerned with the well-being of the people it represents and that has as its goal the long-run development of the nation it heads. The actual form that a government assumes will not be the important factor in determining the success of national development efforts. It can be democratic, socialistic, totalitarian, or some combination of these more traditional forms. The important factor in each developing country will be a government that is motivated to act in the best long-run interests of the nation and its people, that is above all dedicated to economic growth, and that is strong enough to assume a leadership role in unifying the nation and mobilizing the resources for the implementation of whatever programs are needed to confront and solve the particular combination of development problems that each country faces.

Participatory Democracy or Totalitarian Rule

The first aim of the Third World leaders who immediately succeeded colonial rule was to throw off the yoke of colonial oppression and establish a working system of self-government. This had to be done by first gaining control of the administrative apparatus of the state, and then by trying to develop a grass roots identification with and loyalty to the new nation—a process that is still going on in many countries. Once control of the state is established, the new leaders can proceed with their second major aim—that of promoting national economic growth and development. A key problem that had to be confronted in the initial establishment of self-government concerned the issue of participation, or the extent to which the various segments of the populace would be permitted to share in the decision making process. Here there is room for and has been a great deal of diversity. The basic question is one of how much control the central government will assume for itself, as opposed to how much autonomy it will allow at other levels of administration. On a very simple dichotomous level the question resolved itself into a basic choice between a totalitarian or a democratic form of government.

As indicated above, it is the position in this volume that it really doesn't matter what form the government of a particular country takes, as long as it sees its major role as furthering the well-being of the nation and its people, and performs its role accordingly. However, many students of development have different ideas on this subject. In particular, there are those who feel not only that a strong authoritarian government may be necessary to direct national development, but that such a government—an "iron government"—is in fact an inevitable requirement for the poorer countries in today's highly competitive world. Robert Heilbroner (1974), for example, asserts that an authoritarian (totalitarian) form of government may be the only possible alternative for a country that is seriously committed to the goal of national economic development, because it is the only type of government that will be able to force the kind of cooperative efforts that such development requires. Although many Third World governments have evolved out of what have been claimed to be national movements, the post colonial states have often proved to be weak, in part because of the existence of cultural diversity and factionalism and the need to try and satisfy so many different groups. Many of the governments resemble what the Swedish social scientist Gunnar Myrdal characterizes as the "soft state" (Goldthorpe, 1975:265). Soft governments tend to express two public views: they talk of the need for radical social change, and they talk of the need to preserve traditional cultures and maintain ethnic integrity. Often the two conflict, and while policies for radical change may be proposed, the government is reluctant to use its authority to enforce the necessary compliance; when they do institute radical institutional reforms such as land redistribution they often become watered down with numerous exceptions and loopholes that facilitate their acceptance by particular elite power groups but at the same time seriously negate their original intent.

Heilbroner's position is that such soft states will simply not be capable of exacting the kind of obedience needed to ensure participation in the various development programs designed to meet the many difficult challenges it faces. Many of the freedoms that people in countries such as the United States hold sacred and take more or less for granted— freedom of speech, of assembly, and of the press—may well have to be sacrificed for the sake of the common good if many development programs are to succeed. Although Heilbroner makes it quite clear that he does not favor the curtailment of such freedoms, he does see it as a probable precondition to development in many Third World countries. He feels that "we" (meaning the people in the highly developed countries, particularly in the United States) must understand this, and must recognize and accept the fact that the path to development for today's poor countries is going to be much different than it was for the industrialized nations of the Western world. Very likely, the governments of those less developed countries that do succeed in their goal of national development will have a strong military component and a strong socialist revolutionary orientation. At the same time, however, he does recognize the dangers that such totalitarian governments represent. To be effective and exert a positive influence on development they must want national development and must work actively to achieve it: A dictatorship that is interested in its own self-aggrandizement (e.g., the recently ousted Emperor Bokassa I of the Central African Republic or the government of Idi Amin in Uganda), or that looks after the interests of a small group of elites (as is the case with many of the military governments in Latin America) will not contribute much if anything to the development of the country as a whole.

Whatever form a government takes, the one thing that is certain is that if development is to succeed the state has to play a much more active role as an agent of development than it did in the history of the western democracies. Some of the specific functions that the state may perform in this role are discussed more fully in the following sections.

The State as an Agent of Social Change

It is generally agreed that as a very first step the state must provide the basic social and economic infrastructure that is necessary for modernization. In order for economic development to take place there must be efficient systems of transportation and communication; there must be schools and training programs to enhance the quality of the labor force; public utilities and public health facilities are needed to provide energy and basic medical services; and so forth. Education is of particular importance in the process of modernization (see chapter 7); literacy rates are both a measure of the level of development and an indicator of the skill qualifications of the labor force. Hence, where literacy levels are low, or where basic technical skills needed for the development of either agriculture or industry are lacking, investment in educational institutions should be an important component of a national development program.

Another problem facing many underdeveloped areas relates to housing. Many of these countries are presently experiencing a very rapid rate of migration from rural to urban areas. Most of this migration is unplanned and uncontrolled and has led to the haphazard growth and expansion of various types of slum and squatter communities that are full of overcrowded, dilapidated shanties, and that are lacking most if not all of the public services that are commonly associated with adequate housing—energy for heating and lighting,

Table: 8.1 Selected housing characteristics of developed and developing societies.

	Percent of dwelling units with 3 or more persons per room	Percent of urban dwelling units having no piped water
Developed countries	2	2
Developing countries	32	39

Source: E. G. Stockwell, "The Dimensions of Development: An Empirical Analysis," *Population Review*, 18 (1974):35-51.

running water, drainage and waste disposal systems, etc. An indication of the crowding and unsanitary conditions characterizing the housing situation in many underdeveloped countries is provided by the statistics in Table 8.1. Nearly one-third of the dwelling units in the underdeveloped areas can be described as overcrowded, and approximately two out of every five urban housing units lack such a basic service as running water.

The existence of such slum communities in and around the larger cities in many Third World countries points up the failure of local urban authorities to cope with city problems, and outlines still another area where some kind of government intervention and action may be necessary. The need for government programs with respect to housing is further emphasized by the fact that urban land is often scarce and very costly, and by the fact that private developers will be more interested in short-run profits to themselves rather than in meeting national housing needs.

A shortage of medical services and facilities is also a severe problem in most developing nations. The nature of this problem can be illustrated by a simple comparison; as compared to a physician/population ratio of 1 doctor for every 800 persons in the more highly developed countries, the underdeveloped countries have a ratio of 1 physician for every 16,000 people, and among the poorest of the poor countries there is only 1 physician for every 33,000 people (Stockwell, 1974:43). Since the availability of trained doctors is commonly regarded as a useful index of the level of living characterizing a given country, these comparative statistics clearly point to a serious deficiency among the poor countries. In fact, a case can be made that the situation is even worse than that revealed by the statistics. Part of the health service facility problem is created by the fact that many doctors from Third World countries prefer to settle and practice in the more developed countries, but part of it is also a reflection of the fact that those who do stay at home prefer to practice in the larger urban areas where modern hospital facilities are available, and where they can profit more personally by catering to the health care needs of the rich and middle classes. In other words, the situation in many developing countries is often one where the few physicians that are available are concentrated in the urban centers so that the masses of the rural poor have virtually no access to any modern medical facilities or services. Government efforts in this area could entail such things as providing incentives that would encourage service in rural areas or in poorer areas of the cities, or it could require all physicians to devote part of their time (say one day each week) to working in public health clinics. Whatever the efforts, it is clear that the provision of more and better health care to the indigenous population is another of the important tasks facing governments throughout the developing world.

A particularly important aspect of the public health problem in developing societies concerns the provision of family planning services and getting people to use them in order to facilitate the fertility transition that many see as a necessary part of the modernization process. Related to this is the need to provide certain other social services such as unemployment compensation programs and social security programs to provide support for the aged and other economically dependent persons. Such welfare programs are needed to provide the support normally given through the extended family in preindustrial societies. By taking over certain functions previously performed by the family, the government can have a positive effect on reducing the importance of having a large family to ensure one's economic survival. Thus, this is still another area where the state can play a positive role as an agent of social change.

It is a relatively simple task to do as we have just done and discuss several areas where there is a need for some sort of government intervention or control in meeting some of the needs of developing societies. Indeed, such societies have so many problems and needs that virtually every area of human life could be cited and discussed in terms of the potential role that government could exercise in trying to ameliorate the situation. This brings into focus still another dimension of the development problem; there are so many problems and so little money that each country is faced with the task of deciding where and how to allocate scarce capital resources. There is some question, for example, as to how much should be invested in infrastructure at any one time, and as to where such efforts should be concentrated. For example, should efforts be concentrated in and around an existing major city, or should the efforts be dispersed throughout a country? Should education take priority over transportation facilities? How much effort should be devoted to agricultural programs as opposed to manufacturing and industrial development? How much money should be put into housing? Hospitals? Family planning programs? Social welfare? These and other similar questions must be answered in the context of each country's unique resources and growth potential at a particular time. A country with a limited amount of capital, for example, would probably do better to concentrate its efforts in one major area, whereas one with a lot of surplus capital (as is the case with many of the oil-rich nations in the Middle East) can more readily afford to diversify its efforts. Similarly, countries where the surplus population problem is especially acute would do well to invest more heavily in family planning programs and to concentrate on the development of labor intensive as opposed to capital intensive industry. Countries where literacy rates are especially low might want to emphasize primary education; other countries might give higher priority to the expansion of secondary and higher education facilities.

In line with the basic two-dimensional development problem seen by the present approach (the economic and the demographic), and also to give some organization to this discussion of the role of the state as an agent of social change, the remainder of this section will focus on the role of the state with respect to economic development and population growth.

Economic Development

In talking about the role of the state in promoting economic development it is convenient to discuss its potential separately in relation to the two major sectors of the economy: the industrial sector and the agricultural sector. In many if not most underdeveloped countries today, major reforms are needed in both sectors, and the state is going to have to play a major role in implementing these reforms. In the remainder of this section we will discuss some of the problems of instituting reforms in these sectors and show what some countries have tried to do or are in the process of doing in an effort to overcome them.

Industrial Reform One of the problems of development in the Third World today lies in the fact that heavy industrialization, or capital intensive industrialization, is often equated with economic development, and many governments are often very eager to promote the growth of such heavy industry. However, this may not always be the best course for them to follow. Indeed, Heilbroner (1974) suggests that industrial growth may have to be curtailed in many of the newly developing nations because there are limits to the amount of industrialization the world as a whole can handle—not only economic limits but also, perhaps especially, environmental limits. This of course is a very difficult position to take, and one that can be accused of having a selfish ethnocentric bias; it also borders on the unrealistic. One cannot, for example, tell a developing country that it should not have an automobile industry because there are already enough automobile manufacturers in the world, or because there is a growing crisis with respect to the world's supply of petroleum. Not only would such a position be a very selfish one (a classic case of "do as I say, not as I do"); but it would also be difficult to defend in a world where economic development tends to be equated with industrialization. Nevertheless, the resources of the world are finite, and there is a serious need to embark on some kind of global planning program for regulating and conserving their use.

In any case, to the extent that a national government does seek to promote industrial development there are a number of things it can do to facilitate it and to make sure that their particular industrialization program contributes to overall national economic growth. For example, the state can establish a list of priorities with respect to what kinds of products are most essential to the nation. To be more specific, in some cases it may want to place restrictions on the manufacture of such luxury items as automobiles and emphasize the production of items of more immediate need, such as cement and mortar for building construction, or tractors and other farm machinery, that would otherwise have to be imported. Another important consideration in deciding what industry is to produce should be the international competitiveness of the product. In this case the government should try to coordinate its efforts as much as possible with other nations in the region so that countries within a particular trade area are not duplicating efforts. Still another question should be the employment potential of particular industries; in many countries the possibility of encouraging labor-intensive as opposed to capital intensive industry should be given serious consideration. The progress of the People's Republic of China during the past twenty or so years should be a good example of the positive effect that labor intensive programs can have for national economic growth.

As has been noted several times previously, many underdeveloped countries face the problem of having to deal with the effects of past colonial domination, and the fact that much of the potential investment capital that has been generated internally has left the country instead of being used to promote indigenous economic growth. In this respect, national businessmen need to be encouraged to invest in their own country—perhaps by means of tax incentives or some other positive government inducements. Related to this is the need to put more emphasis on the training of nationals, whether it be through the expansion of university facilities, the creation of specialized training institutions, or through the existing corporations. The latter is becoming a more common practice in many Third World countries, particularly within the large multinational corporations, because of growing governmental pressures for businesses and industries to be controlled by the host country, and because such control is virtually impossible when all the high ranking managerial positions are held by foreigners. Related to this trend has been the increasing tendency throughout the developing world to expropriate foreign holdings and to nationalize what the governments feel to be the key industries of the country.

While expropriating foreign owned industry is politically controversial, and may even be detrimental to a country's short-run progress by leading to a curtailment of foreign aid, in many cases it may be the only way to keep profits within the country and to promote economic growth in the long run. An alternative course of action that a government might take, short of complete nationalization, is to try and regulate the manner in which an industry may invest its profits. One recent illustration of this kind of approach is presented by the "Industrial Community" program inaugurated in Peru shortly after the military seized control of the government in 1968. This program has been described by Laidlaw, who notes that its basic objectives were

> . . . to increase worker participation in the directorship of the companies in which they are employed, and to foster the social, cultural, professional and technical development of the workers . . . The means by which the latter is to be achieved is by the distribution of dividends at the beginning of each year and through a system of profit sharing among workers. (1977:2)

The Industrial Community law applied to all industries having six or more workers or a gross annual income of one million *soles*. Any company that met these criteria was expected to form an "industrial community" comprised of all employees of the company, including management level employees. This community would then elect a board of

directors which would function to maintain financial rec-
ords, arrange meetings, and generally keep the workers informed of the state of the company. Under this program, 27
percent of each company's net profit was to be deducted at
the end of each fiscal year and set aside for distribution
within the industrial community: 10 percent for profit sharing, 2 percent for research and development, and 15 percent
for reinvestment to generate dividends. According to the
system of profit sharing, each worker, whether salaried or
hourly, was to receive a cash payment from the 10 percent
set aside for this purpose, with each worker's share being
determined by the number of workers in the industry and by
the number of years each has worked in the company. The 2
percent that was earmarked for research and development
had to be applied toward this purpose, and if a definite
research plan was not drawn up—or if it was judged to be
inadequate—these monies were to be remitted to the central
government for general national use. Finally, the remaining
15 percent was to go to the industrial community to be
reinvested in the company on behalf of the workers. This
latter practice was established as the method of equity accumulation by means of which the industrial community
eventually was to acquire ownership of 50 percent of the
company.

In short, the Industrial Community program in Peru was
one that sought to move gradually toward worker control of
the participating companies, to permit workers to share in
the profits, and to promote research and development. At
the present time, however, it is still too early to judge the
program as either a success or a failure. On the one hand,
there has been some resistance ever since its inception, not
only from management which tends to see it as unwarranted
government interference in private enterprise, but also from
union leaders and left-wing intellectuals who regard it as an
attempt by the government to co-opt the workers and divert
them from more radical activities. On the other hand, recent
(1976) government modifications in the law which have

exempted some industries from participating in the program have tended to create cynicism among the workers as to the strength of the government's commitment, and they have promoted the feeling among management that continued resistance on their part could lead to still further government concessions (as it in fact has). Nevertheless, regardless of whether this particular program succeeds or fails, the Peruvian experiment does have some important implications for Third World development. It illustrates one way in which a developing country can move to gain control of its industrial sector short of complete expropriation and nationalization, and it may provide an example for other countries where the assertion of national autonomy and control over indigenous resources is important for their future economic growth and development.

Agrarian Reform Related to what has often been an overemphasis on the development of industry and manufacturing has been a failure on the part of many governments to place sufficient emphasis on the development of the agricultural sector. Many Third World countries have export economies that are heavily dependent on the production of cash crops. While the capital derived from such export crops may in some cases be beneficial and even necessary to a country's economy, a major problem facing many underdeveloped areas today is a shortage of food for internal consumption. Often the income derived from export crops has to be used to pay for food imports rather than being invested in more productive enterprises. Thus, a major task facing many of the less developed countries today is one of increasing domestic food production—not only to feed their own rapidly growing populations, but also to create a surplus which they can then export as a means of acquiring development capital. In today's world the state is often the only institution with the necessary power and resources to promote actively the development of an independent and self-sufficient agriculture; in many underdeveloped countries the government has to take steps to change the existing system of agricultural production. In many countries this will involve two steps: land reform programs to bring about a more equitable and more economical distribution of agricultural land and modernizing the techniques of agricultural production to bring about an increase in output. The two should occur more or less simultaneously, although the first is in part a prerequisite to the second.

Land reform in many parts of the Third World is a problem of major proportions, and one for which there are no easy solutions. The two basic types of landholding systems which present the greatest obstacles are excessive fragmentation of holdings (most commonly found in Asia and Africa), and the existence of large estates, or *haciendas*, found predominantly in Latin America. Fragmentation is inefficient because it is not amenable to mechanization, and it tends to lead to a subsistence type of farming. Large estates, on the other hand, are often inefficient because they may be poorly managed by absentee landlords, or because they emphasize the production of cash crops for export. Solutions to both of these problems can take the form of government expropriation as a first step. In the case of fragmentation, consolidation would be the second step, whereas for the large estates it would be some form of land subdivision and redistribution. Both solutions present a number of major problems (resistance by present owners, how to compensate former owners for the loss of their land, means of redistributing expropriated land), yet they are problems with which some countries have managed to deal successfully.

An example of a country that has been relatively successful in dealing with the problems of fragmentation is the People's Republic of China. An excellent description of the process of collectivization in China has been given by de Castro (1967) who notes that certain agricultural priorities had been established by the present communist government before it came to power. The Chinese government was conscious of the fact that too much emphasis on industrialization could interfere with the creation of a firm agricultural base, and they took active steps to enhance agricultural production through such things as the consolidation of agricultural lands, the elimination of tenure, and the forcible stopping of rural-to-urban migration and the relocation of urban workers back to their old villages. A heavy reliance on labor intensive activities such as using manual labor to construct irrigation canals, which accomplished the dual purpose of utilizing available manpower at the same time that it increased the acreage available for agriculture, have played an important role in Chinese agricultural development. At least one scholar asserts that the rewards in terms of increased production and rising living standards have been at least as great as the costs in terms of the restrictions on individual freedom (Demerath, 1976:159-60). Other countries (e.g., India), where the government has taken a much less firm hand, have been far less successful in promoting their agricultural development policies and raising the level of living of their populations.

The problem with respect to the existence of large landholdings is particularly acute today in Latin America, and in that part of the world the implementation of land reform programs has proven to be especially difficult—often because there has been an overlap among the owners of the large estates and the members of the government. Some progress in breaking up and redistributing large holdings has been made in a few countries such as Cuba and Mexico, but inequities still exist, particularly in Mexico where again the government has taken a less than firm stand in the promotion of land reform.

Another country in Latin America that had a particularly bad land distribution situation, and that has made some measurable progress in this area, is Peru. The various governments of Peru since the end of World War I, and even more in the post-World War II period, have generally recognized the need for land reform, and most have included it as part of their overall development program. Such efforts, however, have consistently met with stiff opposition from the landowners, and it was not until the present decade that any real progress was made. The most recent agrarian reform program in Peru was initiated by the revolutionary military government of General Juan Velasco which came to power in 1968. According to a law passed in June 1969, there was to be both a breaking up and redistribution of the large estates and a consolidation of very small holdings into medium-sized properties that would be farmed directly by their owners (Laidlaw, 1976:95-98). The law also called for a planned program of government financing of agricultural development through the provision of technical assistance and the operation of agricultural training centers, the regulation of labor contracts in order to eliminate exploitation, and the establishment of an insurance program to protect farmers against drought, floods, frost, etc. However, the success of this program to date, like that of the Industrial Community program cited above, is difficult to evaluate. For one reason, although the majority of the large haciendas have been expropriated, the various sources differ extensively in their estimates of the amount of land that has actually been redistributed—estimates range from 2.5 million to 8 million acres. Nevertheless, it is clear that the Peruvian government has made a positive start on promoting substantial reforms in the agrarian sector. Although all reform programs have slowed down in Peru since 1975, when a more conservative military junta assumed control over the government, the programs that were initiated in the early 1970s will be very difficult to reverse. Thus, Peru is another example of how a government, acting from above, can induce agrarian reform. While it has not been as successful as China, it does serve to illustrate the kind of role that a strong central government can play in promoting economic development programs.

Population Growth

One of the most controversial topics in the Third World today relates to the problem of population growth, and this represents one area where the role of the government will be especially crucial. There are two key considerations concerning the role of government in this respect. The first relates to the extent to which the government of a particular country regards rapid population growth as a problem and as an impediment to its long-run development aspirations. Second, if the government does see population growth as a potential problem, the issue becomes one of how active a role it takes and the kind of program it tries to implement to try to bring about a reduction in fertility and a slowing down in the rate of population growth. These two considerations are discussed below under the headings of Government Policy and Government Activity.

Government Policy Writing in *The Public Interest* several years ago the well-known American demographer Donald Bogue (1967) expressed the view that the present world population crisis is a phenomenon of the twentieth century, and that it will be largely a matter of history by the time we reach the end of the century. One of the arguments he cited in support of this optimistic position was the "aroused political leadership" throughout the developing world. In this argument he suggested that in contrast to the years of fertility decline in the western nations, when birth control was officially regarded as immoral, subversive, and sinful, the situation in the developing countries today is one where the political leadership is both aware of the population problem and openly accepts family planning as a moral and rational solution. While it is true that the governments of many developing countries have adopted family planning programs and have created state agencies or departments to administer them, some of the events of more recent years suggest that there is a need to re-evaluate the strength of the political commitment to population control programs in many Third World countries.

There is a wide range of policies that a government may adopt in an effort to influence the population growth trends of a nation. At one extreme it may adopt an expansionist policy that seeks to promote growth by means of various fertility incentives (baby bonuses, tax allowances, laws against abortion and the manufacture and sale of contraceptive devices, etc.), or by encouraging immigration or outlawing emigration. At the other extreme it may adopt a restrictive policy that seeks to inhibit growth through such means as providing government subsidized family programs, restricting immigration or encouraging emigration, and adopting various kinds of fertility disincentives (withdrawing tax benefits for births that exceed a set number, imposing an excess head tax on excess births, compulsory sterilization of one or both parents when they have achieved a specified family size, etc.). It can adopt some mixture of these two extremes, for example, by providing and encouraging the use of free family planning services while stressing the right of each couple to decide for themselves how many children they will have; or it may take a hands-off attitude, adopting no official policy, and simply let nature take its course.

From the point of view of most western scholars, the logical policy for most of the developing countries would be a restrictive one. They believe the most rational position for the political leaders in such countries to take would be one that recognizes rapid population growth as a potentially serious obstacle to programs of national development and that regards the adoption of a fertility control policy as a major aspect of their overall development plan. However, there are a number of factors that would mitigate against taking such a position. One of these factors is the intense wave of nationalism that has accompanied the attainment of political independence among many Third World countries and the present struggle throughout the developing world to obtain a greater degree of economic independence from the more highly developed countries. One can identify several common ingredients of this new nationalism that represent potential obstacles to programs of fertility control (Stycos, 1963; 1971). First, there is a general "pride in numbers" often associated with independence; many newly arisen political leaders look upon a growing population as a good thing, not only as a precondition to increasing the potential strength of the nation, but also, for more sentimental reasons, as a source of pride in having more people like "us" in the world. In its most extreme form an increase in numbers may constitute a rationale for territorial expansion (as in the case of Germany and Japan prior to World War II), or as a strong argument to justify the need for such things as more foreign aid and greater access to world markets—both of which may be more appealing to Third World peoples than western imposed suggestions that they should have fewer babies.

Not infrequently this "pride in numbers" is related to the anticolonial attitudes that prevail in many countries. This latter attitude often translates itself into a belief that family planning programs are a subtle form of genocide, and that the former western rulers are using population scare tactics to inhibit the growth of the poor nations, thereby keeping them in a subordinate position. In this same vein, as Stycos has noted, the new political leaders may take the position that the lack of development in the past was due entirely to the economic exploitation of the former colonial masters and that now, having thrown off the repressive yoke of colonialism, the nation is prepared to embark on a new course leading to economic growth. To admit that population may be a problem would be like admitting that their past backwardness was not due solely to colonial oppression; it might even be regarded as a sign of a lack of faith in their own new economic policies.

The significance of these potential obstacles to fertility control programs in underdeveloped countries was brought out most clearly at the World Population Conference held in Bucharest during the summer of 1974 (Finkle and Crane, 1975). This conference, which marked the first time official government representatives from all countries got together to confront the question of the relationship between population growth and economic development, was initiated largely by the United States with the support of a small group of Western European and Asian nations that were actively concerned with world population growth and the problems associated with it. As a basis for discussion at the conference the United Nations Secretariat had drawn up a Draft World Population Plan of Action which represented a concerted attack on the problems of world population growth. However, the Draft Plan was never adopted. Instead, led by Algeria and Argentina, a group of Third World countries "attacked both the language and the basic premises of the Draft Plan and, in effect, insisted that it be rewritten to incorporate the principles of the New International Economic Order" (Finkle and Crane, 1975:101). The action of these countries served to change the focus of the conference, shifting it away from the question of population and development policies to the much more politically sensitive issue of restructuring the world economic situation. That is, instead of going along with the proposal to focus on population problems, this group of nations took the position that their underdeveloped status was due largely to their disadvantaged position in world trade and to the economic policies that the rich countries had adopted toward them. Accordingly, they called for a different plan of action that stressed such things as reducing trade barriers and obtaining other economic concessions from the industrialized countries in order to enhance the economic development of the Third World nations.

As a result of this opposition, the delegates at the conference became polarized into two camps: the incrementalist camp, represented by those Western nations that had initiated the conference as a step toward coming to grips with the problem of world population growth; and the redistribution camp, represented by those Third World nations that viewed population problems not as a cause but as a consequence of underdevelopment and that called for a radical restructuring of the international economic situation as the way to solve them. This position can best be summed up by a statement made by the head of the delegation from the

People's Republic of China:

> . . . the primary way of solving the population problem lies in combating the aggression and plunder of the imperialists, colonialists, and neo-colonialists, and particularly the superpowers, breaking down the unequal international economic relations, winning and safeguarding national independence, and developing the national economy and culture independently and self-reliantly in the light of each country's specific conditions and differing circumstances and raising the living standards of the people. (Finkle and Crane, 1975:106)

In an effort to find some area of agreement and prevent the Conference from being a total loss, these two opposing camps gradually merged into a conciliation position which accepted the fact that population growth may be a problem in many developing countries, but which saw the ultimate solution to such problems to be in social and economic transformation. The final plan to come out of the conference was one that stressed the need to accelerate the rate of socio-economic development and to bring about a new and more equitable economic order.

The significance of the 1974 World Population Conference at Bucharest is that it demonstrated quite forcefully to the industrialized western countries that their "rational" view of the relation between population growth and economic development is not shared by many of the Third World countries, and that these latter countries are not going to accept Western-imposed policies of population control as representing the solution to their present economic problems. Rather, the issue of population growth has today become highly politicized within the context of a struggle over the distribution of resources and power between the industrial nations of the West and the developing nations of Asia, Africa, and Latin America. At the same time, however, it is fairly safe to conclude that the poor countries are not going to neglect entirely their population problems just to spite the incrementalist position. To make a simple analogy, underdevelopment can be looked at as a disease for which a cure is being sought while rapid population growth can be looked at as a painful symptom of this disease; no rational argument can be offered for not trying to relieve the symptom while working on the ultimate cure of economic development. Population control policies have already been adopted in many developing countries, and they will likely be adopted in many others. The question now concerns the nature of the policy that is adopted and the means by which the governments of the Third World countries elect to implement them.

Government Activity There are three relevant questions that can be raised in this section: (1) What activities have governments promoted in an effort to influence population growth trends (specifically fertility trends)? (2) How successful have these activities been? (3) What kinds of activities will be necessary to achieve a reduction in fertility and an end to runaway population growth?

Considering the first question, the nature of government activity will obviously depend on its policy position with respect to the seriousness it attaches to its population growth situation and the role it sees population growth playing in relation to economic development. (A recent survey of national population policies and programs is found in *World Population Growth and Response, 1965-1975*, Population Reference Bureau, 1976b.) A government that regards population growth as beneficial for the overall well-being and development of the country will naturally not go to a lot of trouble to promote population control programs. On the contrary, they may act deliberately to frustrate individual efforts to control fertility, as in Saudi Arabia where the government prohibits the import and sale of contraceptives, or in Laos where the government has recently banned the use of all forms of birth control; or they may adopt programs to encourage fertility, as in Argentina which has adopted a wage policy of increasing subsidies and school allowances for each additional child. Such strong pronatalist activities are not widespread among the developing nations, however, and even those countries that play down the seriousness of the population problem give some attention to programs of fertility control. Algeria, for example, is a leading advocate of the position that high birth rates are the result of underdevelopment, not its cause, but has a program that encourages the wider spacing of births and makes contraceptives available to persons who want them.

Although pronatalist programs exist in some Third World countries, the governments in most of them are either neutral in this respect or have adopted some kind of population control policy. According to one recent survey (Nortman and Hofstatter, 1976), sixty-four out of seventy-nine developing countries surveyed (81 percent) either had adopted an official policy to reduce population growth (thirty-three countries) or were providing some level of support for programs aimed at a reduction of fertility (thirty-one countries). On the other hand, roughly one-fifth of the countries surveyed had no known policy with respect to population control. The primary attention in this section will be on those countries that do regard population growth as part of the development problem and that have adopted population control as one of their national goals.

What have these latter countries done in an effort to achieve this goal? Broadly speaking, there are a number of steps that a government can take to influence the level of fertility in the desired downward direction. For the most part these will involve policies aimed at changing individual attitudes regarding fertility and family size and changing those aspects of society that influence individual attitudes (Zeidenstein, 1977).

In the first instance the government could use the educational and mass media institutions of the society to impart new values concerning marriage patterns and sexual behavior outside of marriage, to raise aspirations concerning life styles and increase material expectations, and to exhort the social and economic advantage of smaller families. In the second instance a government could encourage the emergence of low fertility values through such things as manipulating the tax structure to favor smaller families; decrease the economic value of children by passing child labor laws or instituting compulsory education, as well as by increasing parental access to alternatives for old age security; increasing the availability of and access to family planning services and reducing or eliminating the costs of practicing birth control; and increasing employment opportunities for women. This list is certainly not exhaustive, but it does illustrate the kinds of policies that a government might adopt in an effort to reduce fertility and slow down the rate of population growth.

To date, the nature of the activities engaged in by most governments that have adopted population control as a national policy goal can be subsumed under what is referred to as the family planning approach. While the major goal of family planning is clearly one of reducing fertility, it is an entirely voluntary approach that emphasizes the rights of individual couples to decide for themselves how many children they want to have, whether or not they want to practice birth control, and what method to use (Demerath, 1976:18). Moreover, it is largely a public health approach that views family planning as only one component of larger programs for enhancing maternal and child health. As one spokesmen for this position has stated:

> By "family planning programs" we mean deliberate efforts, typically governmental in funding and administration, to provide birth control information and services on a voluntary basis to the target population; to the end of lowered fertility (among other objectives, e.g., maternal health, child health, reduced resort to nonmedically induced abortion). (Berelson, 1970:1)

The countries that have adopted this approach generally have programs that aim to encourage smaller families through education and provide the contraceptive means to achieve the small family goals, but that continue to place a high value on parenthood (albeit "responsible parenthood") and on the rights of every couple to be free to choose how many children they want to have. In Mexico, for example, which has one of the fastest growing populations in the world—in 1974-75 the crude birth rate of Mexico was 42 per

1,000 and the population was increasing at an annual rate of 3.8 percent—family planning has been an official policy for several years, but it is a policy that is based on the rights of each family to act as it chooses in the pursuit of "responsible parenthood":

> The role of the authorities lies in urging responsibility, informing, and facilitating access to medical and supporting services. (Population Reference Bureau, 1976b:148)

Similarly, in Colombia, which had a crude birth rate in 1974-75 of 33 per 1,000 and an annual population growth rate of 3.2 percent, the official government policy is one of extending

> . . . social and medical assistance to all classes of the country in order that *every family may have the liberty and responsibility to determine the number of its children*. (Population Reference Bureau 1976b:141. Italics added)

The program that has evolved in this country is one where independent groups operate within and through existing health agencies to provide family planning education and services, and the position of the government is that:

> It is indispensable to . . . make available objective and sufficient information on family and sex life so that couples make a free decision [and] make available the necessary medical services which will assure medical care and guarantee respect for conscience. (Population Reference Bureau, 1976b:139-40)

In Ghana the official program is one that

> . . . seeks to alter the traditional reproductive habits of Ghanaians by emphasizing the benefits of responsible parenthood and by providing contraceptives to enable couples to regulate the size of their families. (Population Reference Bureau, 1976b:34)

In Bangladesh:

> The 1973-78 campaign for achieving population growth control . . . aims at bringing information, education, and family planning services into every home. (Population Reference Bureau, 1976b:71)

And so forth. In other words, the family planning approach to population control that has been adopted by most developing countries is essentially a noncoercive, education-service approach that seeks to educate people to the social, economic, and health advantages of small families, and to provide contraceptive information and services to enable people to achieve their desired family size.

Turning to the second question—How successful have family planning programs been?—the answer is not encouraging. In fact, one authority has recently concluded that family planning programs in the developing countries have produced no significant decreases in fertility, nor are they likely to do so in the forseable future (Demerath, 1976:86). This conclusion may be a little harsh, as the data that are available clearly indicate that some fertility reduction has taken place in many countries that have fairly well established family planning programs (Tsui and Bogue, 1978). However, even this evidence suggests that the results of fertility control programs in the developing world have at best been mixed. Of the twenty-three countries that can be identified in the mid-1970s as having fairly well established family planning programs (Population Reference Bureau, 1976b) thirteen still had crude birth rates in excess of 35 per 1,000 and eight of these had birth rates of 40 per 1,000 or more (see Table 8.2). On the positive side, six countries had birth rates that have fallen below 30 per 1,000 and three of these were below 25 per 1,000. In many respects, however, the direct influence of the family planning programs on the lowered birth rates in these often cited "success" stories is open to some question. South Korea and Taiwan, for example, have much higher levels of literacy and industrial development than most developing countries, and these two countries have also been the recipients of an unusual large amount of United States foreign aid and technical assistance. In the case of Singapore, which had a 1974-75 crude birth rate of only 18 per 1,000, part of the "success" may be attributed to its relatively small and compact size, as well as to its level of urban-industrial development. Even more significant, however, is the fact that Singapore's program of fertility reduction can be described as having gone beyond family planning. In addition to a conventional family planning program that includes such things as a liberal abortion law, free sterilization, a variety of contraceptive devices available at low cost, and information and education programs in schools and places of work, the government of Singapore has adopted a number of fertility disincentive programs. That is, rather than offering incentives to encourage fewer children (e.g., India's policy of paying men for being sterilized, or the plan being considered by the government of Pakistan to pay bonuses to women who do not take a maternity leave for five years), the program in Singapore threatens to take away certain benefits if parents do not limit the number of their children. Specifically:

> In Singapore tax relief could once be claimed for up to five children. Tax relief can now be claimed only for up to three. Hospital fees for pregnant women are low for the first child but rise steadily for every subsequent pregnancy. Paid maternity leave used to be available up to the third or fourth confinement. It now stops after the second (Moraes, 1974:48).

Perhaps the most effective disincentive, however, is in housing. Being such a small country, Singapore has a serious

Table 8.2 Crude birth rates for countries with established family planning programs: 1974-75.

Country	Crude Birth Rates	Country	Crude Birth Rates
Egypt	36	Bangladesh	47
Ghana	47	China (People's	27
Kenya	49	Republic)	
Morocco	48	China (Taiwan)	23
Tunisia	34	India	34
		Indonesia	38
		Korea, South	24
Columbia	33	Malaysia	35
Costa Rica	29	Pakistan	44
Dominican Republic	46	Philippines	35
Jamaica	30	Singapore	18
Mexico	42	Sri Lanka	28
		Thailand	35
Iran	44		

Source: Population Reference Bureau, *1977 World Population Data Sheet*, Washington, D.C., 1977.

space problem and housing is at a premium. To meet the needs of the population the government is subsidizing housing, and up until 1970 highest priority was given to couples who had several children. But beginning in August 1973, this policy was reversed and highest priority is now given to couples with three children or less. Most recently the government has passed a law that requires foreign workers (both male and female) who wish to marry Singaporeans to agree to undergo sterilization upon the birth of their second child. Failure to comply would mean suspension of permission to work in the country as well as the loss of other privileges. These disincentives must be given a lot of credit for Singapore's present low birth rate.

In spite of the fact that there have been a few notable successes, the overall effect of the family planning approach to date has not been very encouraging. According to Demerath (1976:90-117), there are at least five characteristics of this approach that explain its relative lack of success so far and that also lead to a pessimistic view with respect to immediate future prospects. These are as follows:

1. Obsession with technique—or the naive belief that the solution to high fertility is to be found in the provision of medically tested, clinically approved, effective methods of contraception.

2. Oversimplification of motivation—or the assumption that anyone is capable of planning his life if he so desires, and that all it takes to get people to choose to have fewer children is to make them aware of the advantages to be derived from small families and to provide them with effective techniques for limiting family size.

3. Pseudorealism and societal naivete—or the tendency to overlook or play down the importance of traditional customs and social institutions such as the young age at marriage, especially for girls, the relatively high ideal family size norm found throughout the Third World, and the agrarian economic base that is conducive to large families.

4. Political impotence—or the fact that family planning

administrators are generally outside of the power structure and, with their emphasis on voluntarism, do not tend to view political power as a means to achieve their ends.

5. Weak management—which refers to such things as the inclusion of family planning in broader health programs, the proliferation of several agencies acting independently of one another, the domination of such programs by medical personnel who are more concerned with maternal and child health programs than with fewer births, inadequate funding, and inadequate staffing.

The net effect of the preceding, according to Demerath (1976:115) is that ''no matter how much it may contribute to the health and well-being of individuals and couples, family planning is a boondoggle so far as the growth of population is concerned.''

With the limited success of the traditional family planning approach as background, the key question now becomes ''What kinds of government activities will be necessary to achieve a reduction in fertility and an end to runaway population growth?'' Although many scholars have criticized the family planning approach for its emphasis on health, information, and contraception, few have offered any real alternatives. One recent exception, however, is Nicholas Demerath (1976) who endorses what he calls ''the societal approach to fertility control.'' This is an approach which looks at population control as only one facet of overall socioeconomic development and which essentially sees fertility declining in response to an increase in social and economic well-being. Quoting from William Rich (1973) Demerath notes that

> . . . in every nation where modern goods and services have been distributed to reach a large majority of the population, national birth rates have declined significantly; moreover, in most instances the decline started before the introduction of large-scale family planning programs, which then served to facilitate the continued decline in birth rates (Demerath, 1976:119).

By modern goods and services is meant such things as

education, health, employment, credit systems, and the more equitable distribution of income; the countries that have concentrated on the provision of these goods and services have been most successful in curbing population growth.

The societal approach to fertility control suggested by Demerath is derived from a theory of fertility behavior adapted in part from the "intermediate variable" scheme discussed in chapter 6 and is based on three propositions (Demerath, 1976:128-35):

1. Every human society is composed of four primary institutional sectors: environment, social structure, culture, and polity (ESCUP).
2. The reproductive practices (REPP) of any society gain their regularity and force from the primary institutions of ESCUP.
3. For any given population the fertility behavior (F) is the result of the primary ESCUP institutions operating through the reproductive practices (REPP) of the society.

In other words, Demerath offers a model of societal change in which changes in the primary institutions are seen as leading to changes in reproductive practices which will then be reflected in changes in fertility:

$$ESCUP \rightarrow REPP \rightarrow F$$

In applying the model the action moves from right to left. First, the fertility problem is defined—that is, data are compiled to measure the overall birth rate of the population and to identify major fertility differentials—especially to identify high fertility groups. Second, the reproductive practices are identified—marriage rates, age at marriage, patterns of child spacing, use or nonuse of contraception, frequency of involuntary miscarriage, and prevalence of abortion. Third, the institutional levers that influence the reproductive practices are located. These institutional levers include such things as the natural resource base and the urban-rural distribution of the population (environment); the economic base, distribution of income and wealth, work opportunities for women, opportunities for social mobility (social structure); the status of women in society, family size norms and preferences, religion and the moral order, laws and customs (culture); and the bureaucratic organization of the state, tax structure, and the nature of health, education and welfare services (polity). Finally, once these levers have been identified, it becomes the task of the government to formulate and implement programs of general socioeconomic development that will lead to a modernization of the relevant institution and will achieve, as a by-product, a change in reproductive practices that will be reflected in a lower level of fertility. That is, the task of government becomes one of working to raise the overall level of well-being of the population through modifying the traditional institutional structure; one concomitant of this improved level of well-being will be a reduction in fertility and a slowing down of the rate of population growth.

Models such as the preceding may be useful devices for helping us gain a better understanding of particular facets of human behavior (in this case fertility behavior) and for indicating the general processes through which a change in human behavior can be achieved. However, it is a long way from the model to the real world, and saying that the task of government is to change the institutional foundation of a society is a lot simpler than bringing about such changes. Essentially all this societal model really says is that fertility decline will be a response to socioeconomic development, and that governments who most vigorously pursue programs to even out inequalities in the society and provide a higher level of living to the greatest number of people will be more successful in achieving a reduction in fertility than governments that emphasize the family planning approach. Beyond this it merely identifies general areas (as in preceding chapters) where change may be desirable or even necessary to enhance both economic development and population control.

The ultimate value of any model lies in its applicability to actual situations. In the present case, Demerath finds support for this societal model in the experience of several countries whose progress in achieving a measure of population control is greater than the overall success of countries taking the traditional family planning approach. In Cuba, for example, which has one of the lowest population growth rates in Latin America, the official policies of Castro's revolutionary government have emphasized such things as giving the peasantry urban experiences and greater access to urban styles of consumption, while at the same time exposing city dwellers to rural life by requiring some participation in the agricultural work force (environment and social structure); creating new work opportunities for women (social structure); expanding educational opportunities and making public services, including contraceptive services, better and more readily available to the people (polity).

In Tunisia the government has raised the status of women by abolishing polygamy and taking the traditional Islamic right of divorce away from the husband and making it a matter for the courts (culture). Women have also been encouraged to go to school longer, to get into politics, and to enter the labor force (social structure); the legal age for marriage has been raised to seventeen for women and twenty for men (culture); the number of children for whom a family can get child support has been limited to four, and a comprehensive family planning program—which includes legalized abortion—has been established (polity).

And in "the remarkable case of China" (Demerath, 1976:157-90), the government has enhanced employment through the development of labor intensive activities and has brought about a redistribution of the population from urban to rural areas under a program of planned and enforced migration. It has collectivized agriculture and eliminated tenure as a first step in increasing food production; changed property rights to prevent the accumulation of wealth (an individual and his immediate family may be assigned the use of a house or a plot of land, but such property cannot be passed along to others); expanded employment opportunities for women; and provided educational facilities to raise the literacy level of the population. It has brought about some fundamental changes in the family and kinship structure through raising the status of women, establishing a minimum marriage age (eighteen for women, twenty for men), destroying the old economic base of the extended family, and emphasizing the value of children not as labor inputs for the family but as individuals whose talents are to be developed for the benefit of the larger society; and the state has taken over and utilized the performing arts as instruments of education, political indoctrination and propaganda. Finally, it has reorganized the administrative apparatus of the state, creating an extensive decentralization of decision-making power presided over by a tightly organized ruling cadre which maintains a high degree of control throughout all facets of Chinese life; it has established an educational system in which at least part of the emphasis is on encouraging late marriage and smaller families, and on the provision of adequate birth control knowledge; and it has substantially increased the availability of all types of health and welfare services — including contraceptive services.

As a result of these basic institutional changes the reproductive practices have been altered—age at marriage has risen well above the legal minimum, the use of contraception has become fairly widespread, and the length of time between marriage and the birth of children has increased; even more significantly, the Chinese birth rate has declined substantially from a preindustrial level of 40 or more per 1,000 at the start of the 1960s to a more modern level of 25 to 27 per 1,000 by the early 1970s; and the overall rate of population growth is a relatively slow 1.7 percent annually.

In each of the examples cited above, family planning services were made available, but the emphasis of the development programs was on raising the level of living of the society as a whole through social and economic reforms rather than on curbing population growth. More important, in all three cases the government was able to play an active role in forming and implementing programs designed specifically to modify the traditional institutional structure. It was able to play this active role because it was motivated in a national direction rather than being interested in its own self-aggrandizement or in the advancement of particular class interests, and because it was in a strong enough position to force through changes that would otherwise have come about only very slowly (if at all).

This is not the only conclusion to emerge from this discussion of government activity, however. In those countries that have achieved the most remarkable declines in fertility the efforts of the government with respect to population control have gone well beyond the information service programs characteristic of the traditional family planning approach—either through legislation pertaining to the family and marriage patterns (China), or through the adoption of specific disincentive policies to discourage large families (Singapore). This suggests that as with economic growth in general, population control will be enhanced to the extent that the government takes a more active role in pursuing policies that are more authoritarian than the voluntaristic family planning approach. The key question is how much more authoritarian such policies will be? India's recent experiment with compulsory sterilization legislation when family size reached a certain level, though it did not succeed, is one indication of the extremes to which some governments may decide to go in an attempt to slow down population growth. India's failure in this regard may be explained by the fact that it's democratic form of government was not able to generate the force necessary to implement such a program. This reinforces the position taken in this chapter that a "hard government" (along the lines of the "iron government" discussed by Heilbroner) will be most successful in achieving the interrelated goals of economic growth and population control. Some freedoms may be lost, but one must balance the temporary loss of more esthetic freedoms such as freedom to choose the number of children one wants to have against the more basic freedom from poverty and hunger. In many developing countries time is rapidly running out, and one must confront the question: How laudable is it to preserve freedom of the press and speech, and to encourage participatory democracy (which may in fact be illusory in countries where there is such a wide gulf between the masses and the governing elites) in the face of widespread poverty, illiteracy, hunger, and ill health. The freedoms that the western democracies espouse may in fact be more elitist in nature than were Indira Ghandi's policies before her defeat in 1977, and they may be more harmful in the long run to those developing countries that are today struggling to raise their levels of living. Human rights must be preserved, but we must be careful in defining exactly what human rights are and in dictating our values to others. In the long run, success in achieving a better life for the largest number of people may well depend on the strength of the centralized authority and on its willingness to make the hard decision—to set goals, assign obligation for meeting goals, and resort to the authority of law to bring about the desired changes in human behavior.

Summary

The most important conclusion to be drawn from this chapter is that decisive state intervention will be required to initiate and sustain the development process throughout the Third World today. The problems characterizing so many of the presently developing countries (e.g., factionalism, corruption, maldistribution of incomes, widespread illiteracy, rapid rates of population growth and urbanization, numerous traditionalistic elements in the socio-cultural system, and the dependency legacy of colonialism and the growth of European capitalism) are so formidable that it is difficult to conceive of a way they can begin to be solved without the active participation of the state. This does not necessarily mean that the developing countries need to adopt the rigid state controls characteristic of Soviet or Chinese communism. But, it does mean that the government will have to assume a much more direct and active leadership role than it did during the historical development of the western world. The particular forms of governments can be expected to vary considerably among the Third World nations, but in all of them success in their development efforts will depend in large measure on having a government that is firmly in control of the state, that has national economic development as its major goal, and that takes an active role in formulating and implementing national development policies. Given this situation, it is not surprising to find that many presently developing countries are characterized by governments that are either run by or are highly dependent upon the support of their military establishments. Accordingly, the following chapter will examine more closely the potential role of the military as an agent of development in the Third World today.

9

The Military and Development

In his well-known study of the military in Latin America, Johnson (1964) quoted an old Latin American statement that "Liberty, equality and fraternity gave way to infantry, cavalry and artillery." While the term cavalry may not be exactly appropriate today, the statement reflects not only the essence of Latin American political life since independence in the 1820s but political life in many of the newly independent countries in the rest of the world today. Although the various national independence movements had different structural origins, and although each country and region is unique, it is nevertheless the case that a preponderance of military governments is a fact of life in the Third World today. To illustrate this situation, data contained in the 1976 edition of the CBS News Almanac indicates that at least thirty-six of the developing nations in Asia, Africa, and Latin America were ruled by military governments in 1975 (see Figure 9.1). Even in those underdeveloped countries where military men are not in direct control, the military establishment is often powerful and generally exerts a great deal of influence on national policies. Accordingly, it is desirable to consider more fully the potential influence that the military can exert with respect either to promoting or retarding social change and development.

The emergence of military governments in the modern world is generally associated with Latin America. In this region the historical independence movements were primarily guided by an elite who were not so much interested in full independence for their countries as they were in gaining freedom from Spanish control (Laidlaw, 1979). Thus, the results of the continent's revolution can be viewed in one sense as simply the transfer of rule from one elite (Spain and its rulers) to another (the resident elites of the Latin American countries) and then to the military. After independence had been achieved, there was a pronounced lack of interest among the majority of civilians to participate in politics and, almost by default, military men became the rulers. While it could be argued that much the same thing has occurred in the post-World War II era, the guiding themes in the independence movements in Africa and Asia seem quite different from those of Latin America. Perhaps it has been simply a case of increased sophistication, substitution of political philosophies, and the influence of different types of revolutions—the Latin Americans took as models the American and French revolutions whereas the Russian, Chinese, and most recently Cuban revolutions have had a more profound influence on other Third World nations.

Despite different historical antecedents, there are many striking similarities among military governments in the developing countries today, particularly in terms of rationalizations used for intervention, the aims and goals of such governments especially in regard to economic development, and the types of military leaders that have emerged. One interesting development has been the emergence of strong-arm rulers in Africa, who in some ways seem to resemble the nineteenth century Latin American *caudillos* —for example, Amin in Uganda and Bokassa in the Central African Republic. Other points of similarity are that military rulers seek power to fill what they often perceive to be a failure in civilian institutions, and coups are a common means of acquiring control over the apparatus of government. To illustrate, from 1945 to 1964, twenty out of forty-five African and Asian nations experienced military coups; during the years 1950-1965, there were forty-three changes of governments leading to military control in twenty Latin American countries, and there have been several since then—Argentina, Chile, Ecuador, and two in Peru, to list only a few. From 1962 to 1973 on a worldwide basis there were ninety-one coups which involved thirty-one states (Laidlaw, 1977b).

The reasons for which young men enter military institutions also appear to be uniform throughout the Third World—that is, it is often viewed as an avenue of social mobility in most of the developing nations. Traditionally in many countries, the upper classes have disdained military service, thus leaving it open to the lower-middle classes, who were often blocked from other professional careers as a result of being denied entrance to the more elite secondary schools and universities. The military offers training programs of all kinds, which can lead to implementation of civic action programs within the country and also provide the nations with additional trained manpower in the business and administrative sectors after retirement. This has often led to the argument that the military is the strongest, best organized and most capable force in the country, in terms of governmental and administrative ability. Further, because they have often received some kind of technological training (frequently in overseas developed countries), because military men are regarded as possessing a pragmatic, realistic philosophy of the world, and because they are, therefore, more apt to be oriented toward a rationalistic program of economic development, they and others often view themselves as the best possible group to govern a country.

Although the above may be true, it can also be argued that many civilians possess these same characteristics and should be considered superior because they are not hampered by what is often a rigid militaristic approach to problems. However, while civilians may possess many of the qualifications for governing they often lack the organizational ability and power, as well as the mass support necessary for carrying out development programs. To this must also be added the fact that many potentially influential civilians do not seem to be genuinely interested in national development, at least to the extent that military governments are. Frank (1969) has pointed out, for example, that there are two basic enemies to autonomous economic development in Latin America and the rest of the developing world. One is the external enemy—the neocolonialist or imperialist powers which have been and are guilty of exploiting the less developed countries. The other enemy is the immediate enemy—the nationals or civilian businessmen who are in league with the multinationals and who seek to enrich themselves at the expense of their own countrymen.

One valuable function that the military seems to be performing in all regions of the world is that of socialization and nationalization. Many of the developing nations are sharply divided by regions, by ethnicity, by language, or by tribal affiliations, in short, divisions which inhibit the development of feelings of nationhood. In rural areas loyalty may be defined in terms of family and village, and awareness of the outside world may be limited to those who have sought work elsewhere and have either returned to their origins or have communicated with family and friends. But such outside employment may be limited both in terms of time and socialization. Outside employment may be viewed as a temporary measure, as an opportunity to earn money which can later be used to buy land or to support one's family. There may still exist relatively little awareness of a national government. In order to develop politically, all citizens must feel that they are an integral part of the nation; a first step in this direction is to create awareness of the state, and the military may be one route to accomplishing this task. By moving the recruits who come from a lower class agrarian background into an urban environment, exposure is given to another part of the nation and another way of life. Recruits may receive training both in basic technical skills and in citizenship to enhance feelings of national identity (Laidlaw, 1979).

One of the professed aims and goals of many military governments is economic development (most often in the realm of industrialization). Military governments have a tendency to effect this kind of social change from above; their edicts control the economy and there has been a considerable increase in state planning under military governments. There is reason to argue (see chapter 8) that a certain amount of state planning by a strong centralized government is necessary for today's developing countries (i.e., there is too much to do in too short a time to allow for a laissez-faire type of government, and even the developed western nations have incorporated more state planning and controls than would have been thought possible a century ago), planning and control from above can produce other problems. Many social scientists, particularly political scientists, have stressed the need for growth of political participation and argue that extremely centralized governments, and more specifically military governments, prevent the growth of such participation. Pitt (1976) has argued that change from below is more effective than change from above, implying that a highly centralized government, such as a military one, cannot command true loyalty and participation and thus that changes are liable to be uneven. Instead, change should be initiated at the bottom with some governmental aid, but the basic choices and courses of action should be left to the people. Ideally, perhaps, this should be the case, and admittedly military governments do have a difficult time consolidating popular participation and support, but it is questionable at this point in time how much popular participation is possible, at least in the classical sense. Most westerners who stress the importance of participation have been guilty of employing the term in an ethnocentric manner; they think of encouraging participation in the style of Western models of democracy. Until recently it was rare to utilize the model of China, a country in which a viable base of popular support and participation has been built up under a totalitarian government. The idea of having some kind of totalitarian rule may not be appealing to westerners, yet it is ethnocentric to ignore the advances made by such states. In the remainder of this chapter attention will be focused more directly on the military as a modernizing agent with respect to the two problems of economic development and demographic modernization.

The Military and Economic Development

At one time it was a fairly common belief that military regimes and military personnel—by virtue of their technical training, highly disciplined organization, and generally rational approach to problem-solving—possessed a great potential for enhancing the development process within the have-not nations of the Third World. It is clear today, however, that this potential will not necessarily be fulfilled. Whether or not it is realized will depend largely on the type of role that a particular military establishment adopts for itself, and the degree to which it actively pursues its adopted role. In this section we shall first describe and illustrate the range of roles that the military may assume in relation to a nation's social and economic policies. This will be followed by a brief discussion of the position of the military establishment as it relates to the crucial issue of population size and growth.

Although most military leaders will assert that they are motivated by patriotism or nationalism and that they wish to lead their countries forward to a higher state of social and economic development, the specific approaches that military establishments adopt can vary widely. For purposes of simplification and clarification, one can identify two polar, ideal typical goals that the military may adopt (Laidlaw, 1976:10-34). On the one hand it may adopt a traditionalistic goal of maintaining the status quo; on the other hand it may see itself as a modernizing agent responsible for promoting and guiding socioeconomic development. Within the range laid down by these two polar types, one can further distinguish a broad spectrum of approaches, including direct military rule, coalitions with civilians, indirect behind-the-scenes rule, or a watchdog type of role whereby political influence may be exerted simply by posing the threat of more direct military rule.

In other words, we can identify two basic ideological goals—one which actively seeks change (modernization), and one that is actively concerned with impeding change and maintaining the status quo. Within each we can identify a wide range of specific approaches that a particular military establishment might take to achieve its goals.

Before proceeding any further it should be noted that it is often difficult to fit a given military establishment into one of the two polar categories. One reason for this difficulty is the fact that the two categories are ideal types and do not necessarily represent any real situation. Furthermore, any given military establishment, rather than leaning clearly toward either a modernistic or a traditional role, may be a combination of the two types. Brazil, for example, which has been under military rule since 1964, illustrates such a combination. In Brazil the government has promoted national economic development, and the country as a whole has achieved some social and economic progress. At the same time, however, it is a country in which political dissenters have been severely repressed and where the majority of the Brazilian population has yet to benefit from the accomplishments of the government. That is, the government claims to be committed to modernization, but has so far acted in a way that is conducive to the maintenance of the status quo.

In spite of such limitations, the distinction between the modernizing and the traditional roles has been widely used to characterize the military establishment, and it is this distinction that forms the basis of the following discussion.

The Military as a Modernizing Agent

If the military establishment of a given country sees itself as functioning in the role of modernizing agent, then one can identify a number of characteristics of the military that should contribute to its success (Goldthorpe, 1975:270-71). First of all, there is the fact that the military is generally the strongest and best organized force within a country and is therefore in a good position to get things done. Some of the other characteristics that should enhance its role as a modernizing agent would include the following: (1) The military is a tightly disciplined chain of command in which obedience and success are rewarded while disobedience and failure to perform one's duty are quickly punished; (2) Military officers have often received some kind of formal technical training so that they are used to confronting problems in a logical and systematic manner; (3) The military sense of patriotism and its ''service before self'' mentality may lead to a higher regard for the public good rather than private gain, and it may encourage taking stronger action to control factional rivalries, eliminate corruption, etc; (4) Military personnel tend also to have a pragmatic philosophy and a realistic conception of the world around them; and (5) Military personnel are more likely to be oriented toward a rational program of economic development, particularly industrial development.

As was indicated above, there are a number of different ways in which the military establishment may elect to pursue its role as a modernizing agent. Perhaps one of the longest cases on record of the military being a major agent of modernization is represented by India (Bopagmage, 1971). In that country, the army has been an active participant in numerous development programs since the early road-building efforts of the British colonial administration well over one hundred years ago. Throughout the late nineteenth and early twentieth centuries, in fact, the Indian army played a major role in such things as the construction of city water and drainage systems, the establishment of telephone and telegraph communications, the development of hydroelectric power, the promotion of various medical and public health programs (malaria control, water purification, mass inoculation programs), and the modernization of agricultural practices. Since the end of World War II and the attainment of independence in 1947, the Indian military establishment has played a major role in the development of manufacturing industries in the public sector (such as tool manufacturing, as well as those directly related to defense). It has also acted as an important educational agency—not only by training local peasant peoples in modern agricultural methods, but also by offering courses in industrial management to retiring officers to prepare them for administrative and managerial roles in civilian industries.

Similar kinds of development-oriented civic action programs have recently been undertaken by the military in a number of other developing countries. In Iran, for example, members of the armed forces have been trained to work in that nation's family planning program. In Bolivia the army has been responsible for much of the school construction that has taken place in the postwar period. In Peru the army has instituted a mass literacy training program for its recruits who, it is hoped, will themselves become literacy instructors after their military service has been completed. Finally, a number of countries have followed the Indian example of providing officers with nonmilitary training of one sort or another, both to enhance their awareness and understanding of the problems of social and economic development, and to train them to serve in executive or administrative capacities in civilian enterprises.

Socialization Perhaps one of the more significant modernizing roles that the military plays is as a socialization agent. In many developing countries recruits are generally from a rural-agrarian, lower-class background; for them the military represents a major avenue of social mobility. It also exposes the recruits to widely diverse life styles and often leads to a social transformation in which they acquire a broader view of their society and its problems. As part of their military experience the recruits also generally receive both technical training and citizenship training, which prepare them to be more economically productive in civilian life. This military experience also instills in them a stronger sense of national identity and serves as an important unifying force, particularly in countries that are highly fragmented and contain many diverse social and cultural groups. In the above noted case of India, for example, military service was an important factor leading to a weakening (though not an elimination) of traditional class and caste lines; it also helped create the determination among those who served to raise their standard of living and at the same time provided them with the technical training needed to make the agricultural innovations and establish the small-scale industries that has enabled them to realize their higher aspirations.

Direct Intervention Perhaps the most obvious way in which the military can act as a modernization agent is to take over control of the government and actively plan and direct economic behavior. Because of the earlier noted characteristics (a strong and disciplined organization with a relatively high level of technical training and a pragmatic philosophy), the military is often well qualified to do just this. It should be emphasized, however, that this does not mean the military is the only group capable of guiding economic growth in the poor countries of the world. Nevertheless, to the extent that a strong government exercising tight control over economic activity is likely to be highly desirable, if not necessary, in many of the contemporary developing nations (see chapter 8), the military may have certain advantages over civilian governments. This is especially likely to be the case when the civilian government is one whose continuation in power depends on popular support, and whose program and activities are thus directed less toward economic development than toward maintaining this support. In such cases, large amounts of potential development capital may be invested in outwardly visible signs of social progress such as modern skyscrapers, sports palaces, airports, hotels, department stores, etc. that do not really reflect any economic development. On the other hand, a disproportionate amount of scarce capital might be invested in expanding social welfare programs (unemployment benefits, public health) rather than in more productive activities. The former, in fact, characterized Indonesia during the early 1960s whereas the latter occurred in Peru during the mid-1960s. In both these countries, economically unproductive excesses were among the factors leading to a progressively worsening economic situation that ultimately culminated in military intervention and the overthrow of the existing governments.

When the military does take over the government of an underdeveloped country it is usually because of a fear on the part of the military establishment, either real or imagined, that the country is facing some kind of major crisis (economic collapse or a sociopolitical revolution), and that the existing government is less able to cope with the crisis than a well-organized military government would be. Many of the developing nations have achieved independence only since the end of World War II, and self-government is a new and often frustrating experience for them. In many cases the immature and inexperienced civilian governments have proven to be ineffective in dealing with the complex problems confronting the new nations, and they have failed to meet the demands generated by the revolution of rising expectations that has spread throughout the Third World. The result has often been increasing social, economic, and political instability followed ultimately by the intervention of the military in an attempt to restore order.

The failure of civilian governments to maintain order and to promote social and economic progress has not been confined to the newest nation states. It has also been a factor underlying military intervention in a number of older more established countries. Peru is a good case in point. In Peru, a series of guerrilla uprisings during the 1960s, peasant land invasions, an opposition congress that vetoed nearly all the civilian president's reform programs, and a mounting fiscal deficit were all factors behind the 1968 coup that led to establishment of military rule in that country.

A lack of confidence in the ability of the incumbent civilian president was also a factor behind the re-establishment of military rule in Burma in 1962 and in the 1965 military coup in Algeria. Most recently, the failure of the civilian government to deal effectively with mounting economic and political chaos led to military takeovers in Ethiopia (1975) and Argentina (1976).

In all the examples cited in this section the military has acted, by stepping in and taking direct control of the government, as a positive agent of modernization by reversing (or at least halting) trends toward a deteriorating socio-economic situation. Once in power, however, whether or not it succeeds in its role as a modernizing agent and promotes economic growth will depend entirely on the nature of the specific policies and programs that the military government adopts. The fact that the military can play a positive role as a modernizing agent is clearly illustrated by the experience of Egypt after Nasser and the army ousted the old monarchy (Abdel Malek, 1968), and more recently by the experience of Peru under the revolutionary military government of Juan Velasco during the late 1960s and early 1970s (Laidlaw 1976). In the former case, the Nasser government encouraged the expansion of educational facilities and made them available to a larger segment of the population (notably to women). In addition, the power of the old elite groups and foreign economic interests was substantially reduced through a series of measures involving both the expropriation of land and the nationalization of corporations, and marked progress was made in promoting the growth and development of government owned businesses and industries. Similar efforts of the Peruvian military government to promote economic growth and development in that country following its assumption of power in 1968 included such positive measures as the expansion of economic relations with socialist bloc countries, the launching of a major program of agrarian reform and land redistribution, the expropriation and nationalization of a number of foreign owned multinational corporations, the formation of a cooperative social and economic development program with a number of neighboring Latin American countries, and the passage of a number of industrial reforms aimed at increasing worker participation in and control over Peruvian industry (Laidlaw, 1977).

It needs to be emphasized that not all programs inaugurated by military governments will necessarily lead to economic progress. For example, if its development programs are too one-sided (e.g., if it concentrates too heavily on industrial development to the neglect of other equally important areas such as education, land reform, and agricultural productivity); or if it becomes more concerned with strengthening its own position in a society and diverts capital away from more general development programs into military equipment, then military rule may impede rather than encourage the process of economic development. Similarly, if they are too repressive in their actions, military governments may have a harmful effect. Some specific cases in point here would be the murder of hundreds of thousands of Chinese in Indonesia under Sukarno, and the more recent (since March, 1976) harrassment and jailing of scientists and other intellectuals by the government of General Jorge Videla in Argentina.

There is some evidence that military governments do in fact tend to divert a greater share of the GNP to military expenditures than do civilian governments (Laidlaw, 1979). The reasons for this may be that once a military regime assumes power it is likely to spend more to strengthen and maintain its position. Also, priorities may be re-examined and military leaders may decide that more equipment and training is needed to modernize the military, and to protect the country from internal or external threats, real or imagined. One example of this would be the Peruvian-Chilean ''war.'' For the past several years there has been much speculation that a war would break out between these two countries, and much activity has been devoted to preparing for such a conflict, but so far there has been no war.

There is also evidence to indicate that military governments are likely to invest more heavily in industrial development than civilian regimes. The data in Table 9.1, for example, indicates that although both types spend roughly similar proportions on agriculture, military governments allocate a far greater percentage of capital expenditues to industrial development (30 percent) than the civilian governments (11 percent).

Table 9.1 Percent of total capital expenditures going to ''Industry and Power'' versus ''Agriculture,'' by type of government: circa 1973.

Type of Government	Average percent of capital expenditure going for:	
	Industry and Power	Agriculture
Military (n=24)	30 (9)	17 (15)
Other (n=32)	11 (14)	18 (18)

Source: K. A. Laidlaw, ''The Military in the Third World: A Case for the Convergence Hypothesis,'' *International Review of Modern Sociology*, 9 (January-June 1979): 1-15. Numbers in parentheses indicate number of countries in each group.

The reasons behind this differential are varied. On the one hand, military governments may tend to be more technologically oriented than civilian governments, although this is difficult to verify. On the other hand, it may reflect a view among the military that industrialization may be equated with development. This may be an area in which the developing nations, particularly those led by military regimes, could be imitating the developed world. In other words, they believe that making their countries industrial rather than agricultural in nature is the manner in which one achieves development and world stature. This course is not necessarily a good one for the developing nations to follow, particularly in view of severe food shortages existing in the world today.

While far from being conclusive, these two points do illustrate ways in which the policies of military governments may have a negative influence on the overall development process. Despite possibilities such as these, however, the cases of Egypt and Peru clearly illustrate that where a strong development-oriented military establishment exists, it is potentially capable of playing a major modernizing role and actively promoting national social and economic development.

The Military as an Agent of Tradition

The military establishment does not always view itself as an agent of change and development. On the contrary, it may regard itself as the guardian of the status quo, as an organization whose primary function is to protect and preserve a traditional way of life. Once again there are alternative roles the military can play in performing this type of guardian function. On the one hand, it can exert an indirect influence as the supporting power behind a traditionalistic civilian government. In such cases the military functions largely as a police agency whose primary responsibility is to maintain stability in the society and to suppress those groups and activities that might challenge or otherwise pose a threat to the established order. An example of the military fulfilling this type of role in recent history would be found in the experience of Haiti under Papa Doc Duvalier.

On the other hand, and what is more likely to be the case, the military can exert a direct influence by actively intervening in the normal political process and usurping control of the government for itself. When the military does intervene in this manner it is usually for the purpose of protecting traditional class interests or heading off what it perceives as a potential threat to national stability. Thus, the 1966 military coup which removed Kwame Nkrumah from power in Ghana was in part motivated by a desire to preserve traditional class lines; and the increasing trend toward "socialism" in Mali in the late 1960s and in Chile during the early 1970s may be listed among the factors prompting intervention and the establishment of more conservative military governments in those countries.

The Military and Population Policy

One area in which the military is especially likely to take a traditionalistic stance is in the area of population policy. Specifically, military leaders are apt to be very pro-natalist in their philosophical outlook and are likely to support policies and programs aimed at encouraging population growth. In part this is due to a vaguely defined feeling of pride in numbers that goes along with most nationalistic movements. For the most part, however, it is probably due to an out-dated belief (out-dated in an era of nuclear weapons of mass destruction, not to mention the further lethal potential of chemical and biological warfare) that a large population is a necessary basis for national strength and power and that the larger the population the stronger the nation. This view also overlooks the fact that quantity cannot be equated with quality; a large, poorly nourished, ill-equipped army will be no match for a small, well-nourished, and well-equipped army. If the strength in numbers myth did apply then India and Mainland China, rather than the United States and the Soviet Union, would be the most powerful nations in the world today, and the Arab world would long ago have obliterated the state of Israel.

In spite of contradictions like the preceding, it is not unusual to find philosophies favoring population growth predominating among the military elite in the underdeveloped nations of Asia, Africa, and Latin America. The extent to which this is so is clearly revealed by the classification presented in Figure 9.1. This figure contains a list of thirty-six countries that were identified as having military governments in 1975. The countries are listed in three separate groups based on the general nature of their national population policies. The three groups are as follows:

(1) Pronatalist—countries which do not regard population growth as a national problem and which may in fact

actively encourage rapid growth because of a belief that a larger population will enhance economic development. Many countries in this group may allow voluntary birth control programs to exist (mostly privately operated or closely related to more general maternal health programs), but family planning is not officially encouraged.

(2) Antinatalist — countries which have openly expressed concern over high rates of population growth and which have adopted an official policy to reduce the population growth rate that is reflected in active government participation in and sponsorship of family planning programs.

Figure 9.1 Population policies characterizing thirty-six countries with military governments: circa 1975.

Pronatalist Policies	Mixed	Antinatalist Policies
Argentina	Algeria	Bangladesh
Burma	Benin (Dahomey)	Ghana
Chad	Bolivia	Guatemala
Ethiopia	Brazil	Indonesia
Libya	Burundi	
Malagasy Republic	Central African Republic	
Niger	Chile	
Peru	Congo	
Syria	Ecuador	
Togo	Honduras	
Upper Volta	Iraq	
	Lesotho	
	Mali	
	Nicaragua	
	Nigeria	
	Paraguay	
	Rwanda	
	Somalia	
	Sudan	
	Uganda	
	Zaire	

Source: Military governments were identified by the authors from descriptions contained in the 1976 edition of the *CBS News Almanac*. Population policy classifications were determined partly by the classification made by D. Nortman and E. Hofstatter in *Population and Family Planning Programs: A Factbook* (Population Council, 1975), and partly by the authors using information contained in *World Population Growth and Response, 1965-1975* (Population Reference Bureau, 1976b).

(3) Mixed—a residual category that includes all those countries that do not have an official population policy or who otherwise cannot be classified unambiguously as either pro-natalist or anti-natalist. If countries in this group do have family planning programs, it is for reasons of health, or because it is a basic human right. Any anti-natalist effect is a byproduct of the program, but it is not an objective of the program.

Inspection of Figure 9.1 reveals that eleven (31 percent) of the thirty-six military governments identified had population policies that could be classified as pronatalist and that twenty-one (58 percent) had policies that were mixed. Only four (11 percent) of the nations included in this list of military governments were pursuing population policies that would clearly qualify them for inclusion in the antinatalist group.

Table 9.2 has been added to give some perspective to these figures. Here it can be noted that when all underdeveloped countries are considered (irrespective of the type of government) the proportion having policies identified as pronatalist is substantially less and the corresponding proportion with antinatalist policies substantially greater than among countries identified as having military governments.

Table 9.2 Population policies of underdeveloped countries, by type of government: circa 1975.

Type of Government	Population Policy		
	Pronatalist	Mixed	Antinatalist
Military Government[1] (n=36)	11 (31%)	21 (58%)	4 (11%)
All Countries[2]	11 (15%)	29 (39%)	34 (46%)

Sources: 1. Same as Figure 9.1 Numbers in parentheses indicate percent of countries in each government category falling into each policy classification.

2. D. Nortman and E. Hofstatter, *Population and Family Planning Programs: A Factbook* (Population Council 1974).

What is most disheartening, perhaps, is the fact that those countries that do not have active antinatalist policies are often the ones whose level of development is such that they can barely support their present populations, let alone absorb continued rapid population growth. For example, many of the African nations listed on Figure 9.1 (Chad, Ethiopia, Mali, Niger, and Upper Volta) were especially hard-hit by the drought and food shortages of the early 1970s and the resulting serious deterioration in the economic situation was severly exacerbated by their rapid rate of population growth. To the extent that the military governments in these rapidly growing, poor countries refuse to adopt strong antinatalist positions, they will continue to encourage the persistence of what is a major obstacle to real social and economic progress. In fact, to the extent that any poor, rapidly growing country does not adopt a strong antinatalist policy, their development efforts will continue to be hampered, if not blocked entirely, by the increasing population.

Summary

No matter what forms they assume, military governments are today fairly widespread throughout the underdeveloped world. In Latin America, military governments have been a major factor in the political process for years—the March 1979 military coup in Argentina was the seventh in that country in twenty-one years—and the more recently created nations of Africa and Asia have also found that the building up of a military force since independence has resulted in the emergence of a large number of military rulers. Military governments are widespread throughout the underdeveloped countries of the world, and they are likely to be fairly common in the foreseeable future. In many of these countries people's loyalties to the new state are not yet fully developed and there is no real commitment to the civilian institutions. In particular, when instability and turmoil characterize a civilian regime, it will tend to confirm the military's feeling that they are the best organized group and certainly the most competent ruling force in the country. This seems to be one of the dominant factors leading to military intervention in the political process in many Third

World countries. To this can be added the simple fact that the exercise of power becomes habit forming; once the military establishment takes control of a country and stabilizes the national situation it is likely to be reluctant to relinquish control. Even when it does yield formal control to a civilian administration, the military is likely to remain close in the background acting as a watchdog and prepared to step in at the first sign of any trouble.

The crucial question does not concern whether military governments will prevail, but what their role will be vis-à-vis national development programs. A number of scholars have recently been critical of what they have interpreted to be an overriding emphasis by social scientists on the potentially positive role of the military as a modernizing agent in the developing countries. Military rule, even when it claims to be reformist and development-oriented, has been questioned not only as to its effectiveness versus that of civilian rule, but also as concerns its possible detrimental effects for national economic development. It is obvious that military rule *may* be detrimental to a country's political and economic development, but this need not necessarily be the case. The military can adopt either a traditionalistic or a modernizing role, and the particular way in which it attempts to fulfill its adopted role will vary from country to country, depending on the attitudes and qualifications of a particular military establishment as well as on the special historical circumstances of the given country. Evidence was presented in the preceding chapter to the effect that developing nations need strong central governments and that our constitutional brand of government may not be a viable option for many of them. To the extent that underdeveloped countries are fragmented and abound with competing political and economic interest groups, it is difficult to imagine them making any significant progress on the path to modernization without some kind of strong central direction. Constitutional governments have, for the most part, been found to lack both the political and the physical force required to meet the increasingly complex demands of their emerging societies, and we may just have to reconcile ourselves to the fact that the kind of democracy we have known in the United States and other advanced western nations will not work to solve the pressing social and economic problems of many of the underdeveloped nations in the world today. Further, in the heterogeneous and more highly fragmented underdeveloped countries it may well be that the military establishment represents the most viable alternative to providing the strong leadership needed to promote social change and economic development. The only point at issue concerns the nature of the role the military assumes. If it sees itself as a modernizing agent and acts accordingly, there is no reason why the military cannot be a significant positive force for development among the poor countries of Asia, Africa, and Latin America.

10

Summary and Conclusions

It is difficult if not impossible to cover in depth all the complexities of the Third World development problem in a single volume, and that has not been our aim in the present effort. Rather, what we have tried to do in this volume is provide a broad overview of the general problem in terms of a particular framework that we feel will facilitate the identification of many of the specific facets of the problem, as well as serve as a basis for guiding more thorough analyses of particular countries. The framework presented is one that looks at the overall development problem as having three broad dimensions. It has an *economic* dimension in that the developing areas are characterized by such things as low per capita incomes, widespread poverty, low levels of technology and per capita productivity, a natural resource base that is often inadequate and frequently poorly utilized or exploited by the developed countries, and an inequitable access to world markets that are dominated by the industrialized nations. It has a *demographic* dimension in that most of these poor countries are characterized by high birth

318

rates, rapid rates of population growth (especially in urban areas), and a low ratio of producers to consumers. Finally, it has a *sociocultural* dimension in that the prevailing cultural attitudes and values and the nature of the social structure in many developing countries often contain elements that are not conducive to and are sometimes serious obstacles to either economic development or demographic modernization. The primary aim of this volume has been to elaborate this three-dimensional conception of the problem and to describe some of the more salient economic, demographic, and sociocultural characteristics of the Third World countries in order to provide beginning students with a better understanding and appreciation of the many facets and complexities of the broad problem of world development.

It is important to emphasize that the problem being dealt with is truly one of world development. The developing countries of Africa, Asia, and Latin America do not exist in isolation but are an integral part of the international economic system. Taking an historical view of present world economic inequalities, it is apparent that many of the problems now facing the developing countries can be traced to the growth of the European capitalist economic system in which the developing countries emerged as exploited suppliers of primary products for consumption in the industrializing nations (Wallerstein, 1974). From this it follows that Third World development is going to entail a restructuring of the world economic system, and this is going to require a strong commitment from and the active cooperation of the developed nations. However, while recognizing that world economic development will require the active assistance of the developed countries, it must also be recognized that the assistance must be given in such a way that each nation will have the freedom and autonomy to choose its own path to development.

In spite of the fact that a number of generalizations pertaining to the various dimensions of the problem have been presented in the preceding chapters, it is important to emphasize again that the precise nature of the development problem facing particular countries, and thus its most likely solutions, will be situationally determined. By that we mean that any given underdeveloped country will exhibit its own unique combination of economic, demographic, and socio-cultural circumstances relevant to its level of development, and each such country will have to be considered separately in arriving at an understanding of what its particular problems are and of how these problems can best be solved. Given this situation, it would indeed be presumptious to assert that there is any single solution for a specific problem that would be universally applicable throughout the developing world. At the same time, however, it should be possible to identify in a general way the overall kinds of strategies that are most likely to lead to the development and implementation of successful programs of national economic and demographic modernization. It is to this end that this final chapter is directed.

Theory, Policy, and Strategy

The search for solutions to the problems of world economic development may conveniently be perceived as operating on three broad levels. The first is the theoretical level which seeks to explain or otherwise understand the causes of the inequities that presently exist throughout the world. The second policy level takes off from the first and seeks to develop general plans and proposals for dealing with the problems delineated in the theoretical approach. Finally, there is the level of strategy which concerns the specific programs that are designed for the purpose of implementing general policy decisions. To take a specific illustration, one approach to the problem of underdevelopment sees it as being at least partly related to the dominant personality type prevailing in a country—for example, to a low need for achievement. In this case, the general policy would be to alter the external conditions of a society in order to create a stronger psychic need for achievement. Those who adhere to this position have suggested a number of different strategies for attaining this end such as mass media development to create an informed public opinion, emancipation of women and alteration of the ascribed status structure, and expansion of educational facilities and reorientation of the curricula to teach modern attitudes and values. This is admittedly an oversimplified example, but it does serve to illustrate the general steps to be followed in arriving at solutions to the problem of world economic development.

In reading the preceding chapters it should have become apparent that there is no single theoretical approach that is capable of explaining all the complexities of the multi-dimensional problem of world development. Some of the theoretical models may have limited validity for specific countries at specific times, but there is no universally applicable general theory of development. Nor can there be. What we have tried to do in this volume is bring the several theoretical approaches together in a general perspective that will permit a broader understanding of the many facets of the problem, and provide a framework for identifying some of the general kinds of policies that the developing nations might adopt in their present struggle to eliminate the pronounced economic inequalities that differentiate them from the more advanced nations of the Western world. The crucial element in eliminating these inequalities will of course be the specific strategies that the developing countries adopt, and it is to this topic that the following discussion is devoted.

Strategies for Development

One way to approach this topic would be to follow the general framework presented in this volume and identify various strategies for achieving economic change, demographic change, and sociocultural change. For example, given the economic goal of increasing per capita productivity and raising levels of living, one could suggest strategies relating to agrarian reform (land redistribution, establishment of agricultural cooperatives, improved credit systems,

irrigation projects, etc.); industrial development—
(expropriation and/or nationalization of foreign-controlled
mineral resources, more intensive use of labor, tax incentives, international trade agreements, etc.); tax reform to
alleviate the present maldistribution of income and encourage saving and investment; and so forth. Similarly, given the
policy goal of reducing the birth rate and slowing down the
rate of population growth, one could cite strategies such as
legalizing and providing free access to all kinds of family
planning services, including sterilization and abortion; developing educational programs to emphasize the desirability
of smaller families; and providing economic incentives or
disincentives to encourage adherence to small family norms.
Finally, there are a number of specific strategies that could
be suggested for altering various aspects of the broad sociocultural system to enhance the attainment of economic and
demographic policy goals. These might include expansion of
educational facilities and opportunities and development of
the mass media to reduce illiteracy, to expose people to
modern attitudes, and to acquaint them with national goals
and create a sense of nationhood; legislation to enhance the
position of women in society and make them more equal
partners in the development process; and implementation of
various social welfare programs such as unemployment
compensation and old age retirement pensions to weaken the
sometimes stifling influence of the traditional extended
family.

Such a piecemeal approach is not likely to be very profitable, however, for reasons that have already been discussed
in the preceding chapters. More important, however, although many countries will want to include such strategies as
part of their internal development programs, this approach is
a much too simplistic one and does not come to grips with the
real crux of the problem; namely, the nature of the international economic situation. The developing countries of Africa, Asia, and Latin America exist in a world that has been
and still is dominated by the economic interests of the rich

industrialized nations; their present economic status is at least partially the result of their relative position within the world economic system (Chase-Dunn, 1975; Rubinson, 1976), and they need to adopt policies and strategies to confront this reality. In this endeavor, we would re-emphasize that one of the major prerequisities for the development of the poor countries today is a strong centralized government that has national economic development as its primary goal, and that is intimately involved in the planning and directing of development projects. Stated most simply this means that decisive state intervention will be required to initiate and sustain the development process. The nature of the world today is such that national economic development cannot be separated from international politics, and a strong, perhaps even a highly authoritarian government is necessary in the developing countries, not only to maintain internal stability and coordinate national planning efforts, but also (and more important) to deal effectively with the international situation. Because of the diversity and complexities of the problems of development in the various regions of the world, it is not possible to outline a single global strategy for development. However, one can identify a number of specific strategies that some Third World countries have adopted, and that others may wish to consider, in order to further their own national interests. One recent effort in this direction has identified six such strategies that we feel deserve mentioning (Wriggins and Adler-Karlsson, 1978:43-102).

1. Establish commodity coalitions. Countries that are endowed with particular resources needed by the industrialized nations can form international agreements and band together to control the supply and price of the resource in question. The obvious example here is the Organization of Petroleum Exporting Countries (OPEC). Although initially formed as a means of influencing the policies of the Western nations toward the Middle East, particularly in reference to Israel, the OPEC countries have continued to maintain con-

trol over the price of the bulk of the world's petroleum resources and have significantly increased their capital resources in the process. One problem that this has created is that the developing countries also need petroleum, and the OPEC price increases have seriously hurt the economies of other Third World nations. As was noted earlier, however, this is a problem that could be alleviated by the adoption of a differential pricing structure so that the rich countries would pay more for their oil imports, thereby helping to subsidize the development of the poor countries. Although OPEC is by far the most dramatic example of a commodity coalition in the world today, there are numerous possibilities for similar coalitions throughout the Third World. Many of the mineral resources that the developed countries require for their industrial economies (e.g., bauxite, chromium, copper, nickel, phosphates, tin) are concentrated in various developing countries, and the OPEC case provides a good example of the possibilities of utilizing such resources to further their own national interests.

2. Form regional coalitions. Countries located in the same part of the world can band together and cooperate to promote their own regional development by establishing trade agreements along the lines of the European Common Market. In the Third World today regional coalitions are represented by such groups as the Organization of African Unity, formed to resolve intra-African differences and reduce the frequency and costs of local conflicts in order to forestall outside interference from the major world powers; the Association of Southeast Asian Nations, formed to draw the countries in that part of the world together so that each could become less dependent on the United States; and the Andean Group that was formed as a kind of Latin American common market. Although such regional coalitions have so far had little effect in altering the world economic order, they do have a good potential for enhancing regional control over regional resources and markets.

3. Establish universal coalitions. Instead of trying to control the supply and distribution of particular resources (as in the first strategy) or attempting to develop regional development policies (as on the second), this type of coalition would draw countries together from all over the developing world in a broad attempt to influence relations between rich and poor countries in general. Such coalitions would function both as consciousness raising groups to promote greater solidarity among Third World nations, and as pressure groups to try and influence policies of the more developed countries. A good example of the latter would be the action taken by a large bloc of Third World countries at the 1974 World Population Conference (see chapter 8) in which the World Plan of Action proposed by a group of countries led by the United States was effectively modified to emphasize the goal of achieving economic parity with the western nations through international economic reforms rather than through population control.

4. Form associations with a major world power. A fairly common approach that many Third World countries have taken is to become closely associated with one of the major world powers. Very often these associations have been formed for political reasons (e.g., the association between the United States and Taiwan or the earlier associations between Egypt and the USSR, and that between the USSR and Cuba). However, such associations have also provided the developing countries with industrial equipment, technical advisors, and various economic concessions that have generally had a decidedly beneficial effect for their economies.

5. Threat or precipitation of local wars. Another way in which some Third World countries have gained political and economic support from the more developed countries is to threaten or actually precipitate a local war. In cases where this strategy has been followed the initiating country sought to enhance its own economic position by drawing in one of

the major powers to help. Example of this strategy would be Sukarno's threat to annex New Guinea (West Irian) to Indonesia in the early 1960s, which prompted the United States to use its influence to speed up the peaceful transition from Dutch control, and the continued Arab rumblings in the Middle East, which have substantially altered American foreign policy in that part of the world. Such a strategy has the effect of focusing world attention on the problems of the initiating country and of motivating one or more of the major powers to exert influence on its behalf.

6. Irregular violence. Whereas the preceding strategy is one that a government in power might adopt, the use of irregular extralegal violence is one that can be resorted to by weaker groups to call attention to the plight of their nation. The terrorist activities of the PLO have certainly focused world attention on the problems of the Palestinian refugees, and numerous national liberation movements throughout the Third World (e.g., Rhodesia, Angola, Zaire) have been effective, in varying degrees, in mobilizing support from one or more of the major world powers as well as from other Third World countries.

The preceding is only a brief sketch of some of the kinds of strategies that have been adopted by various Third World nations in their efforts to enhance their own position in the world economic system. All of them have their value, but all of them also have their limitations. Commodity coalitions may hurt other poor countries more than they hurt the rich nations, or they might even prompt retaliatory action by one or more of the major powers (e.g., military intervention or the withholding of food aid). Alignments with a major power or strategies that encourage major power intervention could enhance dependence rather than lead to economic gains. The main point, however, is that all of them have been followed by some countries in the past, and all of them are likely to be followed in one form or another by Third World nations in the years immediately ahead. How the industrialized nations respond to them will largely determine the outcome of the present global struggle to reduce inequities and achieve world economic development.

Concluding Comments

The brief sketch of the dimensions of the development problem presented in this volume has been somewhat pessimistic and may make it appear to be insurmountable. Achieving world economic development will indeed be an enormous task, and while there may be grounds for pessimism we prefer to view the future with guarded optimism. The developing countries of the Third World are not in as weak a position as is often contended, as is aptly illustrated by the relative success of the OPEC coalition and by influence exerted by the developing countries at the 1974 World Population Conference. More and more the industrialized nations are coming to realize this fact and are making efforts to adjust to it. It will require a massive effort on the part of all of us to come to grips with the many dimensions of the development problem. This effort is already underway, and there are some positive signs: progress continues to be made in agricultural research to increase world food production; many of the poor countries have embarked on more vigorous programs of national development; the rich nations are becoming more acutely aware of their responsibilities to assist Third World development; and there are signs that the rate of world population growth is slowing down. We would like to conclude that present efforts will succeed, but instead we choose to say they *must* succeed. The world we live in today is highly interdependent, and becoming more so every year. To ignore this fact is to court disaster. The problem of Third World development has emerged as the most critical problem facing the human race today, and it will continue to be the most critical problem we face for several decades to come. Not just the well-being of the people in the poor countries is at stake; the well-being of all of us hangs in the balance, and it is very much in the best interests of all of us to exert the massive efforts that are and will be required to achieve some semblance of economic parity throughout the world.

Bibliography

Abdel Malek, A. *Egypt: Military Society; The Army Regime, The Left, and Social Change Under Nasser.* Translated by C. L. Markham. Random House, 1968.

Almond, G. A. and G. B. Powell, Jr. *Comparative Politics: A Developmental Approach.* Little, Brown and Co., 1966.

Amin, S. *Neo-Colonialism in West Africa.* Monthly Review Press, 1971.

Anderson, C. W. *Politics and Economic Change in Latin America.* D. Van Nortrand, 1967.

Andrain, C. F. *Political Life and Social Change: An Introduction to Political Science.* Duxbury Press, 1974.

Armer, M., and L. Issac. "Determinants and Behavioral Consequences of Psychological Modernity: Empirical Evidence from Costa Rica." *American Sociological Review,* 43 (June 1978):316-34.

Ayres, R. L. "Political Regimes, Explanatory Variables, and Public Policy in Latin America." *Journal of Developing Areas,* 10 (October 1975):15-35.

Baines, J. M. "U.S. Military Assistance to Latin America: An Assessment." *Journal of InterAmerican Studies and World Affairs,* 14 (November 1972):469-87.

Barber, W. F., and C. N. Ronning. *Internal Security and Military Power: Counterinsurgency and Civic Action in Latin America.* Ohio State University Press, 1966.

Barnett, H. J. "Population Problems—Myths and Realities." *Economic Development and Cultural Change,* 19 (July 1971):545-59.

Beier, G. J. "Can Third World Cities Cope?" *Population Bulletin*, 31 (December 1976):3-34.

Belli, P. "The Economic Implications of Malnutrition: The Dismal Science Revisited." *Economic Development and Cultural Change*, 20 (October 1971):1-23.

Berelson, B. "The Present State of Family Planning Programs." *Studies in Family Planning*, 57 (September 1970):1-11.

Blumberg, R. L. "Fairy Tales and Facts: Economy, Family, Fertility and the Female." In I. Tinker and M. B. Beamsen, eds., *Women and World Development*. Overseas Development Council, 1976. Pp. 12-21.

Bogue, D. J. "The End of the Population Explosion." *The Public Interest* (Spring 1967):11-20.

Bopagamage, A. "The Military as a Modernizing Agent in India." *Economic Development and Cultural Change*, 20 (October 1971):71-79.

Boserup, E. *Women's Role in Economic Development*. St. Martin's Press, 1970.

Brown, L. R. *World Population Trends: Signs of Hope, Signs of Stress*. Watchword Paper 8, Watchword Institute (October 1976).

Browning, H. L. "Migrant Selectivity and the Growth of Large Cities in Developing Societies." In National Academy of Sciences, *Rapid Population Growth: Consequences and Implications*. Johns Hopkins Press, 1971.

Burch, T. K., and G. A. Shea. "Catholic Parish Priests and Birth Control: A Comparative Study of Opinion in Colombia, the United States, and the Netherlands." *Studies in Family Planning*, 6 (June 1971):121-36.

Burke, M. P. "Women: The Missing Piece in the Development Puzzle." *Agenda*, 1 (March 1978):1-5.

Castillo, G. T., et al. "The Concepts of Nuclear and Extended Family: An Exploration of Empirical Referents." *International Journal of Comparative Sociology*, 9 (March 1968):1-40.

CBS News Almanac, 1976. Hammond Almanac, Inc., 1976.

Chandrasekhar, S. "Cultural Barriers to Family Planning in Underdeveloped Countries." *Population Review*, 1 (July 1957):44-51.

Chandrasekhar, S. *American Aid and India's Economic Development*. Praeger, 1965.

Chandrasekhar, S. *Infant Mortality, Population Growth and Family Planning in India*. University of North Carolina Press, 1972.

Chase-Dunn, C. "The Effects of International Economic Dependence on Development and Inequality: A Cross-National Study." *American Sociological Review*, 40 (December 1975):720-38.

Chiang, A. C. "Religion, Proverbs and Economic Mentality." *American Journal of Economics and Sociology*, 20 (April 1961):253-64.

Clark, C. "Do Population and Freedom Go Together?" *Fortune* (December 1960):136ff.

Clinard, M. B., and D. J. Abbott. *Crime in Developing Areas: A Comparative Perspective*. John Wiley and Sons, 1973.

Cockcroft, J. D., et al. *Dependence and Underdevelopment.* Anchor Books, 1972.

Coser, L. *Masters of Sociological Thought.* Harcourt Brace Jovanovich, 1971.

Curle, A. "Education, Politics and Development." *Comparative Education Review,* 7 (February 1964):226-45.

Davis, K. "Institutional Patterns Favoring High Fertility in Underdeveloped Areas." *Eugenics Quarterly,* 2 (March 1955):33-39.

Davis, K. *World Urbanization, 1950-1970,* vol. 2, *Analysis of Trends, Relationships, and Development.* Berkeley: Institute of International Studies, University of California, 1972.

Davis, K. "Asia's Cities: Problems and Options." *Population and Development Review,* 1 (September 1975):71-86.

Davis, K., and J. Blake. "Social Structure and Fertility: An Analytic Framework." *Economic Development and Cultural Change,* 4 (April 1956):211-35.

De Castro, J. *The Black Book of Hunger.* Beacon Press, 1967.

De Gregori, T. R., and O. Pi-Sunyer. *Economic Development: The Cultural Perspective.* John Wiley and Sons, 1969.

Demerath, N. J. *Birth Control and Foreign Policy.* Harper and Row, 1976.

Deyrup, F. J. "Family Dominance as a Factor in Population Growth of Developing Societies." *Social Research,* 2 (Summer 1962):177-89.

Du Bois, V. D. "The Drought in West Africa, Part II: Perception, Evaluation, and Response." *American Universities Field Staff Reports,* West Africa Series, 2 (1974).

Edari, R. S. *Social Change.* W. C. Brown, 1976.

Eisenstadt, S. N. *Tradition, Change, and Modernity.* John Wiley, 1973.

Environmental Fund. *World Population Estimates: 1975.* Washington, D.C. 1975a.

Environmental Fund. *The Real Crisis Behind the "Food Crisis."* Washington, D.C. 1975b.

Fanon, F. *The Wretched of the Earth.* Grove Press, 1963.

Feit, E. *The Armed Bureaucrats: Military Administrative Regimes and Political Development.* Houghton Mifflin, 1973.

Finer, S. E. "The Man on Horseback—1974: Military Regimes." *Armed Forces and Society,* 1 (November 1975):5-27.

Finkle, J. L. and B. B. Crane. "The Politics of Bucharest: Population, Development, and the New International Economic Order." *Population and Development Review,* 1 (September 1975):87-114.

Fitzgerald, F. *Fire in the Lake: The Vietnamese and the Americans in Vietnam.* Vantage Books, 1972.

Foster, G. M. *Traditional Cultures and the Impact of Technological Change.* Harper, 1962.

Foster, G. M. "Peasant Society and the Image of Limited Good." *American Anthropologist,* 67 (April 1965):293-315.

Foster, G. M. "A Second Look at Limited Good." *Anthropological Quarterly,* 45 (April 1972):57-64.

Franda, M. F. "Militant Hindu Opposition to Family Planning in India."

American University Fieldstaff Reports, South Asia Series, 16 (1972).

Frank, A. G. *Latin America: Underdevelopment or Revolution.* Monthly Review Press, 1969.

Freedman, R. *The Sociology of Human Fertility.* Halstead Press, 1975.

Gavitt, A. R. "Impact of Mass Media on Economic Growth of Underdeveloped Countries." *Agricultural College Editors Quarterly,* 54 (April/June, 1971):7-21.

George, E. "Women in Africa." *Agenda,* 1 (February 1978):1-22.

Gill, R. T. *Economic Development: Past and Present.* 2d ed. Prentice-Hall, 1967.

Glick, E. B. *Peaceful Conflict: The Non-Military Use of the Military.* Stackpole Books, 1967.

Golden, H. H. "Literacy and Social Change in Underdeveloped Countries." *Rural Sociology,* 20 (March 1955):1-7.

Goldthorpe, J. E. *The Sociology of the Third World.* Cambridge University Press, 1975.

Goode, W. J. *World Revolution and Family Patterns.* Free Press, 1963.

Gusfield, J. "Tradition and Modernity: Misplaced Polarities in the Study of Social Change." In A. Etzioni and E. Etzioni-Halevy, eds., *Social Change: Sources, Patterns and Consequences,* 2d ed. Basic Books, 1973. Pp. 333-41.

Hagen, E. E. *On the Theory of Social Change.* The Dorsey Press, 1962.

Harbison, F., and C. A. Myers. "Education and Employment in the Newly Developing Economies." *Comparative Education Review,* 8 (June 1964):5-10.

Heer, D. M., and E. S. Turner. "Areal Differences in Latin American Fertility." *Population Studies,* 18 (March 1965):279-92.

Heilbroner, R. *An Inquiry into the Human Prospect.* W. W. Norton and Co., 1974.

Hendershot, G. E. "Population Size, Military Power, and Antinatal Population Policy." *Demography,* 10 (November 1973):517-24.

Horowitz, I. L. *Three Worlds of Development: The Theory and Practice of International Stratification.* 2d ed. Oxford University Press, 1972.

Hoselitz, B. F. *Sociological Aspects of Economic Growth.* The Free Press, 1960.

Huntington, S. *Political Order in Changing Societies.* Yale University Press, 1968.

Hyman, E. H. "Soldiers in Politics: New Insights on Latin American Armed Forces." *Political Science Quarterly,* 87 (September 1972):401-18.

Ilchman, W. F., and N. T. Uphoff. *The Political Economy of Change.* University of California Press, 1971.

Inkeles, A., and D. H. Smith. *Becoming Modern.* Harvard University Press, 1974.

International Bank for Reconstruction and Development. *World Tables, 1976.* Johns Hopkins University Press, 1976.

Jaffe, A. J. "Population Trends and Controls in Underdeveloped Countries,'' *Law and Contemporary Problems,* 25 (Summer 1960):508-35.

Janowitz, M. *The Military in the Political Development of New Nations.* University of Chicago Press, 1964. For an expanded version of this volume, see M. Janowitz, *Military Institutions and Coercion in the Developing Nations.* University of Chicago Press, 1977.

Janowitz, M. ''Preface.'' *Armed Forces and Society,* 1 (Spring 1975):283-86.

Johnson, D. G. ''Food for the Future: A Perspective.'' *Population and Development Review,* 2 (March 1976):1-19.

Johnson, J. J. *The Military and Society in Latin America.* Stanford University Press, 1964.

Jones, G. W. *The Economic Effect of Declining Fertility in Less Developed Countries.* The Population Council, 1969.

Jones, G. W. ''Effect of Population Change on the Attainment of Educational Goals in the Developing Countries.'' In National Academy of Sciences, *Rapid Population Growth: Consequences and Policy Implications.* The Johns Hopkins Press, 1971. Pp. 315-67.

Kahl, J. A. *Modernization, Exploitation and Dependency in Latin America.* Transaction Books, 1976.

Kanthi, M. S., et al. ''Hunger in the Third World.'' Paper presented at the Second Annual Convention of the Eastern Economic Association; Bloomsburg, Penn. (April 1976).

Khalaf, S., and E. Shwayri. ''Family Firms and Industrial Development: The Lebanese Case.'' *Economic Development and Cultural Change,* 15 (October 1966):59-69.

Kirk, D. "Factors Affecting Moslem Natality," In C. B. Nam, ed., *Population and Society.* Houghton Mifflin, 1968. Pp. 230–42.

Kirk, D., "A New Demographic Transition." In National Academy of Sciences, *Rapid Population Growth: Consequences and Policy Implications.* The Johns Hopkins Press, 1971. Pp. 123–47.

Kossok, M. ''The Armed Forces in Latin America: Potential for Changes in Political and Social Functions.'' *Journal of Inter-American Studies and World Affairs,* 14 (November 1972):375-98.

Kunkle, J. H. *Society and Economic Growth.* Oxford University Press, 1970.

Kuznets, S. ''Population and Economic Growth.'' *Proceedings of the American Philosophical Society,* 11 (June 1967):170-93.

Kyemba, H. *A State of Blood.* Ace Books, 1977.

Laidlaw, K. A. *A Comparative Study of Civilian and Military Rule in Peru, 1963-1974: Implications for Economic Development.* Unpublished Ph.D. dissertation, Bowling Green State University, 1976.

Laidlaw, K. A. ''The Industrial Community in Peru: An Experiment in Worker Participation.'' *International Review of Modern Sociology,* 7 (January-June 1977):1-11.

Laidlaw, K. A. "The Military in the Third World: A Case for the Convergence Hypothesis." *International Review of Modern Sociology,* 9 (January-June, 1979).

Lakshmanan, T. R., L. Chatterjee, and P. Roy. ''Housing Requirements and National Resources." *Science,* 192 (June 4, 1976):943-49.

Lerner, D. "Toward a Communication Theory of Modernization." In L. W. Pye, ed., *Communications and Political Development.* Princeton University Press, 1963. Pp. 327-50.

Ling, T. O. "Buddhist Factors in Population Growth and Control," *Population Studies,* 21 (March 1969):53-60.

Longworth, B., and R. Yates. "The Church: A Decade of Change." *Chicago Tribune* (January 23, 1978): 1, 8.

Lopez-Rey, M. *Crime: An Analytical Approach.* Praeger, 1970.

Lopez-Rey, M. "Crime and the Penal System," *Australian and New Zealand Journal of Criminology,* 4 (March 1971):5-21.

Lorimer, F. *Culture and Human Fertility.* UNESCO, 1954.

McClelland, D. C. *The Achieving Society.* D. Van Nostrand, 1961.

McClelland, D. C. "The Achievement Motive in Economic Growth." In B. F. Hoselitz and W. E. Moore, eds., *Industrialization and Society.* UNESCO and Morton, 1963. Pp. 74-96.

McClelland, D. "Does Education Accelerate Economic Growth?" *Economic Development and Cultural Change,* 14 (April 1966):257-78.

McClelland, D. C., and D. G. Winter. *Motivating Economic Achievement.* Free Press, 1969.

McKeown, T. *The Modern Rise of Population.* Academic Press, 1976.

Malthus, T. R. *Population: The First Essay.* University of Michigan Press, 1959. (Originally published in 1798.)

Mead, M. "A Comment on the Role of Women in Agriculture." In I. Tinker and M. B. Bramsen, eds., *Women and World Development.* Overseas Development Council, 1976. Pp. 9-11.

Miller, N. N. "The Dynamics of Population in Uganda," *American Universities Fieldstaff Reports.* East Africa Series, 10 (1971).

Moraes, D. *A Matter of People.* Praeger, 1974.

Nafziger, E. W. "The Effect of the Nigerian Extended Family on Entrepreneurial Activity." *Economic Development and Cultural Change,* 18 (October 1969):25-33.

Nagi, M. H. *Labor Force and Employment in Egypt.* Praeger, 1971.

Nash, M., ed. *Essays on Economic Development and Cultural Change in Honor of Bert F. Hoselitz.* University of Chicago Press, 1977.

National Academy of Sciences. *Rapid Population Growth: Consequences and Implications,* Vol. 1. *Summary and Recommendations.* Johns Hopkins Press, 1971.

Needler, M. C. "Political Development and Military Intervention in Latin America." In G. S. Masannat, ed., *The Dynamics of Modernization and Social Change.* Goodyear Publishing Co., 1973. Pp. 468-87.

Nordlinger, E. A. "Soldiers in Mufti: The Impact of Military Rule Upon Economic and Social Change in the Non-Western States," *American Political Science Review,* 64 (December 1970):1131-48.

Nortman, D., and E. Hofstatter, *Population and Family Planning Programs: A Factbook.* 6th ed. The Population Council, 1974.

Nortman, D., and E. Hofstatter. *Population and Family Planning Pro-*

grams: A Factbook. 7th ed. The Population Council, 1975.

Nortman, D., and E. Hofstatter. *Population and Family Planning Programs: A Factbook.* 8th ed. The Population Council, 1976.

Novack, D. E., and R. Lekachman, eds. *Development and Society: The Dynamics of Economic Change.* St. Martin's Press, 1969.

Nun, José. "The Middle Class Military Coup." In R. I. Rhodes, ed. *Imperialism and Underdevelopment.* Monthly Review Press, 1970.

Okediji, F. O. *Changes in Individual Reproductive Behavior and Cultural Values.* International Union for the Scientific Study of Population, Bucharest, 1974.

Olusanya, P. O. "Cultural Barriers to Family Planning Among the Yorubas." *Studies in Family Planning,* 37 (January 1969):13-16.

Omran, A. R. "Epidemiologic Transition in the U.S." *Population Bulletin,* 32 (May 1977):3-42.

Pala, A. O. "Definitions of Women and Development: An African Perspective," *Signs,* 3 (Autumn 1977):9-13.

Palmer, D. S. *Revolution from Above: Military Government and Popular Participation in Peru, 1968-1972.* Unpublished Ph.D. dissertation, Cornell University, 1973.

Parsons, T. *The Social System.* Free Press, 1951.

Pearson, Lester B., et al. *Partners in Development: Report of the Commission on International Development.* Praeger, 1969.

Peaslee, A. L. "Education's Role in Development," *Economic Development and Cultural Change,* 17 (April 1969):293-318.

Perlmutter, A. "The Praetorian State and the Praetorian Army: Toward a Taxonomy of Civil-Military Relations in Developing Politics." *Comparative Politics,* 1 (April 1969):382-404.

Perlmutter, A. *The Military and Politics in Modern Times.* Yale University Press, 1977.

Peshkin, A., and R. Cohen. "The Values of Modernization," *Journal of Developing Areas,* 2 (October 1967): 7-22.

Petersen, W. *Population.* 3d ed. Macmillan Publishing Co., 1975.

Pierce, B. F. "The Ethnic Factor in Biotechnology," *Economic Development and Cultural Change,* 14 (January 1966):217-29.

Pike, F. B. *The Conflict Between Church and State in Latin America.* Alfred A. Knopf, 1964.

Pike, F. B. *The Modern History of Peru.* Praeger, 1967.

Pitt, D. *The Social Dynamics of Development.* Pergamon Press, 1976.

Population Reference Bureau. "Third World Development: Where Does Population Fit?" *Population Bulletin,* 28 (1972):5-22.

Population Reference Bureau. "Literacy and World Population." *Population Bulletin,* 30 (1976a):3-29.

Population Reference Bureau. *World Population Growth and Response: 1965-1975, A Decade of Global Action.* Washington, D.C., 1976b.

Population Reference Bureau. *1977 World Population Data Sheet.* Washington, D.C., 1977.

Population Reference Bureau. *1978 World Population Data Sheet.* Washington, D.C., 1978a.

Population Reference Bureau, *Intercom*, 6 (June 1978b).

Portes, A. "On the Sociology of National Development: Theories and Issues," *American Journal of Sociology*, 82 (July 1976):55-85.

Potholm, C. P. "The Multiple Roles of the Police as Seen in the African Context." *Journal of Developing Areas*, 3 (January 1969):139-57.

Preston, S. H. "The Changing Relation Between Mortality and Level of Economic Development." *Population Studies*, 29 (July 1975):231-48.

Rapoport, D. C. "Military and Civil Societies: The Contemporary Significance of a Traditional Subject in Political Theory." *Political Studies*, 12 (1964):178-201.

Rich, W. *Smaller Families Through Social and Economic Development*. Overseas Development Council, 1973.

Rogers, E. M. *Communication Strategies for Family Planning*. Free Press, 1973.

Rostow, W. W. *The Stages of Economic Growth: A Non-Communist Manifesto*. Cambridge University Press, 1960.

Rubinson, R. "The World Economy and the Distribution of Income Within States: A Cross-National Study." *American Sociological Review*, 41 (August 1976):638-59.

Ryan, W. *Blaming the Victim*. Vintage Books, 1972.

Sachs, I. *The Discovery of the Third World*. MIT Press, 1976.

Schick, B. "Women: An Untapped Resource in a Hungry World." *Agenda*, 1 (June 1978):1-4.

Schramm, W. *Mass Media and National Development*. Stanford University Press, 1964.

Seavoy, R. E. "Social Restraints on Food Production in Indonesian Subsistence Culture." *Journal of Southeast Asian Studies*, 8 (March 1977):15-30.

Shabtai, S. H. "Army and Economy in Tropical Africa." *Economic Development and Cultural Change*, 23 (July 1975):687-701.

Shea, T. W. "Barriers to Economic Development in Traditional Societies: Malabar, A Case Study." In D. E. Novack and R. Lekachmen, eds., *Development and Society*. St. Martin's Press, 1964. Pp. 233-43.

Silberman, B. S. "Criteria for Recruitment and Success in the Japanese Bureaucracy, 1868-1900: 'Traditional' and 'Modern' Criteria in Bureaucratic Development." *Economic Development and Cultural Change*, 14 (January 1966):158-73.

Smith, G. "What We Got for What We Gave." *American Heritage* (April-May 1978):64-81.

de Sola Pool, I. "Communications and Development." In M. Weiner, ed., *Modernization: The Dynamics of Growth*. Basic Books, 1966. Pp. 98-109.

Spengler, J.J. "Social Structure, the State, and Economic Growth." In S. Kuznets et al., *Economic Growth: Brazil, India, Japan*. Duke University Press, 1955. Pp. 363-87.

Stockwell, E. G. *Population and People*. Quadrangle Books, 1968.

Stockwell, E. G. "Some Observations on the Relationship Between Population Growth and Economic Development During the 1960's." *Rural*

Sociology, 37 (December 1972):628-32.

Stockwell, E. G. "The Dimensions of Development: An Empirical Analysis." *Population Review,* 18 (1974):35-51.

Stockwell, E. G., and B. W. Hutchinson. "A Note on Mortality Correlates of Economic Development." *Population Review,* 19 (1975):46-50.

Stokes, R., and A. Harris. "South African Development and the Paradox of Racial Particularism: Toward a Theory of Modernization from the Center." *Economic Development and Cultural Change,* 26 (January 1978):245-69.

Straus, M. A. "Family Organization and Problem Solving Ability in Relation to Societal Modernization." *Journal of Comparative Family Studies,* 3 (Spring 1972):70-83.

Stycos, J. M. "Obstacles to Programs of Population Control—Facts and Fancies." *Marriage and Family Living,* 25 (February 1963):5-13.

Stycos, J. M. "Opinion, Ideology, and Population Problems—Some Sources of Domestic and Foreign Opposition to Birth Control." In National Academy of Science, *Rapid Population Growth: Consequences and Policy Implications.* The Johns Hopkins Press, 1971. Pp. 533-66.

Stycos, J. M., and R. H. Weller. "Female Working Roles and Fertility," *Demography,* 4 (1967):210-17.

Sullerot, E. *Women, Society and Change.* Translated by M. S. Archer. World University Library, 1971.

Tabbarah, R. B. "Toward a Theory of Demographic Development." *Economic Development and Cultural Change,* 19 (January 1971):257-76.

Teitelbaum, M. S. "Relevance of Demographic Transition Theory for Developing Countries," *Science,* 188 (May 2, 1975):420-25.

Thompson, W. S. *Population Problems.* 4th ed. McGraw-Hill, 1953.

Tietze, C., and M. C. Murstein. *Induced Abortion: 1975 Factbook.* The Population Council, 1975.

Tinker, I. "The Seminar on Women in Development." In I. Tinker and M. B. Bramsen, eds., *Women and World Development.* Overseas Development Council, 1976a. Pp. 1-6.

Tinker, I. "The Adverse Impact of Development on Women." In I. Tinker and M. B. Bramsen, eds. *Women and World Development.* Overseas Development Council, 1976. Pp. 22-34.

Tinker, I., and M. B. Bramsen, eds. *Women and World Development.* Overseas Development Council, 1976.

Tsui, A. O., and D. J. Bogue. "Declining World Fertility: Trends, Causes, Implications." *Population Bulletin, 33 (October 1978).*

United Nations. *1966 Demographic Yearbook.* New York, 1967.

United Nations. *1971 Demographic Yearbook.* New York, 1972.

United Nations. *1973 Demographic Yearbook.* New York, 1974.

UNESCO. "Urbanization and Economic and Social Change." *International Social Development Review,* 1 (1968):21-35.

U.S. Bureau of the Census, International Statistical Programs Center.

World Population, 1973: Recent Demographic Estimates for the Countries and Regions of the World. ISP-WP-73. U.S. Government Printing Office (May 1974).

U.S. Bureau of the Census, International Statistical Programs Center. *World Population, 1975: Recent Demographic Estimates for the Countries and Regions of the World.* ISP-WP-75. U.S. Government Printing Office (June, 1976).

Wallerstein, I. *The Modern World System: Capitalist Agriculture and the Origins of the European World Economy in the Sixteenth Century.* Academic Press, 1974.

Walton, J. *Elites and Economic Development.* University of Texas Press, 1977.

Ware, H. "Ideal Family Size." World Fertility Survey Occasional Paper No. 13 (October 1974).

Weber, M. *The Protestant Ethic and the Spirit of Capitalism.* Charles Scribner's Sons, 1930.

Weinstein, J. A. *Demographic Transition and Social Change.* General Learning Press, 1976.

Weller, R. H. "The Employment of Wives: Role Incompatibility and Fertility." *Milbank Memorial Fund Quarterly,* 46 (October 1968): 507-26.

Weller, R. H., and D. F. Sly. "Modernization and Demographic Change: A World View." *Rural Sociology,* 34 (September 1969):313-26.

Westoff, C. F., and L. Bumpass. "The Revolution in Birth Control Practices of U.S. Roman Catholics." *Science,* 179 (January 5, 1973): 41-44.

Wiarda, H. J. "Toward a Framework for the Study of Political Change in the Iberic-Latin Tradition: The Corporative Model." *World Politics,* 25 (January 1973):206-35.

Wiarda, H. J., ed. *Politics and Social Change in Latin America.* University of Massachusetts Press, 1974.

Wolpin, M. D. *Military Aid and Counterrevolution in the Third World.* D. C. Heath, 1972.

Wriggins, H. "National Integration." In M. Weiner, ed. *Modernization: The Dilemma of Growth.* Basic Books, 1966. Pp. 181-91.

Wriggins, W. H., and G. Adler-Karlsson. *Reducing Global Inequities.* McGraw-Hill, 1978.

Yates, R. "Underground Activist Priests Unite Secretly." *Chicago Tribune* (January 23, 1978):8.

Youseff, N. H. "Social Structure and the Female Labor Force: The Case of Muslim Middle Eastern Countries." *Demography,* 8 (1971):427-39.

Youseff, N. H. "Differential Labor Force Participation of Women in Latin America and Middle Eastern Countries: The Influence of Family Characteristics." *Social Forces,* 5 (1972):135-53.

Youseff, N. H. "Women in Development: Urban Life and Labor." In I. Tinker and M. B. Bramsen, eds., *Women and World Development.* Overseas Development Council, 1976. Pp. 70-77.

Zeidenstein, G. "Strategic Issues in Population," *Population and Development Review*, 3 (September 1977):307-18.

Zeidenstein, G. *Including Women in Development Efforts*. The Population Council, 1978.

Author Index

Subject Index

343